Power in Powerlessness

Power in Powerlessness

A Study of Pentecostal Life Worlds in Urban Chile

By

Martin Lindhardt

BRILL

LEIDEN · BOSTON
2014

This paperback was originally published in hardback under ISBN 978-90-04-21600-6. Reprinted with minor corrections.

Library of Congress Cataloging-in-Publication Data

Lindhardt, Martin.
  Power in powerlessness : a study of Pentecostal life worlds in urban Chile / by Martin Lindhardt.
      p. cm. -- (Religion in the Americas series, ISSN 1542-1279 ; v. 12)
  Includes bibliographical references and index.
  ISBN 978-90-04-21600-6 (hardback : alk. paper) 1. Pentecostalism--Chile--Valpara?so.
2. Valpara?so (Chile)--Religious life and customs. 3. City churches--Chile--Valpara?so.
I. Title.

  BR1644.5.C5L56 2012
  289.9'40983255--dc23

                                                                2011042135

ISBN 978-90-04-26569-1 (paperback)
ISBN 978-90-04-21894-9 (e-book)

Printed by Printforce, the Netherlands

CONTENTS

ACKNOWLEDGEMENTS

I am grateful for the financial support of the Danish Research Council for Culture and Communication, which funded the main field research. I am also indebted to several people for comments on the manuscript. In particular I would like to thank Nils Ole Bubandt for his careful reading of earlier drafts. Thanks are also due to David Lehmann, Ton Otto, Inger Sjørslev, Poul Pedersen, Calvin Smith, Henri Gooren, Jacqueline Ryle and to a few anonymous reviewers. My greatest debt is to all the Chilean Pentecostals who shared their lives with me for a time. My sincerest thanks to all those individuals whose names have been changed together with my apologies for writing a book that is most certainly very different from the one they had hoped I would write.

Parts of chapters have been published elsewhere. A part of chapter 6 appeared in *Suomen Antropologi* No. 34, vol 3, 2009, and some parts of chapter 7 appeared in the volume "*Practising the Faith. The Ritual Life of Pentecostal-Charismatic Christians*" (edited by myself), published by Berghahn Books in 2011. Parts of chapter 9 were published in Spanish in *Revista Cultura y Religion*, No. 3, Vol 2, 2009, and a small part of chapter 10 has appeared in *Nordic Journal of Religion and Society* No. 23, Vol 2. 2010. Permissions to reprint are gratefully acknowledged.

CHAPTER ONE

INTRODUCTION

The Pentecostals had puzzled me since I first visited the city of Valparaíso in Chile in 1992. During late afternoons and on Sundays I had frequently observed them evangelising on the streets and the *plazas* (public squares) in small groups. The energy and enthusiasm with which they preached and sang to an indifferent and ungrateful audience was truly amazing. It sometimes seemed as if the lack of interest from other Chileans who passed by without ever stopping to listen only made the Pentecostals more determined and convinced about the necessity of their mission in a world of misguided sinners.

My curiosity was further stimulated by scholarly literature and frequent trips to Chile (as I married a Chilean Catholic woman from Valparaíso in 1995). In June 1999 I finally set foot in a Chilean Pentecostal church for the first time, having decided that I would conduct a research project on this religious movement. I showed up for a Bible class on a Friday evening in the Evangelical Pentecostal Church (EPC) in Valparaíso and sat down next to an old man who soon started telling me how he used to be a Catholic and a very irresponsible and evil person until the Lord saved him and changed his life forever. When I told him I was married to a Catholic woman and that we had no children, he immediately concluded that God had not blessed us with a child *because* she was a Catholic. He invited both of us to his home for lunch the following Sunday after Sunday school so that he could tell my wife how God had given him and his late wife a child after they converted. When the Bible class finished I struck up conversation with a young man who told me he had been a drug addict before the Lord transformed his life. Being saved and restored was without comparison the most wonderful experience any person could ever have, and he strongly suggested I asked the Lord for salvation. I explained I was an anthropologist intending to do a research project on Chilean Pentecostalism. As we were leaving the church together, he greeted a few older women who asked him who I was and why I had come to the church. 'The Lord brought him here,' my new friend replied, totally ignoring what I had told him, but the women seemed quite content with this answer and did not ask for further explanations.

This was the first but by no means the last time that I experienced how divine intervention and transformative power were invoked in order to make sense of personal biographies and everyday events to the point where more secular explanations could be ignored or dismissed as irrelevant. Whatever I had said about my academic reasons for showing up was clearly secondary to the real reason why I found myself in this church, namely that God had sent me. While I felt my attempts to communicate who I was and why I had come had been undermined, I was also fascinated with the persuasion, ease, and consent with which my new friend disregarded my human projects and made God the main character in his explanation of my presence.

But why is this way of understanding the world, and the roles of human and divine subjects and agency within it, meaningful and appealing to a number of Chileans? And how—or through what processes—do some people living in a modern Latin American society come to think of themselves and the social world in such a way? As the growth and proliferation of Pentecostal denominations have radically altered the face of Chilean and other Latin societies within the last decades, these questions seem as relevant and compelling as ever. In a region where the Catholic Church, from early colonial times and up until the latter half of the twentieth century, has been an all-dominant religious institution and continues to be a highly influential actor on the political scene, recent estimates see Evangelical Protestantism as having some 60 million adherents, approximately 12 per cent of the entire population. At least two-thirds of Latin American Evangelicals are Pentecostals (Bernice Martin 2011*b*: 130). As noted by Paul Freston, within recent decades the religious structure of Latin American societies has moved from a Latin/southern European model with Catholic dominance towards a model of religious pluralism and voluntarism characteristic of the United States (2006: 13, see also Chesnut 2003).

Besides the numerical growth, a noteworthy feature of Pentecostalism in Latin America and elsewhere is the ability of this movement to mobilise and draw its adherents into active, regular participation in ritual, congregational life. While Pentecostalism is still a minority religion all over Latin America, Brian Smith suspects that there may be more Pentecostal than Catholic churchgoers on an ordinary Sunday in several countries (1998: 2). In the EPC in Valparaíso, many congregants participate in meetings or other church activities five to six times a week.

Chile holds a special position in the history of Latin American and world Pentecostalism. Not only was the Methodist Pentecostal Church, which was founded in Chile in 1909, the first Pentecostal church in Latin America; it was also the first indigenous, economically and theologically independent Pentecostal church in the third world. In the second half of the twentieth century, Pentecostalism grew steadily in Chile, and in a national census from 2002, 15.1 per cent of all respondents defined themselves as *Evangelicos* (Evangelicals), a category that includes non-Pentecostal Protestants, such as Lutherans, Anglicans, Presbyterians, Methodists, and Adventists. Estimates have placed Pentecostals at 75–90 per cent of all Chilean Evangelicals (Corvalán 2009: 77; Cleary and Sepúlveda 1997: 101), which makes Chile one of the countries with the highest relative number of Pentecostals in the world. As in other Latin American counties, Pentecostals in Chile mostly belong to the lower socioeconomic sectors of society.

The explosion of Pentecostalism in Latin America has not gone unnoticed by scholars, and the existing literature offers a wide range of explanations and interpretations of causes and consequences of conversion to this movement. Early pioneering studies, based on research in urban Chile and Brazil around 1960, mainly ascribe Pentecostal growth to migration, urbanisation, and the dissolution of rural communities. The Swiss sociologist Christian Lalive d'Epinay (1968) and the German sociologist Emilio Willems (1967) both see Pentecostalism as a mechanism of adaptation in areas that are exposed to intensive social and cultural changes. Lalive d'Epinay places a good deal of emphasis on the ability of urban Pentecostal communities to reproduce rural values such as solidarity, protection, confidence in social relations, and the authoritarian structure of the *hacienda* system (1968: 80–1). Willems, on the other hand, portrays Pentecostalism as a more innovative response to insecure urban life conditions. Though he (wisely) refrains from asserting any classical Weberian connection between Pentecostalism and large-scale capitalist activity, he stresses that the ascetic behaviour and strict personal discipline required of members of Pentecostal communities positively affect physical appearance, job opportunities, family life, and administration of domestic economy (1967: 173–5).

Though it is not very helpful in terms of explaining Pentecostal spread into rural areas, the analytical focus on migration was certainly justified by the historical context of these early studies. In the big cities of Valparaíso, Concepción, and Santiago, Pentecostalism mainly grew among marginal people of rural origin (Willems 1967: 177; Lalive d'Epinay 1968: 69). But half a century later the picture has changed. In the EPC as well as in several other Pentecostal denominations I have visited, a majority of members have been born in a city, and a majority of younger congregants have Pentecostal parents. Besides, many of the congregants who have moved to Valparaíso from a smaller city were practicing Pentecostals before migrating.

Though the works of Lalive D'Epinay and Willems prepared the ground, it was only after 1990 that the boom in the scholarly literature on Latin American Pentecostalism began. While not neglected in recent scholarship, rural–urban migration has ceased to be a dominant focus. Nevertheless, to a large extent, subsequent scholars have followed the line of argument pursued by the two early sociologists by emphasising the ways in which Pentecostalism enables Latin Americans to address permanent (rather than transitory) challenges of impoverished and unstable urban life. While Lalive d'Epinay's view on Pentecostalism as an urban version of the *hacienda* system has found little support, scholars have repeatedly noticed that Pentecostal congregations offer urban residents environments of solidarity and networks of mutual support (Lesley Gill 1990; Canales et. al 1991; Smilde 2007; Orellana Rojas 2009).

The arguments made by Willems have been picked up or at least echoed in a significant body of literature, which is characterised by what might be called a neo-Weberian perspective. The scholars that I refer to as neo-Weberian do not see culture merely as epiphenomenal, that is, as deriving from and reflecting material structures. Rather they share a view on culture (including religion as a cultural phenomena), as a (semi)independent variable or (semi)autonomous sphere from which processes of social change can be initiated. A recurring argument in the literature is that Latin Americans, by participating in Pentecostal communities, acquire new skills or learn new cultural strategies for coping with poverty and social insecurity. By adapting to rigorous standards for personal behaviour and decent physical appearance while at the same time becoming confident of having God on their side, members of Pentecostal denominations develop new self-discipline and optimism, enabling them to confront the work processes of a flexible and insecure labour market (Ossa 1991; Bernice Martin, 1995, 1998; David Martin 1990, 1991, 2001; Mariz 1994).

Some of the most significant work on Latin American Pentecostalism as a source of cultural transformation and mechanism of creative adaptation to difficult life circumstances has focused on gender and family life. Most scholars agree that the conversion of Latin American men to Pentecostalism results in a transformation of the *machismo* personality (Brusco 1995; Burdick 1993; Mariz 1994; Lesley Gill 1990; Stoll 1990; Slootweg 1991; Bernice Martin 1995; Drogus 1997; Cleary & Sepúlveda 1997; Montecino & Obach 2002; Mansilla 2008; Freston 2006). Whereas the traditional Latin American *macho* man mainly finds prestige in the public sphere by spending his money on typical male activities such as drinking, gambling, and womanising, the Pentecostal man becomes a respected congregant by abandoning these activities and being a sober and responsible father and husband. The transformed behaviour and new habits of consumption of a converted man positively affect the distribution of a household income and can therefore be a source of modest social advancement. Research has further shown that Pentecostal women whose husbands remain unconverted learn to ease the tension of marital arguments by avoiding hostility, reacting calmly to aggression, and appearing more obedient (Mariz 1994; Mariz & Campos Machado 1997). Scholars have also argued that Pentecostalism provides Latin American women with forms of social and religious participation through which they develop a new sense of spiritual authority and autonomy (Lesley Gill 1990; Slootweg 1991; Hurtado 1993; Mansilla 2008; Orellana Rojas 2009).

Another argument found in the literature is that Pentecostalism can be seen as a source of symbolic therapy in that it provides people with new conceptual frameworks for making sense of stressful experiences and, more generally, for making sense of a morally chaotic social world (Ossa 1991; Hurtado 1993; Bernice Martin 1998; Mansilla 2008, 2009). The sociologists Cecilia Mariz and Maria Campos Machado found that Brazilian Pentecostal women adopt tolerant attitudes towards aggressive, selfish, and heavy drinking husbands, as they come to see the latter as victims of the Devil (1997: 47; see also Burdick 1996). According to the Chilean Pentecostal pastor and academic scholar Juan Sepúlveda, Pentecostalism offers the losers in society a way to make spiritual sense of their situation and helps them find meaning, purpose, and a sense of community (Bernice Martin 1995: 107). In a similar vein, John Burdick argues that Pentecostals are spiritually equipped to deal with unstable employment and tend to explain unemployment in terms of a Jobian trial (1993: 29; see also Bernice Martin 1995: 113). The Chilean sociologists Manuel Canales, Samuel Palma, and Hugo Viella ascribe the appeal of Pentecostalism to deficits of meaning and feelings of failure and frustration that emerge when people find themselves unable to live up to dominating norms of popular culture. In Pentecostal churches, so they argue, members gain a new sense of self-worth as they learn to reorganise their own biographies and become engaged in new imaginary and meaningful elaborations of social reality (1991: 3–4).

Arguing along similar lines, several scholars have pointed out that Pentecostalism offers Latin Americans from the lower social economic strata new identities and a new sense of dignity by subverting secular or Catholic principles of social status (Lalive d'Epinay 1968; Willems 1967; Rolim 1979; Cleary & Sepúlveda 1997; David Martin 1990, 1995b, 2001; Lehmann 1996). In many Pentecostal churches, pastors have no formal theological training, and different leadership positions can be occupied by men with low levels of education and low-status jobs. With its high degrees of lay participation in congregational life (for example, in street preaching, prophesying, or narrating testimonies during services) and a theological emphasis on each believer's unmediated access to the power and inspiration of the Holy Spirit, Latin American Pentecostalism has—at some levels—succeeded in turning the losers of society into winners, a chosen people that enjoys spiritual privileges and exercises spiritual authority.

What all these explanations share in common is a certain measure of instrumentalism. One way or the other, they suggest that Pentecostalism grows and thrives in Latin America because it provides people with strategies for dealing with different kinds of hardship, whether economical, cultural, or emotional. There are many valuable insights to be found in the existing literature, and the purpose of the present study is not to take issue with instrumentalist approaches. In so far as previous scholarship has shown that Latin Americans convert to Pentecostalism in order to address different life problems or that new-found abilities to cope with life problems are in many cases unintended consequences of conversion that can take us a long way in understanding continued church membership, this book presents no objections. On the contrary, as will become clear, the analysis that I offer does to a large extent build upon the findings of other scholars. And yet, my motivation for pursuing this study and writing up this book stems from the fact that I have felt certain unease with instrumentalist approaches, not because I think they are wrong, but because the scholarly works informed by these approaches only tell a partial story and fail to adequately address what I consider to be a crucial question in the study of Pentecostalism. The question I am thinking of is the second of the two I asked on page 2, though it can be slightly rephrased here in order to avoid mere repetition: how or through what processes does it occur that persons come to relate to themselves and the social world in a particular Pentecostal way? In the existing scholarship on Latin American Pentecostalism, most effort seems to have been put into figuring out *why* people convert to this religious movement. The numerous candidate answers, some of which I have briefly sketched above mainly focus on *what* Pentecostalism does to people—or on *what* people do with Pentecostalism. But *how* does Pentecostalism do what it does (or *how* do people do what they do with Pentecostalism)?

My first significant encounter (that is, as more than a mere observant of street preaching) with Pentecostal-charismatic Christianity did not take place in Chile in 1999 but in Tanzania the year before. Notwithstanding the very different historical, social, and cultural contexts, the similarities and parallels between this variant of Christianity in those two places were plenty. In both places, I was genuinely impressed by the testimonies of persons who had turned around their lives, stopped drinking and smoking, and grown confident of the protecting power of God. But what fascinated me even more and has continued to fascinate me is the ritual-drenched life of Pentecostals/charismatics and the ways in which notions of sacred agency and interference in human affairs pervade their life worlds, shape their everyday experience and interpretation of events, and enable them to cultivate a certain sense of agency. In other words, my fascination with this religious movement does not only stem from my observation of the—to a large extent non-religious—effects or rewards of conversion. It also, and mostly, stems from the ways in which adherents live their religiosity on an everyday basis, and not least from the marked contrast Pentecostal-charismatic lived religiosity provides to the mainline Protestant (Evangelical Lutheran) milieu with which I have some familiarity.

It has been argued more than once in the literature that Latin American Pentecostalism nurtures new types of selfhood. I agree. But the ability of Pentecostalism to do so is often explained rather superficially with brief and passing references to the rigorous disciplines of the churches; the prohibition of drinking, drugs, tobacco, and gambling; the inexorability of a congregation's mutual surveillance; and the provision of new networks that support individuals trying to deal with addictions (David Martin 1990; Bernice Martin 1995; Brusco 1995; Mariz 1994). Surely these are important aspects, and scholars are right in paying attention to them. But while I have absolutely no objections to such explanations, I have found them wanting when trying to figure out how persons like the two men I met during my first visit to a Chilean Pentecostal church begin and continue to think about themselves, and more generally about the role of human and sacred subjects in the social world, in particular ways. Merely pointing out that a man stops drinking or taking drugs because he joins a church where such vices are prohibited and demonized and where congregants mutually supervise each other, or that he becomes more oriented towards the domestic sphere because that is how a Pentecostal man is supposed to behave, does not take us very far in explaining the constitution of new religious self-identities and life worlds. Canales, Palma, and Viella come closer than most others to the kind of analysis I have in mind when they suggest a focus on Pentecostal subjectivity, biographical reconstructions, new self-perceptions, and new organisations of experiences (1991: 3–4). But unfortunately these scholars fail to take full advantage of their own perspective, as they do not provide any analysis of the empirical processes through which autobiographies are reconstructed and new self-perceptions and subjectivities emerge.

I think the British historian David Maxwell hits the nail on the head when he, writing on African Pentecostalism, points out that 'functionalist analysis misses the point that first and foremost of all Pentecostalism is a religious movement and that much of its significance lies in its idioms and practices' (2002: 197). In a similar vein, Joel Robbins has forcefully argued for the necessity of stepping back from instrumentalist approaches since Pentecostalism can only compensate for losses and deprivations once it has succeeded as institutions (2011: 53). Robbins mainly relates its ability to do so to the intensity of people's involvement in church life and more particularly to the effervescence and emotional energy generated in Pentecostal worship (ibid.: 58–9). In this book I adopt a similar perspective. I hope to show that an understanding of Pentecostalism's ability to provide people with sources of identity, empowerment, and alternate world constructions—or in other words, to generate personal and cultural change—can be reached through the fine-grained examination of different aspects of Pentecostal ritual and everyday practice.

What is constituted and nourished through Pentecostal practice is a specific religious life world. Given that this is the third time I use that term (or the fourth if we include the cover of the book), a definition might be in order. Here I follow Alfred Schutz's and Thomas Luckmann's definition of the *life world* as an intersubjective context of meaning, stocks of knowledge, and cultural typifications which actors use to explain the world and orient themselves in it (1973: 7). Inhabiting a Pentecostal life world does not imply living in a parallel world, set apart from wider society. What it does imply is learning a particular religious language and using it in the interpretation and narration of events and individual biographies. And it implies developing an embodied and cognitive sensibility to the sacred or learning to tune the senses to certain experiences and acquiring models for interpreting these experiences in particular ways (see Csordas 1990, 1994, 1997; Luhrmann 2004, 2005, 2006; Lindhardt 2009a, 2011). A substantial part of this book focuses on the ritual and everyday processes and practices, through which a Pentecostal life world is constituted, unfolded, and nourished, that is, on how people learn to think, behave, and orient themselves in the world as Pentecostals.

That being said, the more familiar questions of *why* some people convert to Pentecostalism while others do not and—given the great variety of Pentecostal denominations in contemporary Chile—why some people find particular versions of this religious movement appealing are obviously still important and will also be addressed. I argue that the appeal and cultural dynamics of Chilean Pentecostalism should be seen within a complex societal context of social, cultural differentiation and within a particular historical context of political disenchantment in post-dictatorship Chilean society. Catholic authorities have expressed their concern that religious pluralism in Latin America, generated by the explosion of Pentecostalism, presents a threat to a cultural unity grounded in a common Catholic heritage (see Ruana 1995: 254–5; Smith 1998: 3–4). I think this view is based on an exaggerated notion of Catholic-cultural unity and that social and cultural pluralism has been a dominant feature of Latin American societies since colonial times. The growth of Pentecostalism in the region should be seen as much as a reflection of this pluralism as its cause. What I hope show is that Pentecostalism provides a language and a set of ritual forms by use of which objective structures of social differentiation are renegotiated and reconstituted as religious differences.

A Pentecostal church like the EPC in Valparaíso does not appeal broadly to Chileans from different social sectors. Without exception, first-generation non-native congregants are persons with low levels of education and low-status employment. Most Pentecostals in the world reckon that God can and often does intervene in human affairs and influence the course of events in ways that humans could not do by themselves. But in this particular church a particularly strong theological emphasis is placed on human impotence and total dependence upon divine power. I argue that the appeal of this theology is related to sensations of social impotence shared by people who occupy low positions in social, cultural hierarchies of Chilean society and who feel alienated from the political field. But I also hope to achieve a little more than simply explaining that some people join a particular church because the message preached in that church makes sense to them. In fact, the Pentecostal view on human versus divine power is not just something congregants are explicitly reminded of by a preacher every now and then. On the contrary, what I set out to explore in later chapters is the ways in which the theology of human impotence and dependence upon God is continuously actualised and unfolded, that is, *lived*, by ordinary Pentecostals in their ritual and everyday, discursive/linguistic, reflective, and bodily practice.

In some ways this book joins the chorus of publications that argue that Latin American Pentecostalism, by virtue of its theological egalitarianism and the organisational structures of the churches, subverts secular and Catholic principles of social status. But drawing on insights from anthropological resistance studies (Comaroff 1985) I hope to add nuances to the existing literature by highlighting how congregants from the EPC are engaged in complex and subtle symbolic struggles over categorisations and definitions of social reality. I show how they redefine the social world and not least their own position within it through everyday linguistic practice (chapters 5 and 8); discourses on healing and politics (chapter 5); the narrating of testimonies and life stories (chapter 6); ritual practice, including different kinds of ritual communication where spoken words appear to have a divine authorship (chapter 7); the ritualisation of everyday life (chapter 8); gender politics (chapter 9); discourses on the Devil (chapter 10); and last but not least, the articulation of rumours, conspiracy theories, and apocalyptical readings of world history (chapter 11). I argue that the Pentecostal practices of redefinition contain a critique of different aspects of Chilean society while at the same time represent a re-enchanting defiance of a secular modernist hegemony.

The title of the book, *Power in Powerlessness*, refers to what I consider to be an intriguing paradox, namely that congregants from the EPC, by accepting and even idealizing human powerlessness and total dependence upon God, in fact nurture a certain sense of agency and power. On the one hand, congregants believe that God has a mind of his own. He can influence the course of events whenever and wherever he wishes to do so, and he sometimes works in mysterious ways that only make sense in retrospect and at times only after considerable interpretive effort (see chapter 6). Yet, congregants also believe that transformative divine power mainly works in so far as it is activated by human agents, that is, by born-again Pentecostals who engage in praying, Bible reading, evangelisation, and ritual practice. Hence, they indirectly grant themselves a certain measure of agency, power, and responsibility to act upon the social world. It is my hope that the present study, by shedding light on the ways in which the theology of impotence and dependence is unfolded and actualised through Pentecostal practice, will contribute to our understanding of how this religious movement enables people to negotiate new identities; to gain a sense of authority, autonomy, and control; and to engage in new and meaningful elaborations of social reality.

The Ethnographic Context: A 'Traditional' Pentecostal Church

This book is based on a total of seventeen months of ethnographic fieldwork in the city of Valparaíso in central Chile between 1999 and 2009. Situated approximately 100 kilometres west of the capital Santiago, Valparaíso is one of the poorest cities in Chile. The city alone has around three hundred thousand inhabitants, but within the last decades it has grown together with the equally sized city Viña del Mar, whose centre is located less than five miles north from the centre of Valparaíso. Viña del Mar is a richer city, with giant shopping malls, beautiful beaches, luxury apartments, fancy hotels, a casino, thousands of tourists during summer, fewer stray dogs, and fewer Pentecostal street preachers. For decades Valparaíso has been a bohemian, artistic centre in Chile. It is a beautiful city with colourful houses covering the hills that begin to rise only a few hundred metres from the sea.

Research for the book was mainly conducted in the Evangelical Pentecostal Church (EPC), though I will now and then refer to data from research in other Pentecostal denominations. The EPC is the second largest and one of the oldest and most conservative Pentecostal denominations in the country. It can be distinguished from the majority of Pentecostal denominations by its reluctance to join any interdenominational Evangelical organisations, by not using musical instruments except from an organ during services, and by maintaining strict rules for clothing and physical appearance. Women must wear long skirts or dresses that cover the knees and blouses that cover the shoulders and are not too tight or low necked. Their hair must be long, and they should wear no cosmetics. The men must have short hair and dress decently and modestly. While most practicing Pentecostals in Chile share views on drinking, smoking, dancing, listening to 'worldly' music with sensual rhythms and erotic lyrics, gambling, and pre- and extramarital sex as sinful activities, many members of the EPC, especially from the elder generations, further add watching television and going to the cinema and to the beach to the list. Pentecostals from other and less ascetically focused denominations often refer to the EPC as a 'traditional' Pentecostal church. Members of the EPC rarely use that term to describe their own church, but they do not object to it, either, and do not regard it as offensive and derogatory. On the contrary, they see the term *traditional* as indicating the recognition by others that they are old-school Pentecostals who remain faithful to a moral and ascetic core that has—to different extents—been lost in many contemporary Pentecostal denominations.

Like most Pentecostals in Chile, congregants of the EPC think of themselves as belonging to a wider community of *Evangelicos* (Evangelicals), and they do occasionally refer to friends or acquaintances from other Pentecostal denominations as *hermanos* (brothers/sisters). But whereas many other Pentecostals I have interviewed mainly define themselves as Evangelicals and place little emphasis on their particular institutional affiliation (many of them had shifted churches on more than one occasion and were open to the possibility that they might do so again in the future), congregants from the EPC tend to take particular pride in belonging to one of the most strict and—in their own words—'serious' denominations in the country.

Most active members of the EPC in Valparaíso belong to the lower socioeconomic sectors of society. However, a generational gap in terms of income and education can be observed, as some of the younger 'native' congregants (children of Pentecostal parents) are now university students or professionals and are entering the Chilean middle class. First-generation congregants (that is, ex-Catholics) have low levels of education and modest incomes. Many Pentecostal men are either unskilled workers or self-employed, for example, as owners of small shops or market stalls or independent workmen in areas such as construction. Approximately two-thirds of active members in the church are women, the majority of whom are housewives or work as domestic servants or vendors in small shops or street markets. When I first visited the church in 1999, there was only one person above thirty who held a university degree. In 2008 some of the young congregants—all under thirty-three years of age—had graduated from university or professional institutes.

A theological dualism between the life with God and the godless and corrupted 'world' is important in many Pentecostal churches in Chile and elsewhere, but it is particularly emphasised in the EPC. This dualism has a temporal dimension, as individual testimonies of salvation generally take the standardised cultural form of a story about a journey from the 'world' to the life with God (see chapter 6). And it represents a perceived contemporary tension between the children of God and the remaining society with its political and Catholic institutions, secular status hierarchies, and a decadent mainstream culture.[1]

Active membership of the EPC is time-consuming. In addition to Sunday school from 10 a.m. to 12 p.m., church meetings, starting at 7 or 7.30 p.m. and lasting between one and a half and three hours, are held each night from Sunday to Friday. Most meetings are held in the main building of the EPC in downtown Valparaíso, but twice a week, Monday and Tuesday, meetings take place in ten local church buildings (*los locales*) in different parts of the city. Each of these buildings has its own local leader. Once or twice a month, vigils (late-night meetings) are held in local church buildings on Saturdays, often ending after midnight. Most congregants also participate in street preaching two or three times per week. Other activities include choir practice and excursions, such as visiting congregations in neighbouring cities and evangelisation campaigns in different parts of the country during summers. Besides these activities, most of the women who are married, de facto separated (but hardly ever legally divorced), or widows belong to the female group, the *dorcas*, which meets on Mondays in the afternoon.

Given that congregants live in different parts of city and that much of their social life takes place in the church buildings, this was also where the most substantial part of my fieldwork took place. I showed up for church meetings or sometimes for the preceding preaching on the street on most evenings. A majority of my interviews and informal

---

[1] Whenever I put the term 'world' in quotation marks, it refers to the Pentecostal theological conceptualisation of the 'world' as a state of sin, corruption, and satanic dominance.

social interaction with congregants took place before or after meetings, either in the church or in their private homes, though I also did quite a lot of 'hanging out' at the market stalls of small shops of some of my Pentecostal informants. During my first four periods of fieldwork in 1999, 2000, 2001, and 2002, what is now the main building of the EPC in down town Valparaíso was still being constructed. Five to ten church male members were working on the construction during week days, with one or two of the women preparing the lunch for them. On Saturdays a large group of men spent the day on its construction, and several women worked in the kitchen. This construction site an provided excellent context for hanging out, conducting interviews, engaging in informal conversations, and observing the interaction between congregants. Besides, my presence and occasional assistance (admittedly I tended to spend more time talking than working) was much appreciated by congregants.

As described, I began my research in this church by attending a meeting. As my presence generated curiosity, striking up conversations and establishing contacts with congregants was not very difficult. I was quickly introduced to the pastor who, after some explanation, approved of my presence and my investigations. My position as an anthropologist conducting a research project on Chilean Pentecostals was not, however, simple and straightforward. My own religious background was of central importance for my interaction with Pentecostals. As I will explain in later chapters, many Pentecostals conceive of the Catholic Church as their archenemy and even as the wife of the Antichrist (see especially chapter 11), and if I had been a devoted Catholic, fieldwork in the EPC would have been close to impossible. But being a lifelong member of the Evangelical Lutheran Church in Denmark and the son of a Lutheran minister turned out to be a position that offered some advantages. On the one hand, the Pentecostals who have an opinion about the Lutheran Church in Chile generally see it as too liberal, intellectualist, and spiritually dead. On the other hand, many Pentecostals and especially men have a little knowledge about European church history, and the Protestant reformation, initiated by Martin Luther, is seen as an important and divinely ordained restoration of true biblically grounded and anti-clerical Christianity. For many of my Pentecostal friends and acquaintances, being a Lutheran meant having good anti-Catholic roots and possibly being on the right path, but it also meant having little understanding of the importance of personal salvation and the gifts of the Holy Spirit. Thus, being a Lutheran was a position that facilitated my entrance into the church but also a position that allowed me to portray ignorance—and consequently to ask endless clarifying questions—about a number of issues such as personal experiences of divine power, divine intervention in everyday life, the meaning and experience of salvation, diabolic strategies and attacks on Christians, etc. Adopting different roles in different contexts is a fundamental part of human existence in functionally differentiated societies. Yet, I sometimes overemphasised my identity as a Lutheran from a not too spiritually oriented church to an extent which felt unnatural, as it is a role which, admittedly, seems largely irrelevant to me in most other contexts. Though I never presented my inquiries in terms of a personal search for salvation and religious experiences, I have little doubt that they were perceived as such by a majority of my informants, and this perception probably had a positive influence on their willingness to answer my many questions.

I was under some pressure to seek personal salvation and occasionally found myself in uncomfortable situations when the expectation was voiced up. Sermons in the church sometimes end with an invitation to potential converts to come forward to the pulpit and welcome Christ into their lives. On those occasions I chose to ignore the suggestive gazes of some congregants. Fortunately most of my Pentecostal friends and informants seemed to hold the conviction that they could only guide me and explain me things up to a certain point, but that my personal salvation was ultimately a matter between myself and God. Some congregants expressed the view that my research project and marriage to a Chilean woman were the means that God had used to introduce me to the EPC so that I could go home and bring revivalist power into my own church in Denmark. They further expressed their hopes and expectations that divine truths would reveal themselves through my writings. I am afraid that this book fails to meet the expectations of my Pentecostal friends and informants. While ethnographic knowledge is produced in the intersubjective encounter between researcher and informant (Fabian 1983), an encounter where different projects meet, sometimes overlapping and sometimes clashing, writing up a book or article is usually the sovereign work of the researcher. By including several excerpts from informants I have tried to let their voices be heard, to portray their religious projects and world constructions and to give the reader a glance of the intersubjective processes from which the knowledge I present emerged. But my informants are quoted for my purposes, not their own, and the present work is an

example of how 'the ethnographic project violates the other's project'
(Hastrup 1992: 122).

My contact with Chileans was not confined to lower- or young
middle-class Pentecostals. My wife's family and most of her friends live
in Valparaíso or Viña. Most of them are Catholic or non-believing
middle-class citizens, who are not very likely to convert to Pentecostalism, less to a traditional Pentecostal church. As it became clear to
me that the appeal, dynamics, and contestatory cultural character of
traditional Pentecostalism can only be properly understood within a
context of social differentiation I decided to broaden my focus by inter-
viewing a number of non-Pentecostal middle-class Chileans, most of
whom had higher education. In these interviews we touched upon a
variety of topics such as perceptions of social, cultural, and economic
differentiation, attitudes towards politics, religion, work, leisure, consumption, the mass media, education, sex roles, etc. The purpose of
these interviews was to gain a more detailed knowledge about social
cultural differences in Chilean society and consequently to be able to
figure out why some Chileans are more likely than others to be attracted
to traditional Pentecostal churches.

Outline of the Book

This book explores religious practices through which Pentecostal life
worlds and self-identities are produced, negotiated, and unfolded. In
the first part, I present the theoretical framework and the historical
background of my study. In chapter 2, I introduce and discuss some of
the theoretical perspectives and concepts that will inform the empirical
analysis. I find Thomas Csordas's understanding of charisma as a product of rhetorical apparatuses (1997: 139) particularly helpful. But drawing on the work of Michel Foucault (1972) and Kathleen C. Boone
(1090), I also argue that an analysis of Pentecostal rhetorical practice
needs to consider discursive principles for how statements can be made
and distributed. Finally I introduce a few perspectives of the human
self and argue for their relevance in the study of conversion and of the
constitution of a personal relationship between Pentecostals and the
sacred.

The historical, political, and structural context of the study is highlighted in chapters 3 and 4. Chapter 3 looks at the history of Chilean Pentecostalism and further sheds some light on central political,

economical, and religious processes and dynamics since the return of democracy in Chile in 1990. Chapter 4 examines the social composition of Chilean society and the position of Pentecostals within it.

Chapter 5 shows how Pentecostals, through subtle everyday semantic, discursive, and aesthetic practices, articulate a cultural critique, both of different aspects of Chilean society, such as the health system, the political system, and Catholicism, and more generally of a secular modernist hegemony. Chapter 6 focuses on conversion, addressing the question of how a person learns to think of him- or herself as a born-again Pentecostal who used to be a misguided sinner. I argue for the importance of narrative practice, such as testimonies of salvation, for the constitution of Pentecostal self-identities and for the continuous unfolding of shared life worlds. In chapter 7, attention is focused on Pentecostal ritual. Drawing on recent scholarly perspectives on ritual as an arena of creative social action, resistance, and negotiation of identity, I explore how a Pentecostal anti-modernist theology is actualised and unfolded through different strategies of ritualisation. I further argue that it is mainly through the rhetoric and embodied engagement in different practices of worship that Pentecostal dispositions for orientation towards the sacred are acquired and exercised. Chapter 8 pushes the analysis from chapter 7 further as I explore how ritually cultivated dispositions for experiencing divine presence and for speaking about the world in a certain way and thereby participating in a specific discursive–theological construction of social reality blend into the sphere of everyday life.

Chapter 9 addresses gender politics and the reworking of gendered identities within the EPC. I further explore how a personal relationship with Jesus, often described as an ideal spiritual husband, provides women with a sense of autonomy and self-sufficiency. Finally, I focus on the Pentecostal control of sexuality as a strategy for creating a sense of order and purity in what is perceived as messy world.

The focus of chapter 10 is on the role of a very important figure in the Pentecostal universe, the Devil. I argue that Pentecostal understandings of divine power and blessings are defined and constituted through a symbiotic relationship with satanic resistance and deception. I further demonstrate how Pentecostal diabologies provide a language for speaking about different issues such as intra-church tensions and confrontations with 'worldly' others. Drawing on the concepts of the human self, introduced in chapter 2, I devote the last part of the chapter to an analysis of Pentecostal experiences of diabolic attacks in the form of improper, confusing, and sceptical thoughts. Being a persistent, tireless, and omnipresent sacred other, the Devil reappears in chapter 11. But this chapter moves in new directions by focusing on Pentecostal interpretations of global processes. I argue that Pentecostals, by spiritualizing world history and identifying the hand of Satan behind globally dominant and institutions such as the EU, the Catholic Church, and North American enterprises, constitute a sense of global spiritual agency and project themselves and their own minor struggles against the forces of darkness into a global order. Finally, chapter 12 contains a short summary of the book's main argument and discusses the potential contribution of Pentecostalism to processes of democratization in Latin America.

CHAPTER TWO

ANALYTICAL FRAMEWORK: PENTECOSTALISM, CHARISMA, RHETORIC, AND DISCOURSE

How—or through what processes—are Pentecostal life worlds and self-identities constituted, reproduced, and modified? Or how do people learn to think, behave, and live as Pentecostals? In later chapters, I attempt to answer these questions by examining different aspects of Pentecostal ritual and everyday practice. In this chapter, I introduce and discuss a few relevant theoretical perspectives that will inform my analysis.

Pentecostals belong to a wider family of charismatic Christians that share an emphasis on personal salvation (being born-again) and the continuous manifestations and gifts of the Holy Spirit (the charismata). The first name that comes to mind when speaking of charismatic religiosity is Max Weber. In his tripartite classification of authority Weber distinguishes between (1) legal–rational authority, based on an impersonal, bureaucratic set of rules; (2) traditional authority, based on the belief in the legitimacy of tradition; (3) charismatic authority. Setting itself apart from the economic routines of everyday life, the latter is based on the extraordinary qualities of a leader, qualities which are regarded as of divine origin (1968: 48).

In Pentecostal-charismatic Christianity, extraordinary qualities, for example, the ability to discern spirits, to heal through prayers, to speak in tongues, to give prophecies and inspired sermons and teachings, are ascribed to the power of the Holy Spirit within a person. Given that these qualities are, in principle, equally accessible to any born-again Christian, Weber's definition of charismatic authority can only be applied with some reservations. Some Pentecostal-charismatic churches and movements are organised around leaders with particular charismatic personalities, rhetorical skills, and sometimes the gift of discernment and healing. But every born-again Pentecostal is a charismatic in the sense that he or she can be a channel of the Holy Spirit. The EPC can hardly be categorised as a charismatic movement or church in a strictly Weberian sense, as the authority to preach, lead a meeting, pray for the sick, lead the street preaching, teach in Sunday school, etc. is distributed among a number of congregants. Apart from the main church building in downtown Valparaíso, the EPC has ten local church buildings, *los locales*, in different parts of the city. On Mondays and Tuesdays meetings are held in these local buildings, each of which has its own leader.

For Weber the key to sustaining a charismatic authority lies in the recognition by others that a person possesses charismatic qualities (1968: 51). It follows that charismatic movements (in a strict sense) are unstable, as they can only persist as long as the specific leader delivers. Charismatic movements therefore either die out or undergo processes of routinisation and transform themselves into institutionalised churches over time.

Given the high number of highly institutionalised Pentecostal-charismatic churches on the global scene, routinisation is a process that certainly deserves very careful examination in the study of the history of Pentecostal-charismatic Christianity. But what I want to argue here is that the regular reconfirmation of charismatic qualities and the recognition of extraordinary powers in others continue to be crucial, even in the case of routinised and institutionalised Pentecostal-charismatic churches that are not organised around specific leaders. In the EPC, such confirmation and recognition occurs in ritual life (see chapter 7), through (what is perceived as) divinely inspired sermons and not least through spiritual manifestations such as healing, glossolalia, dancing, screaming, prophecies, etc. In fact, a succession of dull meetings without spiritual manifestations is likely to inspire sensations of spiritual crisis and decay among congregants. Other important practices through which congregants remind themselves and each other of extraordinary powers being at work in their lives include the narrating of personal testimonies of salvation (chapter 6) and of numerous anecdotes about transformative divine intervention in everyday affairs (chapter 8).

As noted by Thomas Csordas (1997: 137), Weber located charisma in the social consensus of the followers concerning the validity of a leader's charismatic powers, but he never really defined what charisma *is*.[1] In his groundbreaking study of ritual practice in a North American Catholic Charismatic movement, Csordas makes up for this deficit by proposing a definition of charisma I have found helpful in

---

[1] It is unlikely that Weber thought that charisma *is* a divine supernatural power invested in particular leaders, since this would imply a theological standpoint that is hardly compatible with the rest of his work.

the context of the present study, partly because it is practice-oriented and partly because it applies to leaderless charismatic movements or churches. Csordas defines charisma as the product of the rhetorical apparatus and persuasive means by use of which both leaders and followers articulate visions and convince themselves and each other that the world is constituted in a certain way (1997: 139). The locus and origin of charisma are among the participants of a charismatic movement, in their performances and interactions. In the words of Csordas:

> Critical for our purposes is that charisma originates in a mobilisation of communal symbolic resources that are realised in a mode of discourse or performed in a genre of ritual language within a particular social setting. (ibid.:141)

According to Csordas, there is no nominal charisma but only charismatic action, which is basically a rhetorical process. Rhetorical charismatic action does not legitimate charisma but creates it (ibid.: 145).

The definition of charisma as a product of a rhetorical apparatus can help us explain the existence of leaderless charismatic movements, since the source of charismatic authority is located outside of individual leaders, while at the same time allowing for the possibility that individuals may have different rhetorical skills. In the case of the EPC, the charismatic (Pentecostal) rhetoric apparatus consists of theological dualisms such God/Satan, light/darkness, saved/redeemed, life with God/the 'world', divine power/human powerlessness as well as a bundle of symbolic and narrative strategies and interpretive schemes by use of which experiences and understandings of the self, God, and the world are organised and transmitted (see also Harding 1994).

A different but, I argue, compatible and complementary, rather than contradictory, approach is found in the work of Kathleen C. Boone (1989) who conceives of North American Protestant Fundamentalism as a particular discourse. Drawing on the work of Foucault, Boone argues that the rules of fundamentalist discourse operate according to a sort of uniform anonymity on all individuals who speak in a fundamentalist discursive field (1989: 82; Foucault 1972: 63). Though they are closely related, discourse should not be reduced to or equated with language or rhetoric. Foucault describes discourse as a violence that we do to things or practices that are imposed on things and that 'systematically form the objects of which they speak' (1972: 49). In order to form objects of which it speaks, language use must be subjected to principles that, unlike grammar, are not inherent within language (as a system) itself. The aim of an analysis of discourse must therefore be to establish *the conditions of possibility* for some speech acts to be taken more seriously than others. As Foucault aptly states:

> In every society the production of discourse is at once controlled, selected, organised and redistributed by a number of procedures whose role is to ward off its powers and dangers, to gain mastery over its chance events, to evade its ponderous formidable materiality.... We know quite well that we do not have the right to say everything, that we cannot speak of just anything in any circumstances whatever, and that not everyone has the right to speak of anything whatever. (1981: 52)

The rules of a discursive formation govern what may be said, by whom, and further define the circumstances (time, place, institutional location) under which it is appropriate to make a given statement. More specifically, a discursive formation consists of rules for the formation of: (1) objects, (2) concepts, (3) strategies, and (4) enunciative modalities including subject positions. The objects of discourse are not pre-given. Rather it is the discourse itself that gives something the status of an object. Foucault gives the example of madness, which was constituted as an object of psychiatry in the nineteenth century by 'all the statements that named it, divided it up, and described it' (1972: 32). In order for statements to constitute new objects, a certain delimitation and specification is required. Mechanisms of delimitation can take the form of non-discursive institutions, which in the case of madness can be medical and juridical. In Pentecostalism, the church, with all its levels of authority, behavioural patterns, and norms, is the main institution that delimits statements. Foucault further argues that discursive objects are constituted through a continuous specification and delimitation, marked in the discourse itself, from other discourses (Østergaard & Ifversen 1996: 30). A religious discourse has to delimit its objects, making it clear that what can be talked about are religious matters. It follows that mechanisms of delimitation and specification produce a scarcity rather than a plenitude of meaning.

The objects of discourse are formed in a conceptual organisation. By *concepts* are meant the types, categories, and elements, which are used in a discursive formation. In traditional Pentecostal discourse the conceptual distinction between the church or the life with God and the 'world' provides an important framework for the narration of personal testimonies of salvation (see chapter 6) as well as for addressing different themes such as politics and healing (see chapter 5). Though the same concepts often appear in different discourses, their meaning is never fixed or pre-given, but is constituted in each specific discourse and may change over time.

By *strategies* Foucault means possibilities for creating the themes of a given discourse. A combination of interdiscursive and non-discursive relations determines the possibilities that are realised. Interdiscursive relations may include complementarity, opposition, analogy, and mutual delimitation (1972: 67). Non-discursive relations define the status of a statement within particular institutional or societal settings.

Objects, concepts, and thematic choices are not created without certain enunciative modalities, that is, without types of discursive activity. In the case of science these may include the forming of hypotheses or formulating regulations. In Pentecostalism, teaching, preaching, prophesying, giving testimony, and healing by prayer are some of the most important types of discursive activity. The analysis of enunciative modalities must address questions such as: Who is allowed to speak? In which situation and (institutional) location is it appropriate for a given subject to make certain statements? In a biomedical discourse, the doctor possesses formal qualifications and holds a specific position within systems of differentiation and hierarchy. According to Foucault, the value, efficacy, and even therapeutic power of medical statements 'cannot be dissociated from the statutorily defined person who has the right to make them' (1972: 51). In the EPC there are different restrictions on access to different modalities. Being allowed to preach on the street requires that a congregant display an exemplary Christian lifestyle. Only men who are known to be committed congregants with a personal testimony of salvation are allowed to preach in the church. In order for a prophecy to be taken seriously by listeners, it should be given by a long-term and respected congregant, male or female, with a testimony of salvation. Each modality is tied to specific situations and locations. Thus the discursive activity of prophesying must take place in the context of a communion in the church or in a home. Foucault stresses that the enunciative position or subject position (role, location, and situation) of each modality is not pre-given, but established in discourse itself. The subjects as well as the objects of discourse are determined by the discursive formation (1972: 52–5).

Boone conceives of Protestant Fundamentalism as a discourse through which objects are constituted and the role of fundamentalist subjects, leaders as well as followers, transcribed. Though individual actors are to some extent able to manipulate a discourse, it mostly works the other way around. Fundamentalist authority is not located in creative and strategically acting individuals but in the discourse as such and is not easily transferable to other fields. Boone argues that the social subject who produces a given statement should not be seen as an autonomous agent existing outside of the discourse. Rather, subjects as well as objects are constituted by discourse. The power of Protestant Fundamentalism, while non-subjective and unlocalisation-able, is intentional, compelling, and omnipresent, 'woven in and through every thread' (ibid.: 3).

Csordas's view of charisma as the product of rhetorical apparatuses invites us to consider the creative linguistic practices and performances through which shared religious realities, meanings, and visions are produced and unfolded. He also defines charisma as a certain way of being-in-the-world or 'a particular mode of interpersonal efficacy: not a quality, but a collective, performative, intersubjective self-process' (Csordas 1997: 140). In the empirical chapters of this book I address different aspects of Pentecostal (charismatic) practice, performance, and interaction. These include the narrating of testimonies and life stories (chapter 6); various kinds of ritual communication (chapter 7 and 8); the sharing of anecdotes and other kinds of informal conversation, praying, internal dialogue with God, and joking (chapter 8); gossiping (chapter 10); and the articulation of rumours and conspiracy theories (chapter 11). I further explore how Pentecostal rhetorical practice follows and is shaped (enabled and constrained) by the rules and principles of a Pentecostal discursive formation. Put another way, I argue that a thorough analysis of the ways in which shared life worlds are constituted through certain kinds of Pentecostal rhetorical practice needs to consider discursive principles for how statements can be distributed.

In July 2002 I was invited to a meeting in a local church building in outer Valparaíso. At the beginning of the meeting I was asked to step forward and say a few words to the congregation. Having become familiar with Pentecostal rhetoric, I decided not to thank any of the congregants for the invitation. Instead I expressed my gratitude to God for giving me the opportunity to visit this local church building. I then said that the room was small and humble, but that one could feel the love of God and a fine spiritual condition.

Afterwards I sensed a clear, albeit unarticulated, approval of my short performance. Members of the EPC insist that the ability to utter wise words is a gift from God. Consequently human speakers should not be given too much credit. When I later had tea with a married couple, Claudio and Liz, they told me that they had sensed the presence of the Holy Spirit when I spoke. They felt my short appearance on the pulpit was a great spiritual blessing for both me and the congregation. Especially my comment that the church building was small and humble but filled with the love of God indicated that the latter was using me in magnificent ways. They encouraged me to regard this experience as an incitement to explore my own relationship with the Lord further. The fact that I was an anthropologist studying the Pentecostals seemed quite unimportant in this moment.

For sure, this incident did not make me a charismatic leader. To be a full member of the Pentecostal community, a testimony of personal salvation and spiritual baptism is required. People with more trusted enunciative positions (preachers, prophets, and Sunday school teachers) have usually been members of the church for some time and portray exemplary Christian lifestyles. But what I did experience was that by being granted a certain enunciative position in a specific enunciative situation—that is, being allowed to address the congregation from the pulpit during a meeting—and by respecting and following the rules of the Pentecostal discursive formation (for instance by limiting my speech to a delimited field of objects—had I started to talk about my great disappointment with Denmark's recent and devastating defeat to England in the 2002 World Cup, I am sure the reactions would have been very different) and applying the Pentecostal rhetoric and conceptual elaborations (for example, a distinction between material humility and spiritual richness), I was taken very seriously. As other congregants were convinced that the power of God was now working in and through me, I could speak with a hitherto unknown (charismatic) authority.

A number of charismatic leaders such as Reinhard Bonnke, Benny Hinn, and Morrris Cerullo, all of whom have large groups of admirers and followers worldwide, have emerged within Pentecostal-charismatic Christianity over the last century. Obviously, it would make little sense to ignore or neglect the importance of the rhetorical skills and seductive personalities of such leaders. However, the point I have tried to establish is that the primary source of Pentecostal (charismatic) authority should not be located in the personality of a given leader nor in the follower's recognition of his gifts but in the Pentecostal discourse and rhetoric apparatus, both of which exist prior to any individual and may be successfully appropriated by particular leaders, but only to a limited extent manipulated by them.

Three Levels of Pentecostal Discourse

A rough distinction can be made between three levels of Pentecostal discourse:

The first level is the kind of discourse that is used when addressing a non-Pentecostal audience, for example, during street preaching, personal conversations, or during church meetings, if a preacher suspects potential converts to be present (see chapter 6). At this level of discourse Pentecostals explain to others how salvation can be achieved through the belief in Christ and how living with Christ enables people to overcome problems and suffering. Little emphasis is placed on the distinction between the life with God and the corrupted 'world' at this level. Living outside of the realm of God is mostly presented as a state of frustration and unhappiness rather than of sin and corruption. Pentecostals never make references to Catholicism when preaching on the street.

The second level of discourse is internal to Pentecostal churches, yet potentially external in that it is often heard and read by non-Pentecostals. This is the discourse of sermons, speeches, teachings, sharing, thanksgiving, testimonies (see chapters 6, 7, and 8), and articles in church magazines. The aim of this type of discourse is not to reach outsiders and convince them of the benefits of salvation, but rather to construct and reproduce shared religious realities. The distinction between the life with God and the 'world' is prevalent and sometimes takes the form of a contrast between fake happiness that comes from consumption and true spiritual happiness. Congregants further remind each other of the return of Christ, which should be preceded by a great spiritual revival. Only cautious and mostly implicit criticisms of Catholicism and other Evangelical churches are articulated at this level of discourse.

The third level of Pentecostal discourse is confined to non-ritual private contexts. This is where the most explicit criticisms of Catholicism and other Evangelical churches are made, for instance in the form of conspiracy theories that present the Catholic Church as the wife of the Antichrist (see chapter 11) and the emergence of neo-Pentecostal prosperity churches as the work of the Devil. The most elaborate stories of miracles such as awakenings of the dead are mainly told in private contexts. Gossiping about fellow congregants—including the articulation of suspicions that others may be manipulated by demonic forces (see chapter 10)—is also confined to private, informal conversations.

Richard Bernstein's distinction between elaborated and restricted language codes (1972) is helpful in terms of explaining the difference between the three levels of Pentecostal discourse. A restricted or condensed code is suitable when addressing insiders who share a set of deeply held values and taken-for-granted knowledge about a topic. When using a restricted code, a speaker can make implicit references to shared values and beliefs and use sub-cultural key terms (such as the 'world' in the Pentecostal-theological sense of the term) without having to explain their meaning. This type of code creates a sense of belonging and includedness. An elaborated code, on the other hand, is more explicit and is used when a plurality of actual or potential listeners with different backgrounds must be considered. Thus statements about values need to be made more explicitly. The first type of Pentecostal discourse is characterised by the use of an elaborated code whereas a more condensed code is applied in the second and especially the third level.

The Pentecostal Sacred Self

As explained, the analytical focus in this work mainly lies on different aspects of Pentecostal religious practice. What are constituted through such a practice are shared life worlds, meanings, and re-enchanted visions of the world as well as new social identities or fundamentally new ways of relating to oneself. Not only does conversion to Pentecostalism imply an autobiographic reconstruction, based on the understanding of oneself as a former 'worldly' sinner who has now become an enlightened, saved subject (see chapter 6). Pentecostal self-transformation also occurs through the powerful experience of divine presence and not least through the constitution and continuous nourishment of a personal and intimate relationship between the subject and the divine (see also Canales et al. 1991). In analysing these phenomena I draw on theoretical perspectives on the human self, as developed by George Herbert Mead (1962) and Csordas (1990, 1994, and 1997).

The basic premises in the work of Mead are that society is prior to the individual and that the development of the self and the ability to think are shaped by human interaction and by the experience of the social group as a whole. The self develops through social processes, where the individual (child) learns to treat itself as an object by taking the attitudes and responses of others towards him or her. It is when taking the attitudes of others becomes an essential part of behaviour that the individual appears as a self in his or her own experience (Mead 1962: 195).

The appropriation of language is crucial for the development of the self in that the child, by taking the attitude of others and seeing itself as an object, becomes able to carry out an inner conversation with itself. Mead argues that it is only through linguistic behaviour that the individual can fully become an object to him- or herself, as it is by use of language that attitudes of others are internalised and come to form subjective attitudes. Reflective thought takes the form of an internal conversation where 'one is talking to one's self as one would talk to another person' (Mead 1962: 139) and hence language is prior to thought. It follows that thought can never be entirely personal, but is always socially shaped, in that it relies on a shared language with socially defined meanings, concepts, and symbols (Mead 1962: 147).

The next phase in the development of the self begins as the child learns to organise the different attitudes of particular others as a unity. Mead calls this unified response 'the generalized other' (1962: 154). The individual must, in his or her own behaviour, respond to the general attitudes of others, not just towards other individuals but also towards different phases or aspects of the common social activity in which people are engaged as members of an organised society (Mead 1962: 154–5). It is in the form of the generalised other that the community or the social process becomes a determining factor of the individual's thinking. In thinking, the individual may take on the roles of specific others over and against him- or herself, but most of the time thinking takes the form of a conversation with the generalised other (1962: 288).

Mead distinguishes between two sides of the social self, the 'I' and the 'me'. The 'me' is the objective presence or the immediate experience of the self, shaped by the attitude of the generalised other, while the 'I' is the subjective attitude of response to and reflection upon this experience. The 'me' can also be described as the individual as an object of consciousness, while the 'I' is the individual as having consciousness. The 'I' and the 'me' are intrinsically connected, as the subjective feeling of the self only develops when the self becomes an object. Without the distance between the 'I' and the 'me', the 'I' would not be able to reflect upon itself from the perspective of the other. Mead also refers to 'I' and 'me' as different phases of the self, as the 'I' can only become an object to itself when it is self-estranged as a 'me' in the past or in an imagined future, but not in the immediacy of an ongoing situation. The inner dialogue of the self is an interaction that takes place when the 'I' reacts to the 'me' that arises through the taking of attitudes of others (Mead 1962: 174). The 'me' belongs to the organisation of the community and mirrors the general values of the group, whereas the response of the 'I' constitutes the individual adjustment to the social environment. The self is constituted out of multiple selves as the objectified 'me' is identified with a number of past actions and experiences with different others. It is the 'I' that creates a unity among different aspects of the self and activates them in different social contexts.

Drawing on the work of Irvin Hallowell (1955), Maurice Merleau-Ponty (1962), and Pierre Bourdieu (1977), Csordas (1990, 1994, and 1997) proposes a more phenomenological approach to self-processes. Hallowell defines the self as reflexive self-awareness, the recognition of oneself as an object in a world of objects. He adds that the cultural context of the self consists of a behavioural environment, which includes natural and cultural reified objects as well as supernatural beings (Csordas 1994: 6). While Csordas finds this understanding of the self helpful, he notes that it is confined to the level of the already objectified self and fails to ground self-processes in embodiment. With Merleau-Ponty, Csordas argues that the human body is not, in the first place, an object but an integral part of the perceiving subject, and that consciousness should be seen as a body projecting itself into the world. The constitution of objects, including the objectification and representation of the body, of the self, and of other humans, is a secondary product of reflective and socially conditioned thinking.

Pre-objective and pre-reflective bodily existence and experience should not be seen as purely natural. Turning to the work of Bourdieu and the concept of habitus Csordas emphasises that culture is grounded in the body and that pre-objective experience is therefore always a culturally constituted mode of being in the world (1994: 14). Bourdieu defines *habitus* as 'systems of durable transposable dispositions ... principles of the generation and structuring of practices and representations' (1977: 72) or as a mediator by which practice is generated in conformity with the objective structures (material, economic, social, and linguistic conditions of existence) that characterise a given group (ibid.: 87). Warning his readers against the 'occasionalist illusion' (ibid.: 81), Bourdieu develops the concept of habitus in order to emphasise that human practice and interaction can never be understood entirely in their own terms, but must always be seen in relation to a system of objective potentialities.

In the work of Bourdieu, the body is seen as a source of encoding memory, to which fundamental principles of culture are entrusted (ibid.: 94). He elaborates this point by introducing the concepts of hexis—referring to the embodiment of social structures, a durable manner of walking, standing, speaking, feeling, and thinking (ibid.: 93)—and 'the socially informed body', in which the five physical senses, which never escape the structuring action of social determinism, cohabit with the sense of duty, morality, necessity, direction, reality, balance, beauty, responsibility, humour, absurdity, common sense, sense of the sacred, etc. (Bourdieu 1977: 124; Csordas 1990: 10).

As they serve to explain commonalities within the pre-objective, Csordas considers Bourdieu's concepts of habitus and the socially informed body to be valuable supplements to Merleau-Ponty's phenomenology of perception. Csordas finds these concepts particularly relevant in analysing Catholic charismatic ritual practice, which is characterised by improvisation, informality, and many apparently spontaneous expressions and experiences of spiritual presence (1990, 1997). In much conventional ritual theory, spontaneity is seen as a source of 'natural' disorder, incompatible with the scriptedness, conventionality, and order characteristic of ritual (e.g. Bloch 1998; Tambiah 1979; Rappaport 1979). For Csordas the concepts of habitus and the socially informed body provide the link that enables us to reconcile ritual with spontaneity. By collapsing well-known dualisms such as mind/body and nature/culture, these concepts are useful in terms of explaining how spontaneous behaviour and pre-objective, pre-reflective bodily sensations never escape social cultural determinism (Csordas 1990: 110–12).

Finally Csordas introduces the term 'the sacred self' (1994) to indicate that the social, cultural world or behavioural environment in which Catholic charismatics orient themselves is not just constituted by human others but, in addition, by non-human divine or satanic/demonic others. Csordas defines the self as sacred 'insofar as it is oriented in the world and defines what it means to be human in terms of the wholly other than human' (1994: 24).

Mead and Csordas both conceive of the self as an ongoing and dynamic process of reflection, self-objectification and adjustment to the social cultural world. In this work I regard their approaches as supplementary. Instead of arguing for the superiority of one perspective over the other, I argue that the phenomenological and the pragmatic perspectives of the human self serve to analyse and highlight different aspects of Pentecostal experience and self-processes. Csordas's view on self-processes as grounded in embodiment is particularly relevant in analysing how dispositions for orientations towards the sacred are cultivated and exercised through the bodily and rhetorical engagement in worship (chapter 7). In the work of Mead, more emphasis is placed on the dynamic interplay between inter- and intra-subjective processes and not least on the acquisition of shared linguistic symbols for the development of the self. This perspective informs my analysis of conversion (chapter 6). I conceive of conversion as a process through which the convert, by interacting with Pentecostal others, requires new linguistic resources for self-objectification. And I argue that conversion, in part, takes place as reflective thought becomes framed as an internal conversation with God. In chapter 10 I draw on both Mead and Csordas as I focus on Pentecostal experiences and cultural identifications of the Devil as an uncanny, intruding other, imposing himself upon their thought activity.

The theoretical perspectives introduced in this chapter enable a multifaceted approach to the themes I set out to explore. By focusing attention on various aspects of linguistic, discursive, embodied, and reflective practice, I intend to portray Pentecostal spirituality, sociality, and self-identities as continuously emerging, unfolding, and negotiated rather than as fixed essences to be represented through expressive behaviour. I further hope to demonstrate that Pentecostal religious practices are shaped by and unfold through a dynamic interplay with wider social forces. In other words, I will do my best to situate creative religious micro processes within a larger structural, historical, and political context. A context-sensitive analysis will allow us to understand traditional Chilean Pentecostals as 'determined, yet determining in their own history' (Comaroff 1985: 1), as structurally positioned within a complex system of social differentiation, yet at the same time actively negotiating social identities and creating new senses of agency and power.

CHAPTER THREE

HISTORICAL BACKGROUND

Early Protestantism in Chile

During the colonial period, the hegemony of the Catholic Church in Latin American public religion was practically unchallenged by other Christian denominations (Chesnut 2003: 17–19). In Chile, as elsewhere on the continent, the church had close ties with the colonial administration, and the contact with the Anglo-Saxon world was limited. The declaration of independence from Spain in 1810 was followed by a war of liberation, and in 1818 a new Chilean republic became a reality. The Catholic Church maintained close relationships with the political elites, but church–state relationships were not totally harmonious. Intellectual creoles, inspired by the French revolution and liberal philosophical streams that followed independence and increased contact with other countries, opposed Catholic conservatism and feared that the failure to keep secular and religious powers apart would pose a threat to economic development (Sørensen 1993: 5). Chilean liberals, including the liberator and first supreme director of the nation, Bernado O'Higgins, were supportive of the introduction of Protestantism as a potential ally against superstition, ignorance, and the excessive powers of the clergy. The first Protestant missionary in Chile was the Scottish Baptist minister James Thomson who arrived in 1821, invited by O'Higgins (Sepúlveda 1999*b*: 42).

Despite liberal sympathies for Protestantism, the position of the Catholic Church was never really threatened during the nineteenth century. After internal political struggles, O'Higgins was forced into exile in 1823, with Thomson leaving the country the same year. In 1833 Catholicism became Chile's official religion (Sepúlveda 1999*b*: 26), and Protestant denominations faced several legal restrictions. Church buildings had to be surrounded by a wall, so that they could not be recognised from the street (Canales Guevara 2000: 276), and Protestants were not allowed to be buried in Catholic graveyards. Only in 1865 were Protestants granted the right to worship publicly and establish their own religious schools (Lalive d'Epinay 1968: 35).

In the 1830s and 1840s, the Protestant, mostly Anglican, missionary activity was focused on the Indian population in Southern Chile. But during the second half of the nineteenth century, an opening to the Anglo-Saxon world through trade was accompanied by new theological waves. Presbyterian and Methodist missionaries began to arrive, in some cases invited directly by liberal political elites. Unlike earlier Anglicans, these new missionaries considered Catholic Chile to be a missionary territory (Sørensen 1993: 8).

Despite liberal sympathies and the missionary effort, the influence of Protestantism on Chilean society in the nineteenth century was insignificant. The upper class as well as the popular masses remained loyal to Catholicism, and even among pupils in Protestant schools few converts were gained. A national census in 1907 showed that Protestants made up 1 per cent of the population, Catholics 98.1 per cent, people of unknown religion 0.8 per cent and non-believers 0.1 per cent (Sepúlveda 1996: 300).

The Birth of Chilean Pentecostalism

Pentecostalism was not a missionary import in Chile, but was born out of a local schism within the Methodist Episcopal Church. The single most important founding figure in history of Chilean Pentecostalism was actually a North American, the Methodist pastor Willis Collins Hoover. But he had no institutional support from other American Methodists. When he, encouraged by Chilean converts, left his church to lead the newly founded Methodist Pentecostal Church, he broke all institutional ties with American Methodists, and the Methodist Pentecostal Church became the first theologically and financially independent Pentecostal church in the third world.

The first Methodist Episcopal Church in Chile was founded in 1877, and Methodism soon turned out to have a greater appeal to lower-class Chileans than other Protestant churches. Up to 1897 the missionaries had to support themselves, and after 1897 they received a smaller salary than their colleagues in the Presbyterian Church. The poverty of the missionaries and the fact that most of them came from the lower class in the United States reduced the social distance to Chilean converts (Kessler 1967: 104).

Born in Freeport, Illinois, in 1958, Hoover grew up as a Methodist. He graduated as a doctor from a university in Chicago in 1884, but five years later he decided to join the Methodist mission in Chile with his wife Mary Anne Hilton Hoover (Hoover 1977: 115). From 1989 to 1902 he lived in Iquique in Northern Chile, serving as a teacher and later as a pastor. During a trip to the United States in 1895 he visited a 'pre-Pentecostal church' in Chicago and was greatly impressed by the 'constant state of revival' in which that church was living (Hoover 1977: 25; Sepúlveda 1999a: 114).

In 1902 Hoover was transferred to the Methodist Episcopal Church of Valparaíso, where he soon got the impression that the congregants, though well organised, had only vague ideas of the meaning of sanctification (Hollenweger 1997: 140). That same year he started to conduct a series of studies on the Acts of the Apostles for the Sunday school teachers. An important moment occurred when they were going trough Acts, chapter 2, and one participant asked: '¿Qué impide que nosotros seamos una iglesia como esta iglesia primitiva?' (what prevents us from being a church like that primitive church?) To this Hoover replied: 'No hay impedimento alguno sino el que esté en nososostros mismos' (there is no impediment except the one that lies in ourselves) (Hoover 1977: 26). According to Hoover this short exchange (which is memorised and frequently cited by members of the EPC and of other Pentecostal denominations more than a century later) was to mark the beginning of a search for sanctification and revival (ibid., see also Sepúvelda 1999b: 92).

In 1907 Mrs. Hoover received a letter from a missionary friend, Minnie Abrams, in Mukti, India, who wrote about a Christian revival, where people had been baptised by the Holy Spirit, spoken in other tongues, fallen to the floor, and had various visions. After this the Hoovers started corresponding with other churches in India, Venezuela, Norway, and the United States, which had had similar experiences. In Hoover's own words: 'se despertó en nosotros una viva hambre de poseer todo lo que Dios tenia para nosotros' (a hunger was awakened in us for possessing all that which God had stored for us) (Hoover 1977: 28).

Revivalist initiatives included all-night prayer meetings and daily prayer groups, during which typical Pentecostal spiritual manifestations occurred. Hoover describes the occurrences as follows:

> Laughing, weeping, shouting, singing, foreign tongues, visions and ecstasies during which the individual fell to the ground and felt himself caught up into another place, to heaven, to paradise, in splendid fields, with various kinds of experience: conversations with God, the angels or the Devil. (Hoover 1977: 41, English translation by Sepúlveda 1999a: 116)

Congregants also started to make incursions into streets and public squares, screaming, 'Alleluia, glory to God', and narrating their

personal testimonies. These incursions and the rather noisy church
meetings made the police intervene (Hoover 1977: 53), and Hoover
had to agree to finish all services no later than 10.00 p.m. (Sepúlveda
1999a: 116). In the national newspapers *El Chileno* and *El Mercurio* the
revival was described as the work of a madman (Lalive d'Epinay 1968:
39; Hollenweger 1997: 143).

Other Methodist pastors disapproved of the revival, fearing it might
be the work of the Devil, and they accused Hoover of practicing hyp-
notism (Hoover 1977: 41). One new convert, Nellie Laidlaw became a
source of considerable controversy. She had originally come to Chile to
work as a maid in the home of the English consul, but according to the
German theologian Walther Hollenweger (1997: 142) it is likely that
she later became an alcoholic and supported herself through prostitu-
tion. After her conversion Hoover was convinced that the Holy Spirit
used this woman in magnificent ways (Hoover 1977: 142). On 12
September 1909 she attended a Sunday morning worship service of a
Methodist Church in Santiago. Though she was carrying a letter of rec-
ommendation from Hoover, the pastor in Santiago did not allow her to
address the congregation. Instead she went outside to speak and was
followed by a number of curious congregants. The pastor was infuri-
ated, and as the incident was followed by a similar one in another
Methodist church in Santiago on the same afternoon, some congregants
in favour of revivalism decided to start holding services in private
homes. In December 1909 Methodist authorities reacted by cutting all
official relations with people who had withdrawn and held private
meetings, and the superintendent declared that spiritual hysteria was a
sign of blasphemy (Hoover 1977: 43).

In February 1910 the revivalist groups from Santiago decided to
found their separate church, *Iglesia Metodista Nacional* (National
Methodist Church) and encouraged Hoover to be their leader. In April
2010 Hoover finally resigned and was followed by four hundred
congregants from Valparaíso, approximately two-thirds of the congregation. He agreed to be the superintendent of the new churches in
Santiago as well but suggested that the name should be changed to
Iglesia Metodista Pentecostal (Methodist Pentecostal Church).
'Methodist' was preserved in the name of the new church, as Hoover
insisted that he was faithfully following the doctrines of John Wesley.[1]

---

[1] Unlike North American Pentecostalism, Chilean Pentecostalism was born
directly out of Methodism and was not mediated by the nineteenth-century Holiness

'Pentecostal' was added to emphasise the belief in the manifestations of the Holy Spirit as they occurred on the day of Pentecost (Hoover 1977: 82).[2] Finally Hoover insisted on erasing the word 'national' in order to stress that the division was not motivated by nationalist sentiments (ibid.: 66; Sepúlveda 1999*b*: 103).

Early historical Protestant churches were clearly foreign imports and only managed to attract very few Chilean converts. With the birth of Pentecostalism in the early twentieth century it makes sense to speak of a Chilenisation of Protestantism. Whereas early Protestantism found sympathy among intellectual liberal elites, Pentecostalism was from the beginning the religion of the *bajo pueblo* (the low or humble people), a common designation for the lower classes in Chile around the turn of the century (Sepúlveda 1996: 314).

The Consolidation and Growth of Pentecostalism: 1910–73

The first twenty years after the birth of Chilean Pentecostalism were a period of organisation and consolidation (see Luis Orellana 2008). In 1929 the Methodist Pentecostal Church counted a total of twenty-two organised churches in Chile, and in addition new denominations were founded after schisms in the 1920s. But according to a national census Protestants only made up 1.4 per cent of the Chilean population in 1930 (Sepúlveda 1996: 317). Many new converts belonged to the absolute margins of Chilean society. Thus it is told that the municipal authorities once sent Hoover a New Year's card with the photographs of twenty-four ex-delinquents, saying that they were convinced that these photographs now belonged to his Hoover's files and not theirs (Kessler 1967: 292).

In the 1930s Chile had become an urban and industrialised nation after three decades of internal migration. The development of the present class structure of Chilean society can also be traced back to the 1920s and 1930s. At the beginning of the twentieth century the main social division in the country was between the upper and the lower class (separated by an enormous gap). But with industrialisation and the rise of the liberal state a significant urban industrial class and a

---

movement. Some Methodist doctrines such as infant baptism still prevail in two biggest denominations in Chile, the Methodist Pentecostal Church and the EPC.

[2] See the New Testament, Acts of the Apostles, chapter 2.

large, though heterogeneous, modernising middle class emerged. The latter was born from the bureaucratic and administrative necessities of industrialisation and became important as taxpayers and consumers and as the main rulers of the permanent apparatus of the state and the party system (Sørensen 1993: 8; Martínez & Díaz 1996: 6–8). Industrialisation did not take place with the same speed as urbanisation, and many marginal migrants who did not find formal employment worked as street vendors, domestic servants, or casual labourers (Martínez & Díaz 1996: 6–8).

In principle, a wide range of organisational options such as labour unions, political parties, and Catholic organisations were available for Chileans who were affected by social transformations. But the Catholic Church was understaffed and oriented towards the middle and upper classes (Smith 1982). The Liberal and Conservative parties were expressions of different factions of the upper classes, whereas the Radical Party and *Falange* (later to become the Christian Democratic Party) gained ground among the growing middle class. Finally the Communist and Socialist parties were expressions of the skilled proletariat of the industrial sector to which labour unions were also restricted (Sepúlveda 1996: 309). According to Sepúlveda, the *bajo pueblo* was mainly left to 'watch the processes of democratisation and modernisation of Chilean society from the sidelines' (1996: 310). In this context of wide-reaching societal transformations, Pentecostalism started growing, especially after 1940. In 1960 Protestants made up 5.6 per cent of the Chilean population (Sepúlveda 1996: 317). Most Pentecostal converts came from the marginal sectors of Chilean society and did not belong to the skilled proletarian working class.

The growth can in part be ascribed to the greater variety of Pentecostal supply on Chile's religious market. In 1934 a major schism occurred within the Methodist Pentecostal Church. A nationalist group within the church, that included the pastor Manuel Umaña from Santiago, wished to get rid of the last remnants of the missionary movement and offered Hoover an early retirement, which he refused. Other sources of conflict and tension within the church included Hoover's refusal to allow for the use of musical instruments during services, which grew from his uncompromising puritanism. His insistence that no congregant should practice sport or go the cinema made him unpopular among younger congregants (Mario Hoover 2002: 237). As Hoover refused to retire, he was expelled. He was followed by a number of congregations and founded the Evangelical Pentecostal Church of which he stayed in charge until his death in 1936. The schism was not a rebellion of a marginal group within the Methodist Pentecostal Church, but a division in two almost equally sized fractions (Lalive d'Epinay 1968: 123). To this day members of the EPC still consider themselves the legitimate heirs of Hoover and the first Pentecostal revival in Chile.

After the schism both churches have proliferated several times, but they remain the two largest Pentecostal denominations in the country. In 1962 the EPC counted six offshoots and the Methodist Pentecostal Church, eighteen (Willems 1967: 112). Between 1930 and 1960 foreign Pentecostal missionaries also arrived in Chile and started founding new churches such as the Assemblies of God from the United States and the Autonomous Assemblies of God from Sweden (Sepúlveda 1999*b*: 111).

The first significant studies of Pentecostalism in Chile and Latin America were the books *El refugio de las masas: Estudio sociológico del protestantismo chileno*, by Lalive d'Epinay (1968),[3] and *Followers of the New Faith: Culture Change and the Rise of Protestantism in Brazil and Chile* by Willems (1967). Both books are based on research conducted in Chile around 1960, and both authors relate the growth of Pentecostalism to migration and urbanisation. For marginal first-generation migrants, many of whom were unskilled domestic workers, porters, watchmen, small self-employed artisans, or journeymen making a living in the informal sector, Pentecostal churches offered new and intimate communities as well as new senses of dignity and spiritual authority (Lalive d'Epinay 1968: 81, 167). Lalive d'Epinay does, however, add that Pentecostalism was not a strictly urban movement. While born in the suburbs of the big cities of Valparaíso, Santiago, and Concepción, Pentecostalism was soon extended into rural areas of southern Chile, especially in the province of Cautín (1968: 69).

Lalive d'Epinay and Willems further share a view on Pentecostalism as being at variance with secular and Catholic hierarchies of Chilean society, in that otherwise marginal people could occupy leader positions within Pentecostal churches (Lalive d'Epinay 1968: 167; Willems 1967: 6, 107). However, the two authors had divergent views on the potential contributions of Pentecostalism to processes of social and

---

[3] An English version of this book, *Haven of the Masses: A Study of the Pentecostal Movement in Chile*, was published in 1969 by Lutterworth Press in London.

political change. Lalive d'Epinay conceived of Pentecostalism as a social strike, arguing that church communities, by virtue of being introverted, apolitical, authoritarian, and spiritually focused, did little to change the political status quo (1968: 170). Willems not only emphasised the functionality of Pentecostal ascetics and personal discipline (for example, abstinence from alcohol, tobacco, and gambling; honesty; decency; responsibility; trustworthiness; and rational spending) for poor urban migrants, trying to make a living on an insecure working market. He further predicted that organisational and rhetorical skills, acquired in Pentecostal communities, might prepare people for future democratic participation (1967: 91–3). As will be shown in the conclusion of this book, this debate has been revived in the 1990s.

In the 1960s Pentecostalism grew at a slower pace than the previous two decades, the total percentage of Protestants in Chile reaching 6.18 in 1970. This decade was characterised by new social dynamics and the integration of hitherto excluded sectors. After the 1964 elections the Christian Democratic Party (founded in 1957) took power. The new government tried to integrate existing grass root movements within the state and encouraged popular mobilisation in labour unions, centers of women, neighbourhood associations, and not least organisations working to provide housing and basic services in poor areas.

The Catholic Church was not a mere spectator to these processes. Following the second Vatican Council from 1962–5, the Vatican started placing more emphasis on human rights, social inequality, and the rights of workers to unite in labour unions. The principles of the Vatican Council were officially adopted into a Latin American context at a 1968 conference in Medelin, Colombia, in which 150 South American bishops expressed a commitment to defend the rights of the poor and oppressed and to instil a Christian conscience in matters of social responsibilities (Smith 1982: 284; Riobó Pioza 2010: 40). In Chile new priests and nuns from Europe and North America arrived in the 1960s to assist the understaffed church in urban and rural working-class areas, where new parishes and social clubs were constituted. The political alliances of the church shifted from the right (the Conservative Party) to the centre (the Christian Democratic Party), and with international financial support the church also became more actively involved in social movements such as labour unions and projects such as new educational and technical training programs for peasants (Smith 1982: 289). It was also during the 1960s that the first Catholic Base Communities were founded in urban lower-class areas. In these communities, weekly meetings were held, with lay people reading and interpreting the Bible in the light of current political circumstances. Though Chilean bishops wished the base communities to be more spiritually than politically oriented, it was mainly through these communities that Catholic lay people were introduced to the Marxist-inspired liberation theology that sees sin in structural and political as well as individual terms and interprets the gospel as a guideline for a struggle for social justice (Riobó Pioza 2010: 40). Through such initiatives and activities the Catholic Church managed to strengthen its bonds with different sectors of society, though it was never able to truly escape its image of a middle- and upper-class institution.

The Pentecostal response to these political developments and the increased competition from other, religious and secular, organisations was diverse. A minority of Pentecostal lay people became engaged in social projects and secular organisations, especially in the rural areas. As the first Pentecostal churches in the world to do so, the Pentecostal Church of Chile (founded in 1946 after a schism in the Methodist Pentecostal Church) and Mission Pentecostal Church (founded in 1952 by ex-members of the EPC) joined the World Council of churches in 1961. Leaders and lay members from both of these churches tried to reconcile Pentecostal faith with active participation in social programmes. But the majority of Pentecostal churches strengthened their traditional position and made a virtue out of not being involved with the 'world'. The EPC strongly discouraged its members from participating in any kinds of social organisational activities outside the church and tried to demonise politics. A protective strategy adopted by many Pentecostal churches in the 1960s was to increase the level of church activities, holding meetings every night so that members would have little free time to engage in other activities (Sepúlveda 1996: 311).

There are no national surveys on religious affiliation during the *Unidad Popular* government, led by President Salvador Allende (1970–3). But Lagos Schuffeneger (1988: 288) refers to a survey from Santiago showing that the percentage of Evangelicals in the city rose from 5.5 to 8 between 1970 and 1973. It should be noted that other scholars, while familiar with the work of Lagos Schuffeneger, hold the conviction that the growth of Pentecostalism during Allende was insignificant (for example, Sepúlveda 1996; Kamsteeg 1998). The political unrest, the increased polarisation of Chilean society, and the fear of political chaos that characterised this period (see Smith 1982; Loveman 2001) may have made membership in apolitical, spiritually oriented Pentecostal churches an attractive option to some Chileans.[4] Research from Santiago in the early 1970s, conducted by the Dutch anthropologist Johannes Tennekes, showed that Pentecostals were less involved in secular social organisations and less interested in politics than other Chileans. In a survey he made in 1971, 82 per cent of Pentecostal respondents considered it inappropriate for an Evangelical to be involved in politics, and 94 per cent believed that Pentecostal churches should not concern themselves with political and social problems (Fediakova 2002: 34). Tennekes further found that Pentecostals were regarded as distinctly odd by their neighbours and that participating in community life was not an option, as it would mean slipping into 'worldly' ways (David Martin 1990: 239). Another survey showed that more Protestants than Catholics and religiously non-affiliated persons refused or were unable to place themselves on a left–right scale (Steigenga & Coleman 1995: 475). Other studies from Santiago indicated that the Protestant population was not particularly unhappy with the government and that they mostly voted according to class interests, though negative attitudes towards Catholicism may also have prevented many from voting for the Christian Democratic Party. The support for Allende was, however, much stronger among Pentecostal lay people than among the pastors (Cleary and Sepúlveda 1997: 104), a fact that may be ascribed to the latter's fear of atheist Marxism (David Martin 1995a: 222).

Military Rule 1973–89

The violent coup d'état on 11 September 1973 turned out to be much more than the end of more than forty years of peaceful democratic tradition in Chile. Much to the surprise of observers who expected a quick return to democracy once peace and order had been restored, the military regime led by General Augusto Pinochet stayed in power for a period seventeen years, during which it radically shook the foundations of society. Apart from torture, systematic persecution, and harassment of political opponents, many of whom were killed or forced

---

[4] This is, admittedly, a highly speculative interpretation of Pentecostal growth during Allende's tenure. I have found no ethnographic or sociological studies shedding light on ordinary people's motives for conversion and continued church membership in this period.

into exile, the most significant achievements of the regime was a depoliticisation of Chilean society and a fundamental reorganisation of the economy along neoliberal lines.

The architects behind the economic reforms in Chile were the so-called 'Chicago boys', a group of national economists who had studied under the influential economist and public neoliberal intellectual Milton Friedman at the University of Chicago. Many of these economists took posts as professors at the Catholic University in Santiago in the 1960s and early 1970s (Klein 2007: 62). In this period they were marginal in national politics and did not even register on the electoral spectrum by the 1970 elections (ibid.: 63). But in the early 1970s a dialogue between the military—plotting to exterminate the Allende government—and the Chicago boys was opened. The latter produced a detailed liberal economic programme to be implanted once Allende was overthrown (ibid.: 71).

The Chicago boys identified state interventionism and protectionism as main obstacles to economic growth. As an alternative the regime implemented new free-market policies, characterised by a removal of trade barriers, encouragement of entrepreneurial culture, the privatisation of almost five hundred state-owned companies and banks, and not least by significant cuts in public spending. Furthermore, the regime introduced the so-called seven modernisations, which included the introduction of free-market principles into the areas of labour, social security, agriculture, education, health, public administration, and the judicial system (Loveman 2001: 265).

At some levels the new policy was a success, with falling inflation and an impressive GDP growth rate (Fleet & Smith 1997: 65). But privatisation and the reduction of the public sector also resulted in thousands of Chileans being thrown out of work and in a significant reduction of real wages. In an attempt to deal with the worst effects of the crisis the regime established emergency work programmes, hiring the unemployed to maintain public infrastructure and paying them one quarter of the already low minimum wage (Paley 2001: 76). But this solution was insufficient, and as a consequence of increased poverty and unemployment, the informal sector expanded. It is estimated that wage employment fell from 65.7 per cent to 48.2 per cent of all labour between 1973 and 1982 (Martínez & Díaz 1996: 108). At the same time an increasing number of women entered the labour market or became engaged in informal income-generating activities, such as domestic service (Paley 2001: 64).

As noted by Judith Paley, the dismantling of the Chilean welfare state 'would have been impossible without demobilisation of the massive social movements making demands for public services throughout the country' (2001: 65). Ironically it was only by actively repressing political citizenry that the regime was able to reorganise the economy along non-interventionist lines. Political parties were outlawed in the 1970s, and the power of negotiation of labour was reduced (Winn 2004). Besides these changes, leadership of important institutions was assigned to people with a military rank (Kristensen 2008: 83). Apart from restricting possibilities of collective negotiation, the regime implemented new labour laws that clearly favoured the employers at the expense of wage earners by allowing high flexibility in the use of labour force, such as the employment of workers without legal contracts or with short-term low or no-benefit contracts (Martínez & Díaz 1996: 113–14; Lavigna 2002: 1).

The privatisation of social security was effectuated in 1979–80. One aim of the privatisation policy was to introduce economic incentives to undermine the capacities of collective action of the Chilean working class (Kristensen 2008: 82, 92). The role of the state in public health was reduced, as the Chilean health system became divided into a public and private system. The latter, which provided superior services, was, and is, mainly covered by private health insurances (ibid.: 92–3). A new university law from 1981 paved the way for the foundation of a number of private universities and professional institutes. Also, the regime cut the economic funding of public universities, which consequently became increasingly dependant upon student fees. Measures were also taken to limit political activism and organisation in the universities. In the 1970s employees with leftist sympathies were fired and in some cases killed or forced into exile, and the institutional independence of state universities was replaced by strict supervision (Rita Cancino n.d.).

The policies of the regime provided favourable and stable conditions for private enterprises and foreign investors. Construction boomed, and with the removal of trade barriers, foreign import goods such as Japanese television sets and radios, Korean cars, French perfumes, and Scotch whisky started arriving on a massive scale. Shopping malls and large supermarkets were constructed, and in 1979 Chile's first credit card (Diners Club de Chile) was introduced. The widespread credit system of payment contributed to a boom in consumerism, and even a yuppie culture abounded in the 1980s. For many Chileans this was a period of optimism and faith in modernisation (Collier & Sater 1996: 374–5).

In the influential book *Chile: La Revolución Silenciosa* (Chile: The Silent Revolution) published in 1987, the neoliberal intellectual Joaquín Lavín who served as a financial advisor for Pinochet and later bid for presidency in 1999 and 2005 praised the neoliberal model and in particular the privatisation and merchandisation of education and health. According to Lavín the policy of the regime had resulted in technological progress, efficiency, and a greater variety of goods and services. Because of these developments Chileans had become active and demanding consumers, exercising a freedom of choice, rather than passive citizens (see Christoffani n.d).

The painfully obvious objection against the views of Lavín is that the freedom of choice that he celebrates is confined to those who have sufficient economic means to buy products and essential services. The other part of the story of what is sometimes referred to as the Chilean miracle is one of reduction of social services and social security, the weakening of social movements and unionised labour, the predominance of flexible labour schemes, and not least of increase in poverty and social insecurity, and in gaps between rich and poor (Lavigna 2002). In the 1980s the unemployment rate fell and reached less than 6 per cent in 1990 (Martínez & Díaz 1996: 49), though a survey from Santiago in 1989 showed an unemployment rate at 16.6 per cent (Ossa 1991: 44). But by 1990 average and minimum wages were still lower than in 1981 and much lower than in 1970. Between 1978 and 1988 the official number of extremely poor rose from 12 to 15 per cent and the numbers of officially poor families rose from 24 to 26. At the other end of the scale the richest 10 per cent controlled 35 per cent of national income in 1978 compared to 42 per cent in 1988 (Martínez & Díaz 1996: 124). Studies have also shown that between 20 and 40 per cent of the working population were engaged in informal occupations in the late 1980s (Collier & Sater 1996: 374), and that between 17 and 30 per cent of the waged labour force had no contract in 1990 (Martínez & Díaz 1996: 127). During Pinochet, poverty and social insecurity were no longer expressed through unemployment and marginality alone but also reproduced in new ways among workers (ibid.: 129).

The Military Regime and the Churches

Due to the chaotic conditions and the increasing fear of a civil war during the last months of Allende's government, the immediate reactions of the Catholic Church to the coup were positive, but also characterised by a clear expectation in a quick return to democracy. Nevertheless the ecumenical organisation, the Committee for Peace in Chile (COPACHI), was founded less than a month after the coup by the Catholic vice-bishop Fernando Aritzía and the Lutheran bishop Helmuth Frenz as leaders. The committee, which was also supported by Baptists, Methodists, Greek orthodox churches, the Jewish society, and even a few Pentecostal churches, worked by providing legal and economic help to the victims of the regime.

As the regime's consistent violation of human rights became too evident to ignore, the tone of the Catholic Church changed, and in April 1974 bishops openly, albeit cautiously, voiced their criticism. But during the 1970s, it became painfully clear that Pinochet had no intentions of restoring democracy in any foreseeable future, and the critique from both bishops and priests escalated. Apart from human rights violations the church authorities also criticised the effects of the regime's neo-liberal policies such as increased poverty and restrictions on collective negotiations. The church also played an important role by providing the only free space for political mobilisation and participation in a society where parties had been outlawed and labour unions restricted (Stewart-Gambino 1992: 25; Winn 2004).

The relationship between the regime and the Catholic Church became tense during the 1970s. In 1975 COPACHI came under hard pressure from the regime when it was known that priests and nuns had helped communists get asylum in foreign embassies. When Helmuth Frenz travelled to Germany to raise money he was informed that he would not be allowed to return to Chile. COPACHI was dissolved and replaced by the organisation *Vicaría de Solidaridad*, which carried out the same work but was more closely connected with the Catholic Church. A number of foreign priests with leftist sympathies, many of whom worked in poor areas, were expelled from Chile in the 1970s (Smith 1982: 332).

A civil religious discourse was invoked by the regime to legitimise its politics. On several occasions Pinochet presented himself as an instrument of God in the struggle against Marxist-atheism and materialism (Lagos Schuffeneger 2001; Cristi & Dawson 1996; Sjørup 2008). Jesus Christ, who preached forgiveness and love for one's enemies, was unsuitable as a religious symbol for the military. Instead the virgin of Carmen, who was the official *patrona* of the armed forces, was presented as Pinochet's personal protector. But the reluctance of the Catholic Church authorities to play along was strikingly evident.

Only unofficial sectors within the church and individual priests supported the regime. The lack of official support from the Catholic Church inspired Pinochet to search for religious-ideological legitimisation elsewhere, and a new scene was soon set for an alliance between the regime and Evangelical leaders.

In some Pentecostal churches the coup was seen as the answer to prayers for peace and order. Some pastors from the Methodist Pentecostal church had even received revelations that Pinochet would convert to Pentecostalism (Sjørup 1995: 22). In 1974 leaders of this church invited Pinochet and other government members to the inauguration of the newly finished Jotabeche Cathedral in Santiago on 15 December. Pinochet responded that he would accept the invitation if given a sufficiently good reason (Lagos Schuffeneger 1988: 191). On 13 December a declaration of support to the regime, signed by thirty-two Evangelical leaders, was published in the national newspaper *El Mercurio*, describing the coup as a response from God to all the believers who considered Marxism to be the most powerful expression of evil. The United Nations that had accused the regime of violating human rights was described an instrument of the atheistic Marxism (Deiros 1991: 141–3).

In July 1975 the Council of Pastors (*El Consejo de Pastores*) was founded by leaders of the Methodist Pentecostal Church and other Evangelical churches, aspiring to challenge the position of the Catholic Church as Chile's only religious institution with close ties to political elites. On 14 September 1975 the council organised the first evangelical *Te Deum* service in the Jotabeche Cathedral in Santiago with the assistance of Pinochet and other government officials. The *Te Deum* had so far been a Catholic thanksgiving service in memory of the declaration of independence (18 September 1810). New governments were usually welcomed by the Catholic Church at the *Te Deum*, but the military regime had been given no such recognition. The Evangelical *Te Deum* in 1975 mainly took the form of a celebration of the coup. Since then Evangelical *Te Deums* have been held almost every year and with the participation of Pinochet until 1989. His absence from Evangelical *Te Deums* after he resigned as the head of state indicates that he was only interested in dealing with Evangelicals as long as he needed them for religious legitimisation (Lagos Schuffeneger 2001: 40). The Catholic Church continued organising *Te Deums* with the participation of Pinochet and other representatives of the state. But the rhetoric was less celebratory, and the archbishop often took the opportunity to assert basic human rights in the sermon (David Martin 1995*a*: 222). Despite the alliance with the Council of Pastors, the regime was careful not to alienate itself too much from the Catholic Church, and several promises of economic support and changed legal status for Evangelical churches were not fulfilled (Sepúlveda 1996: 113). The regime did, however, grant Chile's Evangelicals a few privileges. Pastors from the churches that formed part of the council were given the right to free medical care. In 1983 a decree of the Ministry of Education was passed, allowing for the teaching of Evangelical religion in public schools on the condition that a minimum of twenty pupils would attend the classes. Until then, only Catholic religion had been taught in public schools.

Through the alliance between the Council of Pastors and the regime, Pentecostalism gained a hitherto unknown status as a more official religion in Chile. But the relation between the council and the regime mainly consisted of an exchange of moral–ideological support for more official recognition. Pentecostal churches did not become political actors in the same way as the Catholic Church. Whereas Catholic authorities played an important conciliatory role in the transition to democracy in the late 1980s (Fleet and Smith 1997), Pentecostal leaders did not partake in this process. Unlike the Catholic base communities, which became highly politicized during Pinochet, Pentecostal churches did not provide free spaces for political participation during Pinochet, and lay Pentecostals from the churches that joined the council were not encouraged to become politically active. On a few occasions representatives of the regime praised Pentecostals, Jehovah's Witnesses, and Mormons, describing them as 'true Christians who stayed clear of politics' (Fleet & Smith 1997: 177).

As was the case in the 1960s the Pentecostal response to the political situation was not unified. The Council of Pastors tried to present itself as an official representative of Chile's Evangelical population, but the EPC maintained an apolitical stance and never joined any ecumenical organisation, and neither did church leaders express any political commitment in public. I was told by some of the older members of the EPC in Valparaíso that most lay people and church authorities were in favour of the regime and even regarded the coup as an answer to their prayers.

In 1982 the organisation *Confraternidad Cristiana de Iglesias* (CCI) was founded by leaders of Pentecostal and other Protestant denominations that were critical of the regime. According to the Dutch anthropologist Franz Kamsteeg (1998: 91), the decisions of religious leaders to join ecumenical organisations did not necessarily reflect the views of lay people, who were rarely consulted about the projects of the CCI. The Mission Pentecostal Church, whose leaders were active in the CCI and in the Evangelical NGO, SEPADE, experienced declining membership during Pinochet. Not only did individual members leave to join other churches, but entire congregations separated themselves from the mother church because of the fear of government reprisals.

Pentecostalism grew during Pinochet and most prominently among the lower socioeconomic sectors of Chilean society. According to a 1992 national survey 13.2 per cent of the population defined themselves as Evangelicals (Sepúlveda 1996: 317). A study from Santiago in 1990 showed that 26.1 per cent of citizens from the poorest sector were Evangelicals and that only 13.54 per cent of the Evangelicals had any education beyond primary school, compared to 31.97 per cent of the Catholics (Ossa 1991: 144).

A possible explanation of the growth of Pentecostalism in this period lies in the weakening of civil society and in increased social insecurity. The regime was successful in eliminating or marginalizing social organisations that represented the popular sectors such as political parties, unions, neighbourhood associations, and indigenous organisations (Portales 2000). In the 1960s the social mobilisation and political integration of the popular sectors meant that Pentecostal churches met new competition (Sepúlveda 1999b: 135). The authoritarian system where popular social, political participation was discouraged and restricted turned out to be more nurturing for the growth of Pentecostal churches that mainly define politics as a 'worldly' matter in which believers should not get involved. Studies from 1991, shortly after the transition to democracy, showed that the Evangelical population had less interest in politics and were less willing or able to place themselves on a left–right scale than Catholics and non-affiliated people. When asked why they would not place themselves on the spectrum, a higher number of Evangelicals than Catholics and non-affiliated answered that they were apolitical or that they did not like politics. Of the Evangelical respondents, 62.2 per cent claimed to have no interest in politics, compared to 40.8 per cent of the Catholics and 25.3 per cent of the non-affiliated (Steigenga & Coleman 1995: 475–7).

These numbers could be taken as proof of the depoliticizing effects of Pentecostal church membership. And they can be seen as indications that Pentecostalism mainly appealed to people from the lower social sectors who *already* felt alienated from political life before converting. The Protestants in the two surveys were similar to Catholics in terms of age and gender distribution, but less well-educated and housed (ibid.: 471). Another study, referred to by Ossa (1991: 164) showed that almost 70 per cent of the poorest sectors in Santiago (to which a majority of Pentecostals belong) believed that *los politicos terminan por arreglarse entre ellos* (at the end of the day the politicians make arrangements for themselves). The limited interest that Evangelicals showed in politics in the 1991 survey should probably be ascribed as much to their socioeconomic position as much as to religious socialisation.

As mentioned, the economic policies of the regime resulted in increased poverty, social inequality, and an expansion of the informal economic sector, to which many Pentecostals belong. For marginal groups that did not experience macro-economic growth as personal success stories and for whom the state and secular organisations did not provide much social security, religious movements that defined themselves in opposition to the 'world' were likely to have a certain appeal. The few ethnographic/sociological studies that shed some light on the motives of poor Chileans for conversion and active membership of Pentecostal churches during Pinochet do not tell us much about how lay Pentecostals felt about the regime. The appeal of Pentecostalism in this period is mostly explained in terms of frustrations with the health system (Slootweg 1991),[5] social insecurity, increasing individualism, lack of class solidarity, perceived failures to live up to dominating norms of popular culture, and the search for communities, dignity, and meaning (Canales et. al 1991; Ossa 1991; Reyes 1986).

During military rule Pentecostal leaders were divided between those who actively supported the regime, those who were openly critical, and those who maintained an apolitical stance. Among Pentecostal lay people, the political involvement, either for or against the regime, was limited (see Sjørup 2008: 211). For a number of lower-class Chileans, Pentecostal churches offered new networks, new strategies of survival, and alternative religious narratives in a society that was characterised by social insecurity, inequality, and political demobilisation of the masses.

---

[5] In many cases conversion to Pentecostalism follows healing by prayer.

1990–2008

On 30 June 2002 the Canadian photographer Spencer Tunick, who is known for his photos of big groups of nude people in different parts of the world, visited Chile, with the purpose of photographing nude Chileans in central Santiago at 7 a.m. More than four thousand persons showed up and got undressed, though temperatures were below zero degrees and Brazil and Germany were playing the World Cup final in Japan at the same time. Soon an atmosphere of collective euphoria arose among the nude crowd, and they began running, screaming, and laughing in the streets of Santiago. Pictures and recordings from the happening show a spontaneous and cheerful chaos,[6] quite different from the neat organisation of nude bodies that Tunick has photographed elsewhere in the world.

Interpretations of the event were plenty. Some commentators pointed to a need to rebel against a Catholic culture that oppresses sexuality. Others related the event to a more general rupture with a moral conservative order in Chilean society, especially since 2000 (Tironi 2005: 214). This rupture is also reflected in new gender roles, an increasing number of unmarried couples living together, more nudity and eroticism in the mass media, new reality shows, an increasing acceptance of homosexuality, etc. Others remarked that nudity could momentarily suspend the social differences that are expressed through clothing. A few days after the event, the weekly magazine *Qué Pasa* was released with a picture of some of the nude participants on the front page under the headline 'Portrait of the New Chile'. The magazine included an interview with the Chilean sociologist Eugino Tironi, who related the event to a need for intense communal experiences in a society that has become characterised by increasing individualism and declining faith in social organisations.

The event also clearly testified to the presence of different social and cultural forces in contemporary Chilean society. A number Pentecostals showed up at *Parque Forestal* to protest against what they considered to be an extremely immoral happening. Others such as the members of the EPC in Valparaíso stayed home and prayed for the moral condition of the country. Some even speculated whether the Devil had prevented

---

[6] See 'Spencer Tunick en Chile', *YouTube* <http://www.youtube.com/watch?v=Xwa2kO4GHcQ>

the nude sinners from freezing by covering them with an invisible layer
of warmth.

The remaining part of this chapter sheds light on political, economic,
and cultural processes in post-dictatorship Chile. Since the period covered overlaps with the time of my own fieldwork, conducted between
1999 and 2009, these last sections also present the overall context for
the subsequent empirical chapters.

While the return to democracy in 1990 was, obviously, an important
turning point in Chile's political history, numerous Chilean and
Western scholars have argued that the transition did not mark a radical
break with the policies of the military regime (Moulián 2002; Portales
2000; Larraín 2001; Paley 2001, 2004; Winn 2004). The latter managed
to set profound footprints on the transition, resulting in wide-reaching
institutional continuity. The conditions of a so-called protected democracy under military tutelage had been defined in a 1980 constitution,
which among other things removed the armed forces from civilian
control and submitted future elected governments to a military-
dominated National Security Council (Winn 2004: 30). As the head of
the armed forces, Pinochet continued to be a powerful public figure,
and between 1989 and 1993 he made several threatening declarations
against the new democracy, warning against the legal persecution of
any of his men. The political right, represented by the parties *Renovacion
Nacional* and *Unión Demócrata Independiente*, has presented resistance
to a full democratisation of the government, for example, by defending
a system of designated senators, a system that was only eliminated in
2005. Until then nine out of forty-five senators were appointed rather
than elected, and according to the 1980 constitution all ex-presidents
were entitled to become designated senators. When Pinochet retired as
head of the army in 1998, he took his place in the senate despite public
controversy (Haas 1999: 65). Also, a binominal electoral system has
given the rightist minority an over-representation in the congress.
Throughout the 1990s these factors impeded a constructive public
debate about the military past and the violations of human rights (see
Portales 2000; Lira 2006; Moulián 2002).

The five democratically elected governments[7] have carried on with
the neoliberal economic policy of the regime while at the same time

---

[7] That is, the governments of Patricio Aylwin (Christian Democratic Party) 1990–
94, Eduardo Frei (Christian Democratic Party) 1994–2000, Ricardo Lagos (Socialist
Party) 2000–2006, Michelle Bachelet (Socialist Party) 2006–10, and the right wing government of Sebastián Piñera (*Renovación Nacional*) that took power in 2010.

increasing social expenses. By 1990 the neoliberal model was so profoundly implemented that a return to state interventionism and protectionism never really became a topic of political debate. The democratic governments have been successful in securing macro-economic growth, reducing poverty, and in enabling educational mobility and a continued boom in construction and consumerism. On the other hand, social inequality and segregation were reinforced in the 1990s, and social insecurity persists. The Chilean neoliberal economy is dependant for its competitiveness in part on low wages and laws that favour the employer at the expense of the wage earners, who often have to put up with insecure working conditions. These include arbitrary firings, employment without a contract, contracts with few or no benefits, impediments on collective negotiations and the marginalisation of unions from political decision making. Besides working under such conditions, a substantial part of the work force is engaged in the service sector and/or the informal sector where social security is low (Loveman 2001: 337; Tokman 2001: 19).

As mentioned, the regime privatised the health system and the educational system, and the democratic governments have done little to reverse this process. The entrance of the middle class into the private health systems and private schools was consolidated during the 1990s. According to the Chilean historian Felipe Portales, social insecurity and fear for the future are dominant features in the lives of many Chileans. Unemployment, unforeseen expenses, illness in a system with low social security, or retirement with a minimal pension are some of the risks with which many Chileans have to live (2000: 455). And with the far-reaching privatisation of social security, such risks continue to be individual concerns (Tironi 2005: 176).

The implementation of democracy did not result in a return to previous social dynamics and political integration. The protected democracy is based on the assumption that democracy must be limited in order to avoid the political polarisation and totalitarianism of the 1960s and early 1970s (Pilmark n.d.), and the democratically elected governments have done very little to encourage social political mobilisation in the popular sectors. Organisations that could contribute to a strengthening of Chilean civil society such as workers' unions, health groups, student associations, womens' groups, indigenous organisations, and neighbourhood associations have very little influence in political life and do not present any real challenge to the neoliberal model (Portales 2001: 401). According to Paley, the democratically elected governments have tried to convince the population that living in a democracy implies lowered expectations in the abilities of the state and that too much popular pressure on the state will undermine democracy and might provoke a return to dictatorship (2004: 505–6).

Consumerism continued to boom after the transition to democracy, and the Chilean mass media has contributed to the emergence of a popular culture where status is constituted and communicated through the consumption of prestige goods. Modern technology (cell phones, computers, television) has become more accessible to Chileans, but at the same time the widespread credit card system of payment has resulted in the indebtedness of a growing number of people, especially from the lower social strata. Critical voices have pointed out that such a pattern of consumption and debt is functional for a neoliberal political model, as it tends to foster individualism and conformism rather than associative notions of progress (Moulián 2002: 92; Portales 2000: 447; Larraín 2005: 53; Oviedo 2009: 80).

Surveys on popular perceptions of and confidence in democracy and political institutions and actors are produced in abundance in Chile, making life a little easier for a social scientist. A study from 1994 showed a decreasing popular confidence in political parties and the congress since 1991. Seventy-five per cent of the respondents held the opinion that politicians only pursue personal interests and do not care about the general well-being of the people. In the same survey only 7 per cent of the respondents answered that they were very interested in politics, whereas 73 per cent claimed to have little or no interest. Two-thirds of respondents never or very rarely talked about politics at home (Manzi & Catalán 1998: 540–2). For the parliamentary elections in 1998 more than half million of young people did not register in order to vote.[8] Almost one million persons who did register did not show up to vote, and hundreds of thousands annulled their vote or voted blank. Some of the votes carried written messages like 'corrupt politicians, I am a democrat' or 'I annul the vote, long live democracy' (Bengoa 2000: 37). This was a striking contrast to the plebiscite on 5 October 1988 where a total of 92.2 per cent of the population above 18 were registered to vote. Of these, 2.5 per cent abstained from voting, whereas the annulled or blank notes counted for 2.3 per cent (Portales 2000: 457). In a 2001 national survey, 70 per cent of the respondents

---

[8] In the Chilean electoral system, people have to register beforehand if they wish to vote.

defined themselves as non-political.[9] Another survey, published in the daily newspaper *Las ultimas noticias* on 27 August 2002, showed that only 12 per cent of the respondents had confidence in political parties. To a large extent these numbers can be ascribed to the fact that political parties, not least on the left, have lost contact with the grass roots (Paley 2001; Hugo Cancino n.d.) and for many Chileans appear primarily as instruments for individual aspirations rather than platforms for ideological struggles (Moulián 2002: 64). As political, parliamentarian processes are often characterised by a lack of transparency, many Chileans perceive the world of politics as distant and irrelevant or as a lot of talk but very little action (Portales 2000: 454; Manzi & Catalán 1998: 573).

In the national best seller *Chile Actual: Anatomia de un Mito* (2002), the Chilean sociologist Tomas Moulián argues that the neocapitalist, neoliberal model has gained a hegemonic status in Chilean society and has succeeded in eliminating any cultural space for transformative ideologies (see also Oviedo 2009: 80). Within this social–historical context of democratisation, economic growth, social insecurity, increased individualism and consumerism, and not least, widespread political apathy, Pentecostalism has continued to grow and consolidate itself as the religion of the popular masses. Parallel developments within Chile's religious field include the growth of a Catholic charismatic movement, an indigenous revival, and the increasing popularity of New Age spiritual movements. Reflecting upon this religious/spiritual upsurge, the Chilean sociologist Christian Parker describes the development in Chile in the 1990s as characterised by a dialectic between political disenchantment and religious re-enchantment (1998: 665–6). In a postmodern neoliberal era where seductive political–ideological narratives are on the retreat, a symbolic void emerges that can in many cases be filled by religious narratives and projects.

Chile's Religious Market

Religious pluralism has become more prevalent in Chilean society since 1990. The Evangelical population grew from 13 to 15.1 per cent between 1992 and 2002), and estimates have placed Pentecostals at

---

[9] This survey appears in the research report *Desarollo Humano en Chile: Nosotros los Chilenos. Un desafío cultural*, published by *Programa de las Naciones Unidas para el Desarollo*, Santiago, in 2002.

75–90 per cent of all Chilean Evangelicals (Corvalán 2009: 77; Cleary and Sepúlveda 1997: 101). In a 2001 national survey, 73 per cent of the respondents defined themselves as Catholics, 4 per cent as having other religions (mostly Mormons and Jehovah's Witnesses) and 7 per cent as non-religious. For each Evangelical who converts to Catholicism five make the opposite conversion. But the survey also showed that 79 per cent of all Evangelicals grew up as Evangelicals.[10]

The Evangelical population is distributed among several hundred, mostly Pentecostal, denominations. The Methodist Pentecostal Church is the biggest Evangelical denomination in the country, followed by the EPC. Both denominations have founded missionary churches in other Latin American countries as well as in Europe, Australia, and North America (where most members are Latin American immigrants).

A rough distinction can be made between the traditional Pentecostal churches such as the EPC, characterised by strict rules for clothing and a markedly anti-'worldly' rhetoric, and the neo-Pentecostal churches. The latter tend to be less ascetically focused, and services are some-times reminiscent of rock concerts with electric instruments and up-beat music. Within the last two to three decades the so-called prosperity gospel has also made its entrance in some of Chile's neo-Pentecostal churches (see Oviedo 2009; Mansilla 2007). Central to this gospel is the outspoken conviction that every born-again Christian has the right to receive divine blessings of wealth and health as well as the duty to pay tithes and make donations of money to God through a ministry. The preaching in prosperity churches sometimes resembles motivational speaking. For instance preachers take pains to present congregants as winners (*vencedores*) and in explaining that the belief in Christ is inseparable from a firm belief in oneself. They further emphasise that a born-again Christian should always pursue his or her dreams, for example, by starting a small business, and not allowing him- or herself to be held back by the pessimism of others. Such rhetoric seems to be tailored to the model citizen of neoliberal society, the individual entre-preneur who believes in him- or herself but does not expect too much from the political system.

The 'marketing' or evangelical outreach of Pentecostalism has also become more diverse within recent years. Instead of or in addition to preaching on the street and public squares, several churches (but not

---

[10] *Desarollo Humano en Chile: Nosotros los Chilenos. Un desafío cultural*: 236–7.

the EPC) now make extensive use of the radio. Unlike the Catholic Church, Pentecostal churches have no close associations with the daily press or TV channels,[11] but foreign Evangelical channels can be watched in Chile.

Religious pluralism is accompanied by an increased deinstitutionalisation of religious belonging. As mentioned, 73 per cent of the respondents defined themselves as Catholics in a 2001 survey, but the question asked was: to which religion or church do you feel most related? In a survey from 1996, 15 per cent of all respondents (Catholics and others) defined themselves as *catolica de mi manera* (Catholic in my own way), whereas 25 per cent claimed to be believers without a religion (Parker 1998: 652). Research has shown that a majority of Chilean Catholics disagree with official church positions on several issues such as contraception and divorce (Fleet & Smith 1997: 173; Lies 2006: 71–3). In a study referred to in the *Santiago Times* in April 2007, Christian Parker discovered that 73 per cent of young Chileans, mostly from the middle and upper classes, were not practicing any religion and tended to identify more with individual faith than with particular religious institutions (see also Tan Bercerra 2010). Parker related this tendency to widespread anti-authoritarian attitudes and a search for personal autonomy among Chilean youth.

The detachment of religious identities from particular institutional affiliation and church participation is less prevalent among Pentecostals. A 2001 survey showed that 51 per cent of Chile's Evangelical population attended church at least once a week compared to 30 per cent of the Catholics. In a survey conducted in 2008, 84.3 per cent of Evangelical respondents claimed that they participated in religious activities at least once a week (Fediakova & Parker 2009: 51). Studies have also shown that lay Pentecostals are generally closer to official church positions on morality and sexuality and abortion than lay Catholics (Fleet & Smith 1997: 173; David Martin 1995a: 225; Lies 2006: 74; Fediakova & Parker 2009: 65–6). This is not too surprising, considering the higher degrees of church attendance and the exclusivist and fundamentalist character of Pentecostalism. Whereas many Chilean Catholics see no contradiction between being a Catholic and at the same time reading tarot cards (see Tan Bercerra 2010: 199), being involved in New Age

---

[11] Two newspapers, *El Mercurio* and *La Segunda*, and two TV channels, *Canal 13* and *Canal 9*, are connected with the Catholic Church.

spiritual movements, believing in reincarnation, consulting a shaman, or even being one (see Kristensen 2008), Pentecostals unambiguously categorise such beliefs and practices as the work and deceptions of the Devil.

The more individualistic and less institution-bound forms of religiosity are nevertheless also on the increase among Chile's Pentecostal population (Ossa 1996; Mansilla 2008). Several second- (or more) generation Pentecostals are not active church members but still define themselves as believers. In some of the new and less ascetically focused churches, membership is more fluid and degrees of ritual activities lower than in traditional churches. With the growing supply of Pentecostal denominations and products such as Christian literature, sold in Evangelical bookshops; Pentecostal radio programs; interdenominational seminaries and Bible study programs; web pages; facebook groups; and foreign Evangelical television channels, the religious monopoly of specific churches and pastors is broken. Individual Pentecostals are able to construct their own religious self-identities by 'shopping' around and choosing from a variety of religious inputs and products.

During my latest fieldwork in Chile in 2007 and 2008, I interviewed thirty-five members of new Pentecostal churches, *Ministerio Jesus Cristo para Chile* (the Jesus Christ Ministry for Chile) and the prosperity ministry *Cristo tu Unica Esperanza* (Christ Your Only Hope). More than 85 per cent had previously participated in at least one and in some cases as many as five other Pentecostal churches. Several respondents had for periods of their lives been churchless believers and had visited different Pentecostal churches until they found the right one. Their reasons for shifting church included practical concerns such as a desire to find a church close to their home so that they would not have to spend money on bus fare, loyalty to family members who had found a new church, theological disagreements, conflicts with pastors—sometimes because the latter were involved in sexual scandals—and other congregants, and desires for more personal freedom, for example, with regards to dress and make-up. Others merely explained that they felt the time had come to move on and try something new. Some of the respondents made it clear that they were fond of their present church but did not feel particularly attached to it or to their pastor and did not necessarily expect to stay within the same church for the rest of their lives. It became clear to me that Pentecostals from these churches identified more with individual beliefs, values, and a personal relationship with God than with institutional affiliation.

In the EPC, individual beliefs, values, and a personal communion with God are certainly important, but members also take great pride in belonging to what they consider to be the most serious and strict Pentecostal church in the country. In this church, degrees of ritual activity is high, the dualism between the life with God and the 'world' particularly outspoken, and congregants are encouraged to keep their most important and affective social relationships within the church.

Religion and Politics in Post-Dictatorship Chile

The Catholic Church took a conservative turn after the transition to democracy. Catholic authorities have continued to raise their voice in political debates, but the focus on human rights and social injustice has to a large extent been replaced by a focus on public morality, divorce, moral relativism, abortion, and contraception. Church leaders have tried to influence national policy by putting pressure on congress members, making appearances in the mass media, and publicly encouraging people not to vote for candidates whose politics they consider to be immoral (see Lies 2006).

The political mobilisation of Pentecostals has been modest, though leaders have tried to maintain close relations with the state. The Catholic Church was officially separated from the state in 1925, but it maintained a privileged position, whereas Evangelical churches enjoyed the same legal status as neighborhood associations. When Patricio Aylwin bid for presidency in 1989 he met with representatives of the Council of Pastors and the CCI to discuss the legal status of Evangelical churches. After being elected, he was congratulated by representatives of the Council of Pastors at an official visit (Canales Guevara 2000: 20–1). No Evangelical Te Deum was held in 1990, but the tradition was restored in 1991, and in 1992 representatives of the CCI participated for the first time. Evangelical Te Deum services are still held on the Sunday before 18 September with the presence of democratically elected leaders.

In 1992 the Committee for Evangelical Coordination was founded by Evangelical leaders from a number of churches with the sole purpose of improving the legal status of Evangelical churches. The EPC did not join the committee, as leaders believed that cooperation with other churches with different doctrines would lead to contamination. Despite resistance from Catholic authorities, a law of religious equality was passed in 1999.

Pentecostals have been rather invisible in parliamentarian politics since 1990. According to Freston, there were no Evangelical members of the congress in the 1990s (2004: 141).[12] A few Evangelicals, including Pentecostals, have stood for elections as mayors or local council members, representing different parties. An Evangelical party, *Alizanza National Christiana*, was founded in 1995, but its appearance on Chile's political stage was short-lived. In 1999 the bishop of a small Pentecostal denomination, Salvador Pino Busto, wanted to run for presidency as an independent candidate—according to himself because he had received a divine revelation—but he did not manage to collect enough signatures to register (Freston 2004: 142).

There are different reasons why Evangelical parties and candidates find it difficult to gain a foothold in national politics. The binominal electoral system does not favour new and small parties. Besides, Chile's Evangelical population is so divided that the attempt of single candidates or parties to represent a majority of Evangelicals is doomed to failure. Finally, many Pentecostals are suspicious of any mixture of religion and politics, a theme to which I will return in chapter 5 (see also Fediakova 2004; Fediakova & Parker 2009).

Things may change in the future. In other Latin American countries such as Guatemala, Brazil, and Venezuela, Pentecostals have become more involved in politics than in Chile (Smith 1998; Smilde 2011). A number of young, mostly 'native' Chilean Pentecostals are pursuing higher education or have become professionals and entered the middle class. My own research in different Pentecostal churches has shown that many, especially younger and educated Pentecostals, are in principle supportive of Pentecostal involvement in politics. It remains to be seen whether such principle support will eventually lead to actual political engagement.

In the case of the EPC, active political outreach and involvement seem like a very distant future scenario. What I argue in the subsequent chapters is that the appeal and transformative cultural power of

---

[12] I have found no information on religious affiliation of congress members since 2000.

traditional Pentecostalism does not lie in its potential for political mobilization but in its subtle redefinitions of social reality; in the various ritual, discursive, and narrative practices through which congregants negotiate identities and gain a new sense of empowerment; in the reworking of gender relationships; and not least in a cultural critique of different aspects of Chilean society and more generally of secular modernity.

CHAPTER FOUR

CHILEAN SOCIAL SPACE AND THE POSITIONS OF PENTECOSTALS

The reader who is familiar with Latin American *telenovelas* (multi-episode television serial melodramas) will probably have noticed that social inequality is a dominant theme in this genre. *Telenovelas*, which are mass-produced in countries like Chile, Brazil, Venezuela, Mexico, Argentina, and Colombia, are broadcast daily on evening prime time as well as during the day on several Chilean television channels. The genre typically explores themes such as complicated love relationships between persons from different social classes, inferiority complexes, social resentment, dreams and aspirations for social mobilisation, classism, upper-class arrogance and prejudices, etc.

While people may not consider them to be accurate representations of social reality in Latin American societies, the tremendous popularity of *telenovelas*, especially the national ones, in Chile clearly stems from their treatment of themes, concerns, and problems with which many Chileans identify. Though the percentage of officially poor people has been reduced since the transition to democracy in 1990, social inequality is still one of the most striking features of Chilean society. In a survey from 1994, 67 per cent of the respondents stated that greatest conflict in Chilean society was the gap between rich and poor people or between employers and workers. Unequal access to education and medical attention was also stressed by a number of respondents (Manzi & Catalán 1998: 532–9). Social mobilisation and—in the case of the middle and upper classes—the maintenance of a socioeconomic position is a major concern of many Chileans. Minimum wages for unskilled labour are low, and Chilean scholars have noted that the investment of money in the education of children has become an obsession of many people (Bengoa et al. 2000: 80; Tironi 2005: 261). Andrea, a Catholic woman from the upper middle class who was working as a high school teacher but was married to an engineer, explained the typical priorities and concerns of the middle class to me:

> I am a person from the middle class in Chile; my parents were professionals, and of course, when I started and when I finished high school

I knew all the time that I was going to university, and my parents knew it, because there was no other option…. I would say that for the middle class, the top priority is to study, study a subject that permits you to live. Well, basically you want to study something that permits you to stay within your class.

Chileans commonly distinguish between the upper class (*classe alta*); the middle class (*classe media*), which is subdivided into upper middle, middle middle, and lower middle class; and finally the lower class (*classe baja*) or the poor. In statistics of income distribution, the Chilean population is usually divided into the categories A, B, C1, C2, C3, D, and E. The income distribution in 2002 is shown in table 1.[1]

As can be seen in table 2, which is based on information from a 2001 national survey,[2] most Evangelicals still belong to the lower socioeconomic sectors, a tendency that has been confirmed by a 2008 survey, made by the Chilean sociologist Evguenia Fediakova and Christian Parker (Fediakova & Parker 2009: 52). Poverty has been reduced in Chile since 1990, but economic mobilisation appears to be less prevalent among Evangelicals than among other Chileans (ibid.). The 2001 survey further showed that Evangelicals were more oriented towards their local neighbourhood, whereas Catholics tended to be oriented towards the nation, and non-religious people were more concerned with international matters. Evangelicals were also shown to be more indifferent towards democracy and to have lower levels of education than the other groups.[3] It should, however, be noted that Chile's Evangelical population and in particular the younger and native generations of Evangelicals are now benefitting from the increased access of the popular sectors to secondary and higher education. In 1990, 55.1 per cent of all Evangelicals had no education beyond primary school compared to 17.5 per cent in 2008. And in 1990 only 4.5 per cent had more than 13 years of studies, whereas the number had reached 33.4 per cent in 2008 (Fediakova & Parker 2009: 5).

---

[1] The table draws on information found at 'Descripcion GSE usada en Chile', *Novomerc Chile* <novomerc.cl/gse2.html>; 'Opiniones sobre los GSE', *Novomerc Chile* <novomerc.cl/opinion.html>; 'Mapa Socioeconómico de Chile', *Adimark* <http://www.adimark.cl/medios/estudios/Mapa_Socioeconomico_de_Chile.pdf>; 'Santiago the Segmented', *Notes from Underneath*, 7 July 2010 <http://chileangringa.blogspot.com/2010/07/santiago-segmented.html> (all accessed on 10 January 2011), and in Loveman (2001: 346).

[2] *Desarollo Humano en Chile: Nosotros los Chilenos. Un desafío cultural*, 237.

[3] *Desarollo Humano en Chile: Nosotros los Chilenos. Un desafío cultural*, 237.

Table 1: Chile's social pyramid in 2002

ABC1 7.2 %	Average monthly family income: US$7000	University graduates who hold an executive level or otherwise prestigious jobs. Live in exclusive neighborhoods. Own two or more cars, usually not older than five years. They have live-in domestic household workers. Travel frequently.
C2 15.4 % 'Typical' middle class	Average monthly family income: US$2000	Young professionals, business executives, technicians, salaried employees, proprietors of small businesses, salesmen, merchants. Live in clean well-maintained houses. 80% have relatively new cars. If they have domestic household workers, they are usually not 'live-in'. They travel less than C1.
C3 22.4% Lower middle class	Average monthly family income: US$1200	Salaried employees in public or private sector: specialised workers, teachers, taxi owners; 10–12 years of education. 55% have a car (though not a very expensive one), usually no domestic household workers. Live in neighbourhoods without green areas and sometimes in poorly maintained houses with broken windows and old painting. Households often include people who do not belong to the nuclear family.
D 34.8 % Lower class	Average monthly family income: US$600	Workers, low-level white collar: janitors, messengers, domestic workers, seamstresses. 6–10 years of education. 15% have cars 10 years old or more, almost never have domestic workers. Live in poor areas (often with C3 and E) with many stray dogs and children playing on the street. Extended households are common.
E 20.3 % Poverty	Average monthly family income: US$180	Day workers; earn less than minimum wage; 2–4 years of education; no car, no private phone, no domestic workers. Many families often live together.

Table 2: Religious affiliation in different social sectors

	Catholics	Evangelicals	People belonging to other religions	Non-religious people
B/C1	77%	3%	8%	12%
C2	82%	7%	3%	8%
C3	75%	15%	3%	7%
D	68%	23%	3%	6%

Taste, Distinction and Consumption

For some time, scholars have been emphasising the importance of consumption and cultural style in creating and expressing social differentiation and status (Hebdige 1979; Bourdieu 1986; Ferguson 1999; Liechty 2003; Cole 2008). A focus on consumption is certainly relevant in the study of differentiation in Chile, where consumerism as described in the previous chapter has become a dominant feature of popular culture within the last three decades (Moulián 1998, 2002; Christoffani n.d.). Chilean middle- and upper-class identity is intrinsically related to the consumption of prestige goods and access to services and privileges. In searching for ways of exploring the complexity of social differences in contemporary Chile, I have found that Bourdieu's study of distinction in France is a helpful place to begin.

Bourdieu sees the position occupied by any given actor in a modern class society (France) as defined by his or her amount of economical, social, and cultural (for example, educational) capital—and by the distributions of the total amount of capital among these three types. Actual interactions between actors are formed by invisible structures, which are always inherent in the interaction. In Bourdieu's view taste and habits of consumption function as a sort of social orientation or a 'sense of one's place', guiding actors towards goods and practices, which befit the occupants of a given position (1986: 466). Such orientation is not guided by distanced reflection as much as by 'practical knowledge of the social world' (ibid.: 468), rooted in the embodied dispositions and schemes of perception that constitute the habitus. Through choices of consumption, actors will habitually and almost inevitably adapt to their position within social space.

Taste, in Bourdieu's famous expression, 'classifies, and it classifies the classifier' (ibid.: 6). It is the means whereby actors classify themselves.

And at the same time, classifying practices, whether or not they are inspired by a desire to get oneself noticed, are the basis by which actors can be classified by others. Any classifying practice of consumption is already classified within a hierarchical system. Bourdieu distinguishes between three kinds of taste within this system: legitimate, middle-brow, and popular taste (ibid.: 16). These can partly be distinguished by their levels of abstraction. Thus functionality and concrete appreciability are dominant features of popular taste or the working class aesthetics whereas the legitimate taste is characterised by a preference for non-functional aesthetics.

According to Bourdieu the working class aesthetic is a dominated aesthetic and bound to define itself by reference to the dominant aesthetic (legitimate taste). Thus he presents a top-down view of cultural production, where actors in lower positions can at best aspire for partly successful appropriation of the dominant aesthetic. In his own words:

> the strategies aimed at transforming the basic dispositions of a life-style into a system of aesthetic principles, objective differences into elective distinctions, passive options into conscious, elective choices are in fact reserved for members of a dominant class (ibid.: 57).

Bourdieu's analytical focus on taste, classification, and different kinds of capital has influenced the work of subsequent scholars of social differentiation, as has his understanding of the internalisation of social positions as a kind of practical knowledge or embodied disposition. However, there is a tendency in his work to portray social positions as over-determined and more or less mechanically enacted. His top-down view of cultural production and his understanding of the dominated class as rather passive and unsuccessful appropriators of the dominant aesthetics allows little room for creative practices through which the dominated actively oppose the dominant aesthetic and symbolically invert and reject the principles of the classificatory system. While inspired by Bourdieu, other scholars have found that Judith Butler's notion of performance (1990, 1993) provides an important supplement to his theory as it facilitates an exploration of cultural differences and identities as continually produced, tested, negotiated, and confirmed (Ferguson 1999; Liechty 2003; Cole 2008). As noted by James Ferguson, Butler's discussion of the relation between subjectivity and performance allows more room for ambiguity, irony, and play. But Ferguson also emphasises that people cannot simply choose to perform any identity stylistically. Pulling off a performance involves not only abstract know-how but a certain ease acquired through internalised capabilities of performative competence (1999: 96). What I argue in this work is that traditional Chilean Pentecostals, though clearly positioned and constrained with regards to performative repertoires, find various strategies or negotiating social identities and power relationships, or, in other words, of redefining their passive options as conscious, elective choices.

Differentiation and Distinction in Chile

Class-consciousness in a Marxist sense of the term is by no means a dominant feature in Chilean society, where labour unions are weak and new categories of workers who are not proletarians in the classical sense have emerged. Also, democratically elected governments, including the ones led by socialist presidents, have basically administered the neoliberal economic model they inherited from the regime. But most Chileans I have talked to about social differences expressed a striking class awareness. In addition to members of the EPC, I interviewed or had informal conversations with a number of other Pentecostal and non-Pentecostal Chileans from different classes, where we touched upon themes such as perceptions of social–cultural differences. A majority of my informants from the EPC and lower-class Chileans from other Pentecostal churches mainly conceived of social differences in terms of income and access to goods and services such as private schools and the privatised health system. Non-Pentecostal middle-class informants with higher education generally had more complex views. Though most of them were not familiar with the work of Bourdieu, they almost unanimously emphasised that social differentiation has to do with a number of factors such as level of education, the extent to which higher education is valued, knowledge of art and culture (*cultura*), ways of speaking, personal style, and interest in international matters.

Gloria is a Catholic woman who belonged to the upper middle class when she was married. Having been abandoned by her husband she was now working as a cashier, earning only a little more than minimum wage. When I interviewed her, she was very open about her financial situation, but nevertheless she persistently defined herself as a middle-class person and took great pains to distance herself from the poor. Gloria felt like a middle-class person because of her level of education (she had gone to university, but not finished, which was why she had to work as a cashier), because certain kinds of jobs such as cleaning or domestic service were unthinkable for her, because she valued education and wanted her daughter to go to university at any cost, because she had travelled and was concerned with international politics, because she spoke a proper and decent Spanish without using slang, because most of her friends belonged to the middle or upper classes and were *gente que tiene cultura* (people who have culture) like herself. It was clear from her descriptions that middle class and poverty are not perceived in purely economic terms. On the contrary her statements illustrated how these are culturally loaded and continuously negotiated and contested categories of social identification. Several other non-Pentecostal middle-class informants with university degrees in the humanities and low-income jobs echoed her views and descriptions. It was common for these informants to define themselves in opposition to *la gente humilde* (the humble people). Humility generally implies a modest or simple appearance, a low income and lack of familiarity with elite culture. Many lower and lower middle class Chileans prefer *humilde* to *pobre* (poor) as an auto-designation. In some Pentecostal churches, including the EPC, humility and simplicity (*sencillez*)—as opposed to extravagance, ostentation, and arrogance—are considered important Christian virtues.[4]

Taste and physical appearance are important indicators of social position in Chile. Several Catholic middle-class informants who held university degrees explained to me that the poor and poorly educated people are distinguishable by their clothing, which was characterised as simple, unoriginal, or in poor taste (the use of trainers by men and tight clothes by overweight women was often mentioned), and in the case of women, by use of inexpensive and indiscreet make-up. 'Official' ideals of physical beauty and style in Chile mainly reflect the taste, style, or aspirations of the middle and upper classes. This does not only apply to clothing and cosmetics but also to physical traits. The ideal of being tall, light skinned, and without any trace of Indian ancestors is constantly reproduced in the mass media. According to Teres Valdes,

---

[4] In 2007 an old woman from the EPC confessed to me that she thought that constructing a new and impressive church building had been a mistake. She felt that the spiritual condition of the church had been superior in the old and more humble church building. She suspected that the reason for the spiritual decline was that '*el Señor prefiere las cosas humildes*' (the Lord prefers humble things).

people whose appearance does not reflect this ideal have become marginalised from parts of the Chilean work market (1998: 476).

This view was echoed by Marcela, a Catholic woman in her early thirties who holds a university degree in the humanities. She defines herself as having an upper middle-class appearance. Her hair is brown, whereas most Chileans have black hair, and her cosmetics and clothes are notably expensive. When I interviewed her about perceptions of social differences, she told me that she felt different from most other people when walking around in downtown Valparaíso. She would usually not dress up in the same way when going to downtown Valparaíso as she would when going to the Mall or the centre of Viña del Mar. She further explained to me how she perceived the importance of physical appearance in Chilean society:

> If you go to the restaurants in Viña, all the persons who serve are persons like, well, they are kind of beautiful. You never see persons with an Indian face working in a place like that. Maybe they will be working in the kitchen, washing the dishes. Or they may clean the place after it has closed. These people are the lowest in the social hierarchy. It is sad but that's the way it is. Also if you go to Falabella and Ripley,[5] you will see that all the workers have a good appearance. I have never felt this social stigma. Obviously it serves me well that the system works like that. A person with Indian blood has to work harder to achieve the same. I feel free to do whatever I want here in Chile. I feel that here in Chile, I generally get a very good treatment. When I go to the bank to withdraw money, the guard always hurries to help me. If I had black hair, I probably wouldn't get such a treatment.

Marcela added that her obvious upper middle-class appearance sometimes caused reverse reactions. She had recently taken a local bus and not received her change when she paid for the ticket. The driver was very impolite to her, but when a few women, who were obviously of a more humble origin got on the bus, he was much nicer and these women got their change. Marcela's conclusion was that the inferiority complexes and social resentment of the driver were the reasons why he had treated her impolitely, whereas he probably felt more comfortable with humble women.

A majority of congregants from the EPC, and especially of those above thirty, have what would commonly be characterised as humble

---

[5] Falabella and Ripley are two of the biggest clothes retail chains in Chile, with giant shops in all major cities.

or modest appearances. In the EPC, choice of clothing and hair cuts are restricted by church rules, dictating that women wear long skirts, have long hair, and wear no make-up. Men are supposed to have short hair and be decently dressed, always wearing a suit for the Sunday meeting. In most other Pentecostal churches dress codes are more flexible, but women are expected to wear decent clothes that do not display or enhance the contours of the body. By maintaining strict dress codes and banning the use of make-up, members of the EPC emphasise the Christian virtues of modesty, humility, and simplicity in their outward appearance while at the same time avoiding being associated with bad taste. Thus, to a certain extent they succeed in transforming objective differences into elective distinctions. But congregants are also strikingly aware that their options do not include a physical appearance that corresponds to public mass-mediated ideals of beauty. This awareness is sometimes articulated in humorous comments like the following:

> Josefina (housewife, aged 44 and half Mapuche. She is short, overweight, dark skinned, and has Indian traits): Martin, if you show your mother the photo you took of me, you must tell her that even though this sister is ugly on the outside, she is beautiful on the inside.

> José (referring to Mauricio, an unskilled worker from Northern Chile in his forties who clearly has Indian ancestors. He is not too tall and has dark skin): I don't think that there are any racial differences in heaven; there we will all be the same. Who knows, maybe brother Mauricio will even be beautiful in heaven. Nothing is impossible for the Lord (laughs).

> Pablo (self-employed, unskilled photographer who is only around 1.60 meters high): We in the church are ugly, we are small and dark, but we have God in our hearts. We are poor, but at the same time we are covered with gold. When the people of the 'world' say that they are covered with gold, they mean that they are rich, that they have a lot of money, but when we say that we are covered with gold, we mean that we have a spiritual blessing.

A large group of male congregants belong to an evangelisation group called the cyclists (*los ciclistas*). During summers they go biking and evangelising in different parts of the country. But no congregant ever told me that they would go biking for the sake of mere exercise, as did some non-Pentecostal middle class informants as well as some Pentecostal university students from the Assemblies of God whom I interviewed. Teenage boys and young men in the EPC occasionally get together to play football. But more distinctive and expensive kinds of sport such as skiing, tennis, or aerobics were not practiced by any members of the EPC. In a similar vein congregants have very little interest in and knowledge about fine art, classical music, and non-Christian literature. When I visited congregants in their homes we almost exclusively listened to Evangelical music or radio programmes. Some of the women in the EPC confessed to me that they did not use expensive skin care products and rarely if ever visited the malls in Viña del Mar but bought most of their clothes in cheaper shops in Valparaíso.

Applying the terminology of Bourdieu, most members of the EPC and next to all members above thirty (we will, however, meet one exception in chapter 10) can be categorised as persons with popular taste and low amounts of economic, social, and cultural capital. The argument I pursue in the subsequent chapters is that the appeal and cultural dynamics of traditional Pentecostalism, the rejection of the 'world' of sin; the inversion of secular social hierarchies, and the different ritual and everyday practices through which congregants construct and negotiate identities can only be properly understood if situated within a complex system of social–cultural differentiation in Chilean society.

CHAPTER FIVE

PENTECOSTALISM AS A CULTURAL CRITIQUE

We are the light in this corrupt 'world', brothers [and sisters]. We used to be outsiders, marginal in society, and now we are sitting here as princes. (*Quoted from a sermon in the EPC*)

I only talk about spiritual matters, not about politics or other 'worldly' things. I don't even like to read the newspapers! I don't want to know anything about what goes on in the 'world'. (*Quoted from a sermon in the EPC*)

Politics is bad, very bad. The Lord is true, but politics won't do you any good at all, nothing, nothing! I don't understand politics; I don't understand. I don't understand politics! I don't understand the things of the 'world'! I know that things happen, but we are with the Lord; the best news is found in the word of the Lord. (*Claudio, unskilled worker in his mid-forties from the EPC*)

This Sunday God cured me; I was feeling sick, but I then I felt that a power came upon me, and I started feeling better. I don't go to the doctors; I don't trust any doctor. The Lord is the doctor of all doctors. (*Silvia, widow in her seventies from the EPC*)

Teresa: How are you doing, brother Martin?
ML: I am fine!
Teresa: Don't you mean that you are fine, thanks to the Lord?
ML: Eeh, yeah, of course!
Teresa: Good!
(*Conversation between the author and an old woman from the EPC*)

In much of the existing literature, the appeal of Pentecostalism to poor Latin Americans has, in part, been explained in terms of the movement's contestatory cultural character. Scholars have pointed out how spiritual egalitarianism, active lay participation in services and certain organisational aspects of Pentecostal churches not only provide a marked contrast to the traditional Catholic differentiation between producers and consumers of religious products, but also reverse the whole structure of classist societies (e.g. Lalive d'Epinay 1968; Willems 1967; Rolim 1979; David Martin 1990, 1996, 2001; Cleary & Sepúlveda 1997). In many Pentecostal churches, any saved man can, regardless of income, level of education and other kinds of social status, occupy

leadership positions or may even become a pastor. And though they do
not occupy formal positions, except as leaders of female groups (the
dorcas), Pentecostal women enjoy spiritual authority and are encouraged to preach on the street, pray for the sick, and give testimonies in
the churches (see chapter 9, see also Drogus 1997; Cleary & Sepúlveda
1997; Freston 2006).

Such arguments certainly ring true in the case of the EPC, where a
majority of the congregants who hold official positions are persons
with little formal education and low-status jobs. Besides, the high level
of lay participation in ritual life clearly contrasts with the Catholic ritual division of labour. However, the Pentecostal symbolic inversion of
Chilean public space is far too complex and multifaceted to be aptly
captured by a narrow focus on organisational principles and the priesthood of all believers. In this and in later chapters I intend to push the
analysis of the contestatory cultural character of traditional Chilean
Pentecostalism a few steps further by demonstrating how congregants
from the EPC are engaged in everyday subtle symbolic struggles over
categorisations and definitions of social reality. Focus in this chapter is
on the ways in which these struggles are fought in the domains of style,
everyday linguistic–semantic practice, healing, and discourses on politics. I show theological understandings of human powerlessness and
total dependence upon God inform Pentecostal discourses and practices, through which congregants redefine their own position and
agency in the social world. Such redefinitions represent a critique of
different aspects of Chilean society such as Catholicism, popular culture, national politics, and the public health system, but also more generally of a secular modernist hegemony. In subsequent chapters I
explore how a Pentecostal re-enchanted world ordering is constituted
and unfolded through ritual practice and the ritualisation of everyday
life (chapter 7 and 8), gender politics (chapter 9), and eschatological
readings of world history (chapter 11).

Pentecostal Inversive Practices

For some time, anthropologists and other scholars have been arguing
that a proper conceptualisation of resistance should not be confined to
open, conscious confrontation and mobilisation aiming at overall
structural political transformations but include less organised and subtle tactics of everyday life through which people defy dominant ideologies and discourses (Willis 1977; Comaroff 1985; Scott 1985, 1990;

Abu-Lughod 1990; Keesing 1992; Ortner 1995; Tripp 1997). For actors who do not occupy central positions in dominant public fields such as politics, economics, education, and cultural production, resistance and protest are often enacted from alternative and less public sites. In a study of Zionist churches in South Africa during apartheid, Jean Comaroff demonstrates how religious institutions can serve as platforms from which marginal actors symbolically defy an established social order. Comaroff conceives of Zionism as 'a systematic counter culture, a modus operandi explicitly associated with those estranged from the centres of power and communication' (1985: 191). Rather than representing a direct challenge to economical and political mechanisms of dominance, Zionists have contested the very logic of the neo-colonial socio-cultural system:

> The marginalised in the shantytowns of neo-colonial modernity still seek the spirit in the wilderness, striving to appropriate its unorthodox power to their project of self-realisation and resistance. They do not cent their defiance in the arenas of combat defined by the established culture but in loci diffused in the everyday world, jarring the eye of the orthodox observer with their defiant reformulations of mundane practice. (ibid.: 259)

Comaroff explores how an alternative system of knowledge and practice outside the terms of the neo-colonial culture is constituted through ritual practice, religious language use, bodily attitudes, and clothing. Drawing on the work of Hebdige on British youth cultures (1979), she argues that symbolic resistance against a dominant social order can be enacted through the reworking of signs which extend into the most mundane areas of everyday life (Comaroff 1985: 196).

In a similar way, congregants from the EPC are engaged in subtle symbolic struggles over definitions and categorisations of social reality. Such struggles are in large part fought in the domain of everyday linguistic practice where congregants tend to alter common relationships between signifiers and signified. For members of the EPC, as for most Chilean Pentecostals, the term 'Christian' is used exclusively to refer to born-again Pentecostals and maybe to other Evangelicals but not to Jehovah's Witnesses or Mormons, and certainly not to Catholics. Even Pentecostals who used to be devoted and practicing Catholics often describe conversion as a process of becoming Christians. By using the term in an exclusive and restricted way, Pentecostals make an implicit statement about what it means or takes to be a proper Christian and at the same time defy widespread Catholic and political definitions of Christianity (making a more explicit statement, a Pentecostal friend once told me that 'there is absolutely nothing Christian about the Christian Democratic Party'). In the EPC as in other Pentecostal communities the terms 'brothers' and 'sisters' are given new meaning, as they refer to all other congregants (children of the same heavenly father). Biological siblings are referred to as 'brothers or sisters in the flesh' (*hermano o hermana carnal*). The term 'world' is sometimes used in a secular value-free sense, referring to the planet Earth. But in internal Pentecostal discourse, the 'world' most commonly refers to a state (rather than a place) of sin and human corruption. 'Amen' is often used instead of 'yes' as a confirming response to a question or to mark a question. Thus an exchange could sound like this: A: 'You are coming to church today, amen?' B: 'Amen!' The term 'amen' may also be used as a way of saying 'that is great.' When I arrived in Valparaíso in November 2008 and told a man from the EPC that my wife had recently given birth to our second child, his response was, '*Amén, gloria a Dios*' (amen, glory to God).

When members of the EPC say that someone has gone to Egypt, what is meant is that a congregant has left the church and slid back into the 'world'. I also frequently heard members of the EPC complain that their children or other family members were not walking. They were not referring to any physical disabilities. 'To walk' (*caminar*) means to walk the paths of the Lord, that is, to be a saved and committed congregant. Members of the EPC rarely say that another congregant has died or is dead. Instead they say that the Lord took him or her (*el Señor se lo/la llevó*) or that he or she is with the Lord (*está con el Señor*).

As with most Pentecostals in Chile, members of the EPC insist that they do not have masses and rituals like the Catholics, but meetings, vigils (late-night meetings), Bible studies, prayer sessions, and Sunday schools. Masses, rituals, and liturgy are associated with the impersonal scriptedness, confining formulae, and empty routine of Catholic worship, where there is no room for the spontaneous intervention of the Holy Spirit. Expulsion of evil spirits from possessed persons or houses is practised, though only on rare occasions, in many Pentecostal churches. But instead of calling this practice 'exorcism' as Catholics would do, Pentecostals refer to it as liberation (*liberación*) or simply healing (*sanación*). Pentecostal deliverance is also distinguished from Catholic exorcism in that many lay Pentecostals are authorised to pray for the sick. Besides, the use of Holy Water is regarded as a pagan practice, and the Brazilian neo-Pentecostal ministry, the Universal Church of the Kingdom of God, where holy water, salt, roses, and oil are used and distributed to members, is viewed with considerable suspicion by most other Chilean Pentecostals.

The moral conservatism of Chilean society and the Catholic repression of sexuality outside of marriage, which have influenced the views of many parents on the sexuality of teenage and even adult children, are counterweighted by a popular erotic culture that finds its articulation in music, dance and literature, jokes, swearwords, and common sayings. Especially the 'double sense' (*el doble sentido*), where expressions and sentences have an underlying sexual message, is very common in Chile. This erotic popular culture is explicitly rejected by Pentecostals. Dancing or listening to 'worldly' songs with erotic texts and sensual rhythms is strongly discouraged in the EPC as in most other Pentecostal churches, even those such as the Assembly of God where young congregants see themselves as more moderate and modern. Testimonies of conversion often include accounts of how ways of speaking have changed, and Pentecostals in general make a virtue out of never swearing, making sexually related jokes, or using the double sense. Thus one woman from the EPC explained to me that a proper Christian should avoid using the word *enchufar*, which means 'to plug in the light,' because people from the 'world' sometime use this word to refer to sexual penetration. A Christian should rather say *arreglar la luz* (fix the light) in order to avoid any misunderstandings.

The way Spanish is spoken is an important sign of distinction in Chile. For many middle-class Chileans, belonging to popular sectors is associated with speaking bad or piquant Spanish (*español picante*), characterised by swearing, the use of slang, and not least bad pronunciation, including 'eating' the last part of a word. For many Chileans being a decent person (*una persona decente*) implies speaking proper Spanish. Though middle- and upper-class Chileans also swear and use slang, they often insist on having more sense of when and how it is appropriate to do so. With a Bourdieuan vocabulary, we might call this a practical sense of appropriate language use. Like most rules, these ones have numerous exceptions, as there are Chileans in all social classes who speak without much slang and swearing, and men generally swear a little more than women. But the general perception of different class-related ways of speaking Spanish is nevertheless powerful in Chile. By avoiding the double sense, swearwords, and slang expressions, Pentecostals are able to break with a linguistic class stigma and thus appear as humble but decent people rather than as *rotos* (a term commonly used to refer to people with bad manners).

Apart from language use, architecture constitutes an important domain of ideological symbolic struggles. In a study of the Universal Church of the Kingdom of God in Brazil, David Lehmann challenges Bourdieu's view of popular taste as having an intrinsically subordinate and dependant character, as he argues that Pentecostals are involved in a frontal attack on dominant tenets and practices of their own culture (ibid.: 18). Pentecostal architecture is better seen as a demonstration of indifference to the exigencies of modern sophisticated taste than as poor imitations of its Catholic counterpart. The church buildings of the EPC as of other Pentecostal churches in Chile, Brazil, and elsewhere (see Coleman 2000a for Sweden) are characterised by intended simplicity and functionality. In the church buildings of the EPC there are no external decorations, and internal decoration is limited to a photo or a painting behind the pulpit with a written quote from the Bible. An arrangement of flowers is often placed in front of the pulpit on Sundays. The new church building of the EPC in Valparaíso is big and impressive, but the building is no more decorated than small humble church buildings in outer Valparaíso. As noted by Lehmann, Pentecostals tend to avoid aesthetic practice, which is a part of a secularised culture (1996: 168). Besides, too many church decorations are associated with Catholic idolatry and worship of dead images rather than a living God. Rather than re-appropriations of principles of Catholicism and secular erudite culture, the aesthetic and consumptive practices of Pentecostals represent an active inversion, rejection, and transcendence of such principles (ibid.: 173).

How to Talk about Politics

Pentecostal attitudes to politics have been a recurrent topic in the scholarly literature. Recent research has challenged older views of Latin American Pentecostalism as a religious movement that fosters political quietism by providing the alienated with a refuge, exercising authoritarian control over the time and conduct of lay members, and emphasising spiritual rather than structural causality. Authors have argued that membership in Pentecostal churches not only enables Latin Americans to cope with limiting social and cultural conditions but may in fact prepare them for future democratic participation by cultivating rhetoric, organisational skills, egalitarian values, and a sense of personal autonomy (Willems 1967; David Martin 1990; Mariz 1994; Christian Smith 1994; Dodson 1997). Research also shows that Chilean and Latin American Pentecostals do not necessarily regard their religious commitment and beliefs as incompatible with political involvement and that they often vote according to class interest (Ossa 1991; Canales et al. 1991; Freston 1993; Smilde 1998; Fediakova & Parker 2009).[1] As mentioned in chapter 3, a few Pentecostals have attempted to gain a foothold in Chilean national and local politics since the return to democracy in 1990.

The diversity of Chilean Pentecostalism is reflected in the attitudes of pastors and lay people towards political, democratic participation. During my last field trips to Chile in 2007 and 2008–9 I interviewed thirty-five young members and a few elder members of the Assembly of God and of a newer church, 'Christ Your Only Hope' (*Cristo tu Unica Esperanza*). While acknowledging the danger of getting caught up in a political culture of corruption, hypocrisy, and dishonesty, many of them were in theory supportive of Pentecostal involvement in politics. When asked why a Christian should get involved in politics, a majority answered that the main purpose should be to facilitate Evangelical goals. But quite a few respondents also believed that Pentecostals should try to bring values, morality, and integrity into Chilean political life, and more particularly to publicly manifest Evangelical positions on ethical questions such as abortion and homosexual marriages. Nevertheless none of them considered becoming politically active.

Such positions towards political participation are by no means dominant in the EPC. The church is known for its historically persistent apolitical stance (Mansilla 2009: 29) and has never joined any ecumenical organisations such as the Committee for Evangelical Co-ordination, founded in 1992 with the purpose of improving the legal status of Evangelical churches. Surely, congregants consider abortion and homosexuality to be serious sins. But they generally consider praying, evangelisation, and the salvation of souls as the most efficient means of bringing about changes in public morality. While not formally forbidden, political involvement is clearly not an actual option in the EPC.

---

[1] The fear of the political influence of the Catholic Church also seems to influence the voting behaviour of Pentecostals. During presidential election campaigns in 1999, both candidates, the socialist Ricardo Lagos and his right wing opponent Joaquín Lavín, tried to court the Evangelical population. The latter did so by presenting himself as a man with profound religious values. But when his links with the conservative Catholic organisation Catholic Opus Dei became known his popularity among Evangelicals decreased. Some analysts felt that the victory of Lagos after a very close run-off was decided by Evangelicals (Freston 2001: 226).

Not only is participation in church activities time-consuming, but most members hold the conviction that politics is a corrupt and 'worldly' matter in which it is highly inappropriate to get involved.

In the EPC a classical Christian distinction between the 'world' and the church or the life with God is particularly outspoken as compared to other Pentecostal churches in Chile and elsewhere. Another theological principle, which is more dominant and pervasive in this church than in any other church I have ever visited or heard of, is the emphasis on human powerlessness and total dependence upon an almighty God as the source of all good things. But transformative divine power must be activated by born-again Pentecostals through praying, fasting, sanctification, Bible reading, and participation in ritual life (see chapter 7). Hence, congregants indirectly grant themselves and each other a certain measure of agency to act upon the world.

Such notions of powerlessness, dependency, and agency inform Pentecostal discourses on politics. On more than one occasion I heard preachers from the EPC explain that the relative prosperity in Chile compared to neighbouring countries was a result of divine blessings because of the high number of praying Pentecostals and should *not* be ascribed to sound decisions made by intelligent and hard working politicians. In a similar vein, Ricardo, a retired worker from the EPC gave me the following explanation of the uselessness of political action:

> I pray for all the presidents, but no president will ever give me food or a roof over my head. He is the one who gives me that "[pointing his index finger upwards].... You know Martin, when you finish your studies, if you don't find a job, neither the president nor anyone else will help you, only the Lord. The politicians just take all the money and help themselves and each other. They don't work very much; they have all these benefits. You know, a worker earns 90,000 pesos each month, and those, the politicians, 10–12 million [at this point he raises his voice in anger]. So how can politics be good? It is bad!

Pentecostal perceptions of the efficacy of political action are clearly shaped by a theistic religious frame. As David Smilde puts it, the sense of agency in such a frame comes from the conviction that the source of alteration of undesirable conditions lies in the relationship between human behaviour and supernatural agents (1998: 290). Thus congregants like Ricardo see sanctification and praying to God so that he may send his blessings to the world as the most efficacious way of securing human well-being. However, that is not to say that Pentecostal attitudes towards political participation should merely be explained in terms of religious or ideational determinism. In chapter 3 I described the political climate in post-dictatorship neo-liberal Chile as character-ised by low levels of popular participation, declining confidence in political parties and organisations, and not least by widespread percep-tions of politicians as constituting an elite that profits from privileges and connections but has little interest in the general well-being of the people. The view of politics and politicians that Ricardo expresses in the second half of the excerpt is not too different from the views held by many other Chileans, Pentecostal and Catholic. Pentecostal atti-tudes to politics should, in other words, be seen as emerging through a complex interplay between religious discourses or frames and wider societal tendencies. Of course one may add that this interplay is shaped and facilitated by a neat ideological congruence and practical compat-ibility between Pentecostal theistic understandings of transformative agency and a neo-liberal model where the popular sectors are in large part excluded and discouraged from political participation. Hence it could very well be argued that traditional Pentecostalism, while not being a key motor in the process, contributes to the political disen-chantment in Chilean society.

Processes of censuring, disqualifying, and determining that which is irrelevant or even unthinkable are of central importance for the social–discursive construction of reality. Congregants from the EPC some-times condemn politics in general terms as a corrupt and 'worldly' matter. Like Ricardo, a number of congregants told me that they remembered to pray for divine guidance of presidents and the govern-ment, but that politicians in general are not to be trusted. But specific political topics and events are to a large extent ignored or discursively marginalised. I was repeatedly struck when political events that had taken headlines were simply not mentioned by congregants.[2] At other times congregants found subtle ways of indirectly referring to political issues and events in a way that demonstrates that they were not really worth talking about. In July 1999, workers organised a big strike and major demonstrations in Valparaíso because of the announced privati-sation of the harbour. While this privatisation was generally considered necessary in order to modernise the harbour and enhance its competi-tiveness with the harbour of San Antonio further south, it was also

---

[2] In the 2008 survey only 3.5 per cent of Evangelical respondents claimed to be very interested in discussing politics whereas 70.4 per cent had little or no interest (Fediakova and Parker 2009: 62).

quite polemical as it would leave many workers without a job. The strike and the demonstrations received a good deal of national media coverage. But in the EPC, the subject only emerged in conversations when I brought it up, and it never became a topic of long discussions. When I mentioned the strike the day before it took place to a friend in the EPC, he simply replied that congregants did not concern themselves with such 'worldly' matters and then immediately changed the subject of our conversation. The night before the demonstrations, I went to a meeting the EPC. Only one indirect comment about the events of the coming day was made when the preacher briefly reminded the congregation of the church activities of the week:

> Tomorrow we will meet in the church at 7.30 p.m. as usual and we will let the 'world' mind its own business.

The latter part of this excerpt ('we will let the "world" mind its own business') is not a standard utterance during announcements of coming church activities. Here the preacher was apparently assuming that listeners were aware that something unordinary was about to occur in the 'world'. But by avoiding specific references to the strike or by mentioning it without really mentioning it he also made it painstakingly clear that such 'worldly' events did not deserve much attention. Through such strategies political events are defined as irrelevant and placed at the outer margins of religious discourse in a display of demonstrative indifference.

According to Bourdieu, indifference towards politics should mainly be seen as a manifestation of impotence, a subjective exclusion or sense of place within the social space that follows from an objective exclusion. Being concerned with politics is dependant upon a sense of being entitled or authorised to be concerned with and talk about politics (1984: 406).[3] In 2008 the Chilean sociologists Evguenia Fediakova and Christian Parker conducted a survey among Evangelicals, touching

---

[3] Bourdieu notes that the objective division of labour between those who feel entitled to talk about politics and those who do not is based on both social class and gender. He found that French women were less likely than men to answer abstract political questions in political opinion polls but he also notices that this difference diminishes among people with higher education (ibid.: 405). In Chile I found similar patterns. Whereas many educated, mostly Catholic, women I spoke with enthusiastically engaged themselves in discussions about national and international politics, lower class women, Pentecostal and Catholic, were generally more oriented towards the private sphere (see chapter 9). I very rarely heard women from the EPC talk about politics.

upon themes such as democracy, citizenship, and political participation. The scholars noted that the percentage of 'I neither agree nor disagree' answers was remarkably high (between 16 and 40 per cent). In Pentecostal discourses, indifference towards politics becomes theologically grounded and justified. By conceiving of divine power, activated through praying, as a superior alternative to political power in terms of this-worldly social transformation, congregants symbolically invert secular social hierarchies and transform their 'passive options into conscious elective choices' (Bourdieu 1984: 57).

God or the Doctor

Healing constitutes another important domain of symbolic definitional struggles. Especially elder congregants in the EPC take great pains to stress that Jesus or God is the doctor of all doctors and in presenting divine power as a superior alternative or absolutely necessary supplement to modern biomedicine. Congregants also commonly stress that it is, in fact, the power and intervention of God that makes biomedical treatment work. Praying for the sick with the imposition of hands, a common Pentecostal practice in Chile as elsewhere, takes place at the end of church meetings, or sometimes in hospitals or private homes. However, the physical co-presence of the afflicted and the one who prays is not considered strictly necessary in order for healing to work, and congregants frequently ask God to heal absent others when they pray.

The ability of God to heal is confirmed through numerous stories, first- and second-hand (or more) accounts of persons who were healed from different illnesses or conditions such as infertility, diabetes, cancer, schizophrenia, and pain in different parts of the body. In many stories, miraculous divine healing occurred after human doctors had given up all hope. I even heard a few stories of persons who had been declared clinically dead but were afterwards revived by the Lord. Such stories are obviously difficult to verify, and apart from noting that I do take my informants seriously when they claim that they sometimes feel better and relieved after being prayed for, and that participation in Pentecostal worship can have certain energizing effects (see chapter 7), I shall, conveniently, ignore questions concerning the efficacy of healing.

Members of the EPC distinguish between natural and spiritual causes of illness. Most bodily illnesses, including cancer, diabetes, back pain, heart problems, etc. are categorised as natural whereas especially mental problems such as schizophrenia, depression, and suicidal tendencies are ascribed to demonic manipulation. Other widely recognised unnatural causes of illness are the evil eye (*mal del ojo*), referring to the malevolent power of an envious human gaze, and sorcery. Evil eyes attacks are foremost believed to be directed at newborn children and may be deathly. Some Catholics believe that children who have not yet been baptised are particularly vulnerable to the evil eye but can be protected if a small medal with a picture of Christ or the Virgin Mary is tied to their clothes. Pentecostals, on the other hand, prescribe prayer as the only source of protection against the evil eye. In the EPC the evil eye was by no means presented to me as a major present concern, but a few elder congregants told me how they had originally converted to Pentecostalism because God had saved their children from illnesses that were caused by evil eye attacks. Sorcery, referring to the use and mixture of certain mystical substances or to the use of evil spirits by humans with the aim of doing harm to others, may also cause deathly disease or curses. Actual stories of recent sorcery attacks are a rarity in the EPC, but one single woman in her mid-thirties explained to me that she had only recently learnt that her failure to find a man was due to a curse or sorcery attack of a former boyfriend, the only one she had ever had, whom she had been with as an unsaved teenager.

A good deal of work within the field of medical anthropology has been informed by the multiple rationalities perspective of Evans-Pritchard (1937). According to this view, actors make use of different rationalities or systems of knowledge to deal with different aspects of social reality. A crucial point made by Evans-Pritchard (and part of his implicit argument with Levy Bruhl who argued that the primitive mind does not differentiate the supernatural from reality) is that different rationalities can coexist and complement each other. Thus Evans-Pritchard's Azande informants understood perfectly well that a granary roof had fallen down because it had been eaten by termites. Yet they *also* believed that this had occurred at a particularly unfortunate time, namely when some people were sitting under the roof, because of witchcraft (1937/1973). Drawing on the legacy of Evans-Pritchard (though not always referring directly to his work) medical anthropologists have pointed out how people in different parts of the world often distinguish between immediate (mundane) causes and underlying origin (for example, witchcraft, sorcery) of a medical condition (Ingstad 1990).

While different rationalities or systems of knowledge can harmoniously supplement each other, navigation between them may also involve symbolic struggles over definitions of social reality. As Dorthe Brogaard Kristensen argues in a brilliant and path-breaking study of medical pluralism in southern Chile, medical choices can reflect negotiations of social identities and power relationships (2008: 61). This point can very easily be extended to include medical diagnosis. Diagnosing a given condition as caused by demonic disturbance, evil eye, or sorcery and prescribing prayer, either as the only efficient remedy or as an absolutely necessary supplement to biomedical treatment, can also be seen as a moment of resistance to a secular modernist hegemony. Making such a diagnosis is ultimately an assertion of authority and power, a claim that a humble Pentecostal 'brother' or 'sister' with little formal education is, in fact, in possession of a superior knowledge and is therefore in a better position than the medical doctor with years of academic training to understand what is *really* going on and consequently to take the appropriate action.

If a medical condition is ascribed to demonic disturbance it should come as no surprise that prayer is preferred over biomedical treatment. But what struck me during my fieldwork was that many, especially elder, members of the EPC, repeatedly emphasised that divine power was the only efficient source of healing, even in cases of sickness where no demonic presence was perceived or deduced. Many of the older members of the EPC are generally reluctant to consult medical doctors in the case of sickness. Such reluctance can be ascribed to the unequal access to proper medical attention in Chile and to frustrations with the public health system. Private clinics are both expensive,[4] efficient, well equipped, and located in newly painted buildings, but an overwhelming majority of congregants have to rely on public hospitals. Less aesthetic surroundings, long waiting lists, long waiting time before consultations, endless bureaucracy, lack of personnel and proper equipment (Borzutsky 2006: 152), and occasional gaps between biomedical diagnosis and the subjective experiences of patients (see Kristensen 2008: 124) are all factors that may produce frustrations and

---

[4] Members of the EPC often stress that divine healing is free of charge.

distrust in the public health system and make the healing power of God seem like an attractive alternative, even when no spiritual cause of illness is diagnosed.

Ana Maria, a widow in her late sixties, once told me how she had recently fallen and hurt her leg. A doctor, whom she, after all, went to see, wanted to put her leg in a plaster, but she refused, feeling confident that her only true doctor, the Lord, would cure her. After a church meeting where she was prayed for, her leg recovered completely. In this case, interpretation of a condition was informed by purely mundane attribution schemes. At no point did Ana Maria ascribe her accident to spiritual disturbance, whereas recovery, on the other hand, was clearly seen as the result of divine action. In a similar fashion, Victor, an unmarried street vendor in his fifties, described how God had once cured him of back pains:

> I was sick. I had terrible pains in my back. And I did not have anyone who could give me a glass of water. So I said to the Lord, 'Lord, you are my doctor, why don't you cure me. I don't trust the doctors of the "world".' And one day I was in bed and I felt that someone was knocking on my door. Because the Lord is very polite, very educated, he does not enter without knocking first, I felt that the door was opened and closed, but I didn't see anyone, but I felt the presence of someone in the house. So I said, 'Lord, if it is you, welcome to my home,' and I felt that he came to the bed and put his hand on my back and he started to cure me.

When I later asked Victor what had caused his back pain, he made no references to demonic forces but instead mentioned his many years of hard physical work. Rather than a supplementary or ultimate source of healing, corresponding to a supplementary diagnosis of the underlying or ultimate (for example, demonic or social) origin of a medical condition, divine power is simply presented as a superior and sufficient alternative to the biomedical system, which is rejected all together, no matter the diagnosis. In a similar vein God is sometimes presented as a superior alternative, rather than a supplement, to modern psychology. On one occasion a preacher in the EPC made the following statement:

> We don't need psychologists, because we have the best of all psychologists! We have the Lord. According to the 'world' we are crazy but not according to the Lord.

This statement produced some excitement and several listeners responded by shouting 'amen!' On the one hand, the view held by 'world', namely that Pentecostals are crazy, is rejected in favour of God's opinion. But at the same time the preacher adopts the perspective of the 'world', arguing that Pentecostals are also better off according to 'worldly' standards since they have a superior psychologist, namely the Lord. The 'world' is defeated at home as well as away.

Elaborate explanations of how divine power effectuates healing are not very common in the EPC. However, some congregants present divine power as a very explicit alternative to biomedical surgery by describing how Jesus or God has performed surgery on them. Gloria, a woman in her mid-sixties, explained to me how she had once needed surgery in her head because of the severe beatings she regularly took from her heavy-drinking husband (who was not a congregant). She was unwilling to see a human doctor. In her own words:

> Why would I go to see a 'worldly' doctor? The Lord created us, he saved us, he knows us better than anyone, and he will cure us. I don't like the doctors. He died for my sake! So who could cure me better than him?

She prepared herself for spiritual surgery by putting some boiled water in a bottle and then 'added the blood of Jesus to the bottle through an act of faith'. After drinking the water she received a vision. Jesus, whom she described as beautiful and precious man, placed her in a white chair and shaved the hair of her head. He then opened her head, performed the surgery by removing the source of her pain and dizziness and finally closed her head again. Afterwards she started feeling much better, though the continuous beatings of her husband had made a total of three further spiritual operations necessary over the last decade.

Though elder congregants have a particularly distrustful relationship to biomedicine and medical doctors, the superiority of divine power as a healing alternative is also frequently emphasised by younger congregants. Eloisa, a woman in her late thirties, who had recently given birth to her first child, explained to me how she had tried to get pregnant for more than ten years. After three years of marriage she had asked God if she would ever get pregnant. She then opened the Bible at random with her eyes closed thrusting that he would lead her to a relevant passage. She found the first part of the gospel of Luke where an angel informs Zechariah that his wife Elizabeth will bear a son and that they should name him John (later to be known as John the Baptist). After that Eloisa never doubted that she would one day become pregnant:

> I never lost my faith; whenever someone asked me if I had children, I answered, 'No, the Lord has not given me a child yet,' but I knew that the day would come. I cannot deny that I went to see a doctor two times, but after that I did not go again; we decided to leave it all in the hands of the

> Lord. My husband said to me, 'We are searching in vain; don't go to see
> that doctor anymore, because that will do us no good; he won't help you.
> If the Lord wants to give us a child, he will give us a child.' So I never went
> to the doctor again.

In this story, biomedical expertise and knowledge are clearly devalued
in favour of divine power. It seems as if Eloisa is almost trying to excuse
herself for having seen a human doctor ('I cannot deny that I went to
see a doctor two times') as if this failure to rely exclusively on God was
a sin.

There is more to medical diagnosis and the pursuit of healing than a
search for the most efficient relief of a given condition. Apart from
being an assertion of possession of a superior knowledge, the presenta-
tion of God as the only truly efficient healer also introduces Pentecostal
agency into healing. Transformative divine power must be activated by
born-again human agents, and hence healing is ultimately dependant
upon the persistent praying of Pentecostals themselves. This understanding of human responsibility in healing was clearly articulated
during a church meeting in the EPC, where the preacher encouraged
all participants to pray for an absent 'sister', Cecilia who was ill and had
to undergo surgery:

> We all have to pray for our sister Cecilia who is sick so that God can help
> her. Because if she is only to rely on the doctors, it is unlikely that she will
> get better.

Once more, God is presented as the only efficient source of healing. But
it is also striking how the most important and influential human agency
involved in the recovery of Cecilia seems to be that of faithfully praying
Pentecostals. Members of the EPC very frequently remind each other
of the absolute necessity of persistent praying for the sick, whether or
not a biomedical treatment has been sought.

Despite the frequently articulated distrust in biomedicine, an overwhelming majority of congregants do consult doctors and consume
medicine when they are sick. I was often told that God sometimes prefers to use human doctors as instruments in order to cure people, and
that modern medicine is in fact a divine gift to humans. Thus congregants do not hesitate in describing a successful biomedical treatment
as nothing less than a divine miracle. Stories about recovery through
biomedical treatment often start with a phrase like 'the Lord cured me'
or 'the Lord performed a miracle in my life.' Pointing out incon-
sistencies in the explanations of informants would be an analytical

endeavour of little interest to congregants whose main concern is to remain faithful to the understanding of total dependency on God in all interpretations of healing. As one old Pentecostal woman put it, 'Sure, I go to the doctor sometimes, for instance for a check-up, or if I need antibiotics. But I know that the one who cures me is not the doctor, but Jesus.' When healing occurs without the intervention of a doctor, biomedicine can be seen as an insufficient human solution to problems that only God can solve. And when people are cured by doctors and medicine, these are seen as the means that God sometimes chooses to use.

Modernity and Trust

According to Anthony Giddens, modern existence is characterised by a basic trust in abstract principles and especially expert systems such as technical knowledge and medical science. This trust relies on a faith in the validity and correctness of principles of which most individuals have no or very limited knowledge (1994: 36). Thus a majority of people in modern societies believe in the ability of medical doctors to cure diseases though only a minority possesses detailed knowledge of bio-medical science. And most of us feel relatively confident that we will arrive safely when we take an aeroplane even though we do not understand the mechanisms that prevent the plane from falling down. Giddens does not claim that modern individuals have blind trust in expert systems, but stresses that our trust is often accompanied by scepticism and suspicion (ibid.: 80–1). He further argues that critical reflexivity is a main feature of modernity because of the hypothetical form of modern scientific knowledge (1996: 33) and the dis-embedding processes that foster feelings of loss of control over local events (1994: 26). Nevertheless daily conduct is mostly guided by a pragmatic acceptance of expert systems (ibid.: 81).

Giddens further suggests that the basic trust that characterises modernity must be seen in relation to (a) a context of general awareness that human activity, including the impact of technology, is socially created and not given by nature or divine influence and (b) the increased transformative potential of human agency and dynamic social institutions. Thus a distinguishing feature of modernity is new perceptions of determination and ambiguity, which means that human moral imperatives, natural causes, and mere coincidences are seen as main determining factors in history and everyday life (1994: 36). However, the global emergence of religious revivalism and fundamentalism points to the complexity of the modern world. The Pentecostal symbolic rejection of the 'world' and the emphasis on transformative power as originating from God not only testify to sensations of social impotence, to a widespread political apathy in Chilean society or to frustrated experiences with the public health system. It also contains a more general critique of secular modernist thought. This is not to deny that members of the EPC do in many situations have the same pragmatic confidence as most other people in technical, scientific principles they do not fully understand. But among members of the EPC, I also noticed a remarkably distrustful relationship to some of the main aspects of modernity, as described by Giddens.

In this chapter attention has been focused on Pentecostal inversive practices. I demonstrated how members of the EPC alter established relationships between signifier and signified, challenge popular perceptions of class-related ways of speaking Spanish, and through certain aesthetic practices, reject and transcend principles of Catholicism and secular erudite culture. Focusing on discourses and understandings of politics and healing, I further explored how congregants continuously attempt to downplay the determining power of human agency, social institutions, and mere coincidence. The Pentecostal procedures of everyday creativity (de Certeau 1984: xiv) escape scientific reasoning and secular notions of transformative power and instead posit divine power, accessible to and activated by human agents as the only true source of social and personal transformation.

CHAPTER SIX

CONVERSION

I praise the Lord because he gave his life for me. He washed me with his precious blood, he forgave all my sins! He made me a new creature. He cured me of many diseases. And since that precious day, he has never left me. He is so good! I know that he takes care of me. I am not short of anything at home. God is great and wonderful. I know that he was with us during the meeting last Sunday. I know that he lives. I know that he will do something marvellous with all his people. I know that his house [the church] will be filled with blessings. (*Carmen, Pentecostal widow in her early seventies*)

I had come to the church for the first time in years. I didn't like going to the church, I felt that the church was not a place for me. Well, I sat down with the young women in the back of the church, and they were all wearing skirts. I sat down, and the pastor started speaking. And the sisters looked at me, and I said to myself, 'Are these persons right? Is their opinion the right one?' And I asked myself if it was really worth it. That was my question. I didn't understand too much, so I prayed to the Lord and asked him why he didn't give me something. And I said to the Lord, 'If this is really what you want for me, I will do it!' I had this thing in me. And then suddenly, the pastor quotes a passage from the Bible, where Mary Magdalene dries Jesus' feet with her hair. And I felt that the Lord was trying to tell me something. And when the meeting finished, when they were singing the last hymn, I realised that I was crying. I was crying with joy; I could not control myself! And the sisters looked at me and said, 'It seems like the Lord saved you!' I came home, and I felt strange, as if there was something new in me. (*Ingrid, single unemployed woman in her mid-twenties, daughter of Pentecostal parents*)

There are good reasons for paying attention to conversion in the study of Chilean Pentecostalism. Firstly, the growth of Protestantism in Chile from 1 per cent of the total population in 1907 to 15.1 per cent in 2002 should mainly be ascribed to the conversion of a good number of mostly Catholic and lower- or lower middle-class Chileans to Pentecostalism. Secondly, the experience of conversion is foundational to Pentecostal religiosity and the subsequent narrating of that experience constitutive of Pentecostal self-identity.

Dwelling for a moment at the first observation, the first question that comes to mind is *why* so many Chileans have converted. Addressing this question requires an exploration of the specific historical, cultural, and social circumstances that have made a significant number of Chileans prone to conversion. And, equally importantly, we must ask what Pentecostalism has to offer. As previously mentioned a bulk of scholarly literature on Chilean and Latin American Pentecostalism focuses on motives for conversion and long-term consequences of church membership (sometimes unintended and therefore not to be confused with motives for initial conversion). Authors have demonstrated how participation in Pentecostal churches provides people with cultural strategies for coping with material and emotional hardships or deficits of meaning in contemporary Latin American societies. In the previous chapter I argued that traditional Pentecostal discourses and practices provide actors from specific social sectors with a sense of agency while at the same time articulating a critique of different aspects of Chilean society. In chapter 9 I look at the ways in which Pentecostalism helps believers in everyday life by redefining gender relationships and altering economic priorities.

But in this chapter I adopt a different perspective as I mainly focus on *how* people convert rather than *why*. The Japanese sociologist Shimazono Susumu has suggested that scholars of religious conversion should not limit their analytical focus to the moment when an individual chooses to join a religious movement and the preceding processes of tension and seekership. The study of conversion, he argues, should also be concerned with continuing growth in faith over time (1986: 158). Concurring wholeheartedly with this view, I will address a couple of important questions: How—or through what processes—do people come to perceive themselves as born-again Pentecostals who were formerly misguided sinners? And how are religious self-identities as born-again Christians—whose lives are pervaded by divine presence, protection, and planning—nourished, confirmed, reproduced, and modified over time?

In the following, I argue for the importance of narrative practice for the constitution of Pentecostal self-identities and shared realities. Attention will in particular be focused on the narrating of personal testimonies of salvation as a cultural process through which converts reconstruct their autobiographic pasts by use of new rhetorical, conceptual resources while at the same time empowering themselves. I further focus on post-conversion life stories as a way of continuously re-narrating the engagement of the Pentecostal subject with divine others. In addition to reorganizing the past I argue that Pentecostal narrative practice also provides converts with symbolic structure and a temporal schema for future action.

In the last part of the chapter I suggest that the narrating of testimonies should also be seen as a specific kind of social interaction, constituting a religious reality to be shared by narrator and listener alike. I examine different rhetoric and non-linguistic strategies by use of which the listeners are invited to inhabit or project themselves into the world of the story and live out its plots themselves. By embracing listeners, the narrating of testimonies becomes an important strategy of converting others. And it is a means by use of which already converted Pentecostals repeatedly invite each other to relive the original conversion experience and to continue to inhabit a shared world, which is pervaded by the sacred.

Converting from What?

A distinction can be made between three types of conversion: (1) from Catholic to Pentecostal, (2) from nominal, non-saved to saved/born-again Pentecostal, (3) from non-religious to Pentecostal. Converts in the second category are second- (or more) generation Pentecostals who at some point in their lives made a personal choice to receive Christ as a saviour. The boundaries between the first two categories and the third are fuzzy. Pentecostals often define previous religious affiliation in terms of confessed belief and practice, but in many cases those who report having been non-religious did have some contact with Catholicism or Pentecostalism. Besides, the range of ex-Catholics I met in the EPC as in other Pentecostal churches spanned from persons who hardly ever set foot in a Catholic church to a couple of young men who had entered the Catholic Theological Seminary to be trained as priests. But as a general tendency Pentecostal ex-Catholics never had very strong ties to the Catholic Church.[1]

In the EPC an overwhelming majority of active congregants below forty have Pentecostal parents, whereas the number of ex-Catholics

---

[1] Other scholars confirm this tendency. According to Brian Smith, Pentecostals in Latin America make most of their converts from the "cultural" Catholics (numbering in the range of 300 million) with weak ties to the church (1998: 75), and a similar observation is made by Steigenga and Cleary (2007: 9) and Chesnut (2003: 41).

increases among the older members. Differences in pre-conversion religious affiliation are not reflected in radically different testimonies. The saving power of the Holy Spirit is acquired rather than inherited, and being born and raised within a Pentecostal family does not make anyone a child of God. Salvation must follow repentance of sins and a personal decision to ask Christ to enter one's life. In Pentecostal terminology, Catholics, non-saved Pentecostals, and non-religious people all belong to the 'world'. Most testimonies, including those of second- (or more) generation congregants, include accounts of an unsatisfying life in the 'world' followed by salvation. In several testimonies, told to me personally or during meetings, congregants did not even mention to which of the three categories they had belonged unless I asked them directly.

Defining Conversion

A classical Pauline model of religious conversion as instant, total, and caused by a moment of revelation has been subject to considerable scholarly scrutiny. While this model often informs the narratives of Pentecostal and other religious converts who place a good deal of emphasis on one particular turning point, anthropologists, sociologists, and other scholars mostly conceive of conversion as a gradual and sometimes ambiguous process of socialisation into shared linguistic and ritual practices (Coleman 2003: 16; Rambo 1993; Stromberg 1993; Harding 1987; Gooren 2010).[2] Echoing the views of Susumu, scholars have further argued that this process continues long after the original event, and that conversion as a movement away from something and towards something new is continuously re-enacted in different ritual and quotidian practices (Lindhardt 2009a, 2011; Stromberg 1993; Robbins 2004b). Lewis Rambo suggests that the word *converting* might capture the phenomenology of the process better (1993: 7) and in a similar vein Simon Coleman refers to rhetorical and other

---

[2] I fully share the view of scholars such as Diane Austin-Broos (2003) and Rebecca Sachs Norris (2003) that religious conversion involves both the assimilation of new meanings *and* the development of new ritual dispositions or of new embodied, holistic knowledge, acquired through participation in ritual. Ritual practice is the theme of the two subsequent chapters, but in the present chapter I focus more narrowly on narrative practices.

practices of Swedish charismatic Christians as 'continuous conversion' (2003).

While conversion to Pentecostal-charismatic Christianity is experienced as reorientation to new belief systems, the extent to which such reorientation constitutes a radical break with the past or—to use a rather hackneyed expression—is better seen as 'new wine in old wineskins', has been vividly debated in recent years (Robbins 2003, 2004*a*, 2004*b*, 2007; Meyer 1998, 1999*a*; Engelke 2004; Lindhardt 2009*a*), with most scholars placing themselves somewhere on a continuum between these two positions. What appears to be beyond scholarly dispute is that new identities, beliefs, and dispositions cannot be created totally *de novo* but always build up from existing beliefs and practices. As mentioned, most 'saved' Pentecostals that I have met in Chile were already Christians in some sense, either nominal Pentecostals or (mostly nominal) Catholics, before they decided to receive Christ as their personal saviour. In the case of nominal Pentecostals who convert or become saved, a Pentecostal world view and rhetorical system already existed as a latent resource to be mobilised in a given situation (often some kind of life crisis).

I do not think that a rigid dichotomy between believer and non-believer is a very fruitful point of departure in the study of conversion to Pentecostalism in Chile. Instead I want to argue for the usefulness of Joel Robbins's distinction between two senses of the word 'belief' in analysing the kind of transformation that occurs when nominal Christians become 'saved' or born-again. To 'believe in' something implies trusting it and committing oneself to act in a certain way towards it, whereas 'belief that' is usually applied to propositional statements like: 'I believe that God exists' (Robbins 2007: 14). None of my Pentecostal informants described their conversion as a process of coming to realise or believe that God existed. Conversion or salvation was rather conceptualised as a question of establishing an intimate relationship with God. One young Pentecostal man described the difference between 'before' and 'now' as follows: 'I have always believed that God exists. But before, well, I was minding my own business and he was minding his own business. There was no relation.' What I hope to demonstrate in this chapter is that conversion to Pentecostalism can in large part be seen as a process through which the belief *in* a powerful and caring God who can and frequently does intervene in human affairs begins to inform reflection upon oneself and the social world.

Focus in the remaining part of this chapter mainly lies on different aspects of Pentecostal narrative practice and their role in conversion processes. However, I will start out by highlighting a few differences in terms of pre-conversion religious affiliation and point out different motives of conversion among men and women. I will then briefly discuss a few structural preconditions or predisposing factors for conversion and continued church membership.

Variations between Sexes

It has become commonplace to argue that testimonies of religious converts are better seen as interpretive reconstructions than transparent representations of the objective truth of conversion (Snow & Phillips 1980; Greil & Rudy 1984; Rambo 1993; Peel 1995; Pfeil 2011). I fully share this view, and my purpose of analysing Pentecostal testimonies a little later in this chapter is foremost to explore reconstructive processes rather than to produce objective, quantitative data of factors that lead people to convert. However, assuming that testimonies are not pure fiction or total distortions of actual conversion processes, I will in the following section dare to make a few cautious generalisations, based on Pentecostal testimonies, about conditions and motives of conversion and point out some differences between the sexes and between first- and second- (or more) generation Pentecostals.

Second- (or more) generation Pentecostal women tend to have the least dramatic testimonies. Many of them do not describe their conversion as motivated by particular difficult life circumstances but merely explain that they, at some point in their young lives, felt the need to establish a personal relationship with God instead of just coming to church in order to accompany their parents. Testimonies of men, even young second- (or more) generation Pentecostals, more often include accounts of a sinful and unsatisfying life in the 'world'.

In the case of first-generation Pentecostals (ex-Catholics and non-religious persons), the decision to convert was usually motivated by particular factors such as illness, domestic problems, abuse, often combined with pressure from Pentecostal significant others. The themes of illness and healing figure most prominently in the testimonies of women. Approximately half of all first-generation Pentecostal women first came to a church because they or some family member and mostly children had been sick. Pre-conversion alcohol and drug abuse problems were, on the other hand, exclusively reported by men. A high number of women relate their conversion to family problems such as domestic conflicts, illness of children, etc., whereas men tend to ascribe their conversion to individualistic problems such as alcohol and drug abuse, financial and work related problems, unemployment, etc.

Guisela, a woman in her early twenties explained to me how she, her parents, and her younger brother all converted at the same time from nominal non-practicing to saved/born-again and practicing Pentecostals. They had been persuaded to come to church by a Pentecostal friend after going through serious domestic problems. Guisela's father had problems at work, he started drinking, and it was implied though not said directly that he had been cheating on her mother. Her parents were arguing all the time and the domestic environment had become so unbearable that Guisela spent most of the day away from home. Her personal decision to seek Christ was further motivated by problems with a boyfriend. But throughout my interview with her, she related her personal conversion to the conversion of her whole family. Her testimony was framed in terms of a marked contrast between the pre- and the post-conversion domestic environments. When I later interviewed her father, he narrated his own conversion in much more individualistic terms. He had been possessed by a spirit of laziness, making him tired and unable to work. His testimony included no account of how this possession had affected his family. The domestic turbulence, a dominant theme in Guisela's testimony, was not mentioned. Such differences can be ascribed to particular cultural constructions of gendered identities, a topic that I address in chapter 9. Chilean women, especially in the lower classes, tend to be more oriented towards the domestic sphere, whereas men generally seek prestige in the public sphere and have more individualistic patterns of consumption. For women, conversion often has to do with the well-being of the family whereas for men conversion is rather a matter of individual well-being.

Structural Availability

A majority of first-generation congregants and a majority of second- (or more) generation male congregants convert because of some kind of problem. Yet as Smilde points out, significant life problems are too widely distributed to adequately explain why some people address them through religious solutions (2007: 180). Many men in Chile as elsewhere have alcohol or drug abuse problems, but conceiving of Pentecostal religion as a possible solution to a problem is, to a very large extent, dependant upon the structural availability of the afflicted.

Structural availability refers to social networks with people inside and outside of a religious group. Scholars have been more or less unanimous in asserting that conversion to and continued membership within a religious group is unlikely in the absence of affective bonds to one or more members (Lofland & Stark 1965; Berger & Luckmann 1972; Snow & Phillips 1980; Gooren 2007). The EPC is not successful in attracting new converts through street preaching and does not use the mass media for evangelisation. The only real channel of recruitment is congregants' personal networks. With very few exceptions, active, converted congregants have been introduced to the church by family members, friends, or neighbours. Close family ties or strong friendships with Pentecostals, combined with the absence of strong affective bonds to non-Pentecostals, not only reduce the consequences of conversion in terms of social rupture but also makes the 'Pentecostal solution' to a given problem more readily available.

Conversion to and continued membership within a religious group is further facilitated by weak affective bonds to non-members. In an intriguing study of Venezuelan Pentecostalism, Smilde highlights the complex role of networks in conversion. Emphasizing the importance of family ties for the sustention of identity in Venezuela he points out that male conversion is largely precluded when a man lives with his non-Pentecostal family of origin (2007: 158). In the EPC, many women have Catholic husbands—mostly because they converted before getting married—and children who are not church-goers. But all young and single congregants are either living alone or with Pentecostal relatives or friends. No first-generation congregants reported having experienced strong family support at the time of the distress that lead to conversion. A few congregants—first- and second-generation Pentecostals—converted after leaving their hometown and moving to Valparaíso. I never heard any one ascribe his or her own conversion to being alone in a new town, but in the case of second-generation Pentecostals the decision to join the EPC could very well be motivated by an awareness of the church as a potential source of new networks.

David Snow and Cynthia L. Phillips (1980: 431) have argued that the extent to which weak affective bonds to non-members are required depends on the character of a given religious group. In communal groups such as the Hare Krishna or the Amish, where members live together, affective bonds to outsiders must be limited. Most Pentecostal churches including the EPC are not communal groups or total institutions. Congregants live, work, and study outside of the church, and most of them have family members, colleagues, fellow students, and in some cases even a few friends who are not Pentecostals or nominal Pentecostals. But marriage with other congregants is strongly encouraged in order to avoid clashes between Pentecostal and 'worldly' values. Accepting certain dress codes and refraining from drinking, smoking, gambling, doing drugs, and non-marital sex is easiest if intense social interaction with people who do not live according to such rules is avoided. Keeping congregants' social interaction within the church is partly achieved by maintaining a very high level of church activities.

In the case of many male converts, refraining from partying and womanizing implies distancing oneself from previous friendships and acquaintances (see also Montecino and Obach 2002: 80). For many of the young men in the EPC, conversion resulted in social rupture with previous friends. Some of the university students in the church told me that they rarely participated in social activities with their fellow students. The fact that they did not drink, dance, and party and never participated in university political life made them outsiders. One young man felt further excluded, as he studied biology and was the only creationist in his class. In such cases continued church membership is facilitated by friendships and social participation. In the EPC a group of youth often hangs out in private homes after church meetings or choir practice, having tea and chatting. During weekends they occasionally play soccer, have meals together, or go on evangelisation excursions to neighbouring cities. On Saturdays they sometimes hold vigils (late-night meetings) followed by a meal. To conceive of vigils as a direct alternative to a night out in town might be pushing analysis over the edge. But they do provide a compensation for 'worldly' Saturday night activities in terms of intense social participation and bodily, rhythmic involvement (see chapter 7).[3]

---

[3] In the Assemblies of God youth meetings on Saturdays are actually very reminiscent of rock concerts. A band performs with electric instruments, and the audience stand, dance, clap, and sway with the rhythm. In the EPC no electric instruments are used, and the hymns sung are slower and less 'up-beat' than in the Assemblies of God.

*The Economic and Educational Capital of Conversion: Variations
between First- and Second-Generation Congregants*

In the EPC practically all first-generation congregants are persons with
little formal education and low-status low-income jobs, many self-
employed in the informal economic sector. Some of them have experienced economic advancement after converting and have entered the
lower middle classes after years of hard work, but an overwhelming
majority reported living in poverty at the time of conversion. All university students and degree holders are second- (or more) generation
Pentecostals. When I first visited the EPC in Valparaíso in 1999, there
was only one person in the church who held a university degree. He
was a man in his fifties and a third-generation Pentecostal who considered himself to be quite atypical (we will meet him again in chapter 10).
A number of younger 'native' congregants have entered university, and
when I last returned in 2008 I counted a total of six new graduates, all
less than thirty-three years old, among the active congregants in
Valparaíso.

Pentecostal churches in Chile and elsewhere in Latin America have
problems in keeping young people and middle-class citizens, who are
frustrated because of the low level of the sermons and the teachings in
the churches, and who find the rigorous moral demands unnecessary
and difficult to live up to (Cleary & Sepúlveda 1997; Smith 1998: 99).
Some churches like the Assemblies of God in Valparaíso have successfully coped with this challenge by being more flexible with regards to
dress and hair codes and make-up, allowing youthful services with
rock music, allowing the youth to *pololear* (have boyfriends or girl-
friends) provided that they do not have sex, organizing excursions for
the youth, and offering Bible lessons taught by theologically trained
pastors. The Assemblies of God in Valparaíso has a youth group with
approximately thirty-five members between seventeen and thirty-five.
The majority of these are university students or hold degrees. In the
Assemblies I actually met and interviewed three persons who had converted from Catholicism to Pentecostalism after starting or finishing
university. Two of them were still living with their non-Pentecostal
parents at the time of conversion.[4] Some young congregants told me

---

[4] They were both men who converted after having drug problems and going through
severe depressions. They both reported having received little emotional support from
their parents at the time of distress and had both been introduced to the Assemblies by
friends.

that they had been touring different churches in search for the right one and eventually decided for the Assemblies because of the youth group.

The EPC is known by other Pentecostals as one of the most conservative and old-fashioned Pentecostal churches in Chile, and few attempts have been made to adapt church norms to popular youth culture or middle-class intellectual standards. Dress and hair codes are strict, and no electric instruments are used in services. The pastor has no theological training, and sermons and Bible classes rarely include sophisticated theological arguments.

The message of human impotence and total dependence upon God is most appealing to people in particular social positions. As Smilde notes, people who experience upward social mobility are more likely to adopt a religious frame containing a more mundane sense of agency (1998: 300). In the EPC in Valparaíso there are no ex-Catholics or ex-members of other Pentecostal churches among the university students or young professionals, who all have very strong affective bonds, mainly in the form of family ties within the church.[5] This is not to say that students or young professionals are not committed, devoted, and firmly believing Pentecostals, or that they only stay within the church in order to avoid family conflicts. But the inability of the EPC to appeal to middle-class, well-educated Catholic Chileans is striking, and the presence of young students and professionals within the church must be ascribed to a variety of factors including affective bonds to other members.

Testimonies of Salvation: A Few Theoretical Perspectives

The personal narrative or testimony of salvation (*testimoneo de salvación*) is central to Pentecostal religiosity. It is in large part through the narrating of testimonies that believers construct and reaffirm their own religious self-identities and position themselves within a Pentecostal community. Pentecostal services provide rich opportunities for narrating of individual testimonies. If members of the EPC from another Chilean city visit the church in Valparaíso, they will usually be encouraged to come forward and introduce themselves

---

[5] A few university students moved to Valparaíso in order to study and do not have family bonds within the church. But they have family bonds with members of the EPC in their hometowns, strong friendships in the church in Valparaíso and weak affective bonds to non-Pentecostals in Valparaíso.

to the congregation during a church meeting. In these contexts self-presentation mainly consists in the narrating of a testimony of salvation.

Through the construction of a testimony believers learn to organise and situate their own life course and experiences within a biblical narrative and timeline. John D. Y. Peel defines the narrative as a critical instrument of human agency in that it enables agents to 'integrate the temporal flow of their activities' or provides a sociocultural form in which an arc of memories, actions, and intentions 'may be expressed, rehearsed, shared and communicated' (1995: 582–3). Narratives, he continues, are informed by a superior knowledge, which gives the author an advantage over the chronicler. Unlike the latter, the former has knowledge of an outcome that is used to define incidents as relevant or irrelevant (ibid.: 593). In a similar fashion Wayne Booth claims that the teller of a narrative dwells at the point of arrival, which is implicit throughout the story and forms all details (1995: 372–3). The relation between narrativity and lived time has also and quite thoroughly been examined by Paul Ricoeur, who conceives of the construction of narratives as a process of emplotment. This process mediates between individual events and the story as a whole as the narrator flashes back and forth between the two (1984: 81–5; Carr 1991: 167). It is through emplotment that a subjective identity with a felt unity of experiences or a sense of self-sameness is constituted (Ricoeur 1988: 246).

Peel further argues that the narrative is both an expression of power and works to empower those who can achieve it (1995: 593). Dwelling at the point of arrival and possessing a superior knowledge, the narrator exercises a certain definitional and categorical control of his or her past. This point is echoed in the literature of religious conversion, with several scholars arguing that conversion should foremost be seen as a process of autobiographic reconstruction that—unlike the ongoing reorganisations of biographies that we all engage in on an everyday basis—is informed by radically *new* knowledge and stories (Berger and Luckmann 1972; Rambo 1993). Pointing out that people's consciousness of themselves and the world is to a large extent structured by language, scholars have also emphasised the role of language transformation in conversion (Rambo 1993: 137; Beckford 1978). David Snow and Richard Machaleck define conversion as a process by which a new or former peripheral universe of discourse, defined as a system of common and interpretative frameworks, rooted in language, becomes central. They further suggest that conversion involves the adoption of a new 'master attribution scheme', informing casual interpretations of self, other, and the world (1983: 269).

While testimonies and other narratives are instruments of individual autobiographic reconstruction they are also inherently social in that they tend to follow culturally accepted plots. As Erving Goffman argues in his study of asylums, institutions may exercise power over people by providing a restricted formula for the construction of self-stories (1961). A standard testimony in the EPC takes the form of a story about a journey from the 'world' of sin to the encounter with God, through which a certain sense of control, clarity, and power is gained. The distance between the point of departure and the point of arrival and the obstacles that are met on the way provide the main plot of the story. Through the construction of a personal testimony of salvation, cultural religious knowledge becomes self-knowledge, and congregants learn to objectify experience in particular ways. Thus 'belonging to the "world"' is a cultural linguistic typification that can summarise a wide range of individual pre-conversion experiences and states.

By being personal and stereotypical at the same time, testimonies connect individual stories to a common story of the religious community, that is the metanarrative of an ongoing movement, struggle, and tension between God and the 'world' of sin. Hence the construction and narrating of individual testimonies contribute to the creation and reaffirmation of shared realities and values. The institutional constraints and guidelines for the construction of a personal testimony were highlighted during a sermon in the EPC, when the preacher posed a question to the listeners:

> I have never heard a testimony from a brother who said that he was happy when he lived in the 'world'. Have any of you ever heard such a testimony?

The question was answered with a loud and unanimous 'no' from the congregation. The construction of a testimony of salvation with a happy past in the 'world' is simply not a narrative possibility. What are sometimes reported in testimonies are pre-conversion illusions of happiness while living in the 'world'.

Having introduced some relevant perspectives on testimonies and more generally on narratives, I will, in the following sections, introduce a few members of the EPC and quote parts of their testimonies and life stories as they were narrated to me.

Manuel

When I first met him in July 1999, Manuel was in his early twenties, unemployed, and living with his parents, who were both active congregants, and his brothers (not active congregants). He spent a fair amount of time working in the construction of a new church building, claiming that this was the least he could do considering all that which the Lord had done for him. Before converting he had developed a drug abuse problem and spent most of his time hanging out with friends, some of whom were criminals, and occasionally got into fights. He had now left all that behind and considered himself to be a new man. One of the first questions I asked him was if he had been a Catholic before converting:

> Manuel: No, I just belonged to the 'world'. I did many bad things. I was really bad. I was very aggressive with my parents; I went to parties all the time, drugs, women. But then, when the Lord enters into your life he changes your mind, and he changes everything. You really start realising; the Lord takes your mind away; it is as if you have a blindfold put over your eyes. Before you are not really aware of the things you do. You think that you are doing fine in the 'world'. Or maybe you are aware but this evil thing inside you is haunting you. But when the Lord takes this thing away, you start realising all the bad things you did, that you were really wrong. Now with my parents, there is a big difference. Now we have good communication. Before, I hardly communicated with them. Because the enemy [Satan] puts so much anger and resentment in you, he turns you against your own parents. They are Christians, so I didn't talk to them. There was no dialogue at home. And now, uuuuh, there is so much peace in my home, he changed everything. He even took my television away, now I don't have a television anymore.... Now I have been saved and forgiven for almost four months. Five months ago I started asking the Lord for salvation, and with my human mind I thought that it would take the Lord at least a year to forgive me and save me, considering all my sins. But he saved me after only three weeks. You know, when the affliction is greatest, that's when you most seek the Lord. I came to the Lord with depression, with affliction in my soul, and I became possessed by a suicidal spirit; I wanted to kill myself; the enemy was really working hard with me. Then, I started to go to church, but when I came home, I would turn on the television, and it is true that the television steals all spiritual things from you; the enemy steals it all with the screen. So when I was in my room, the enemy made me terrified; it wasn't fear that I was feeling, it was more like terror. I had to go to my parent's room. So you see, Martin, the best thing you can do is to seek the Lord, to ask the Lord for salvation.

ML: Yeah, well, so you said that a suicidal spirit had possessed you?
Manuel: Yes, it was terrible, and you cannot fight this thing. Since the Lord had not saved me yet, I had no strength, I could not fight against this thing. It was too strong. I had to ask my father for help, so he prayed for me in the name of the Lord.

A little later Manuel explained how his behaviour and personality had changed after salvation:

Yesterday, for instance, I took the bus with my younger brother. I paid for the tickets, and the driver asked me where I was going. But there was too much noise in the bus, so I couldn't hear him properly, and I thought he was telling me I had to pay more, and I didn't have more money. So I said, 'Well, then I'll just have to get off the bus.' But it was because I hadn't understood him. So he scolded me; he became very aggressive: 'Who do you think you are,' and he almost threw my money in my face. And I, if it had been for my human part, if Christ had not been present in my heart, I would have taken him by the hair and hit him. Before I met the Lord, I was violent. I would act without thinking. But thanks to the Lord, I could resist this. I just got off the bus in silence. I didn't say anything to anyone. So I feel that the Holy Spirit of God is guiding me. It is something beautiful.

Manuel uses a standard Pentecostal linguistic typification, belonging to the 'world', to describe his own pre-converted condition. In his description, this condition is partly characterised by ignorance and an illusion of happiness ('you think that you are doing fine in the "world"'). When things were very bad and he was considering suicide, he was obviously aware that something was wrong. But he told me that he did not know that he was being possessed by a suicidal spirit, and that his father had been the first to reach this conclusion. In retrospect Manuel now explains his problems, including domestic disharmony and poor communication with his parents, in terms of diabolic manipulation. His pre-conversion condition is further characterised by lack of strength and incapability of dealing with his problems. In the second excerpt Manuel adds that he used to be violent and dominated by his human part, which implied inability to control his own aggressions. Now, on the other hand, he is able to control himself, as Christ or the Holy Spirit is dwelling in him.

Manuel's conversion and autobiographic reconstruction can be seen as an example of 'alternation', defined by Berger and Luckmann as a transformative process through which an individual comes to see him- or herself and his or her past within a whole new structure of plausibility (1972: 181–5). In his own description Manuel changes from being an object, haunted and manipulated by the Devil and a suicidal spirit, dominated by a violent 'human part', ignorant of the causes of his conditions and—to the extent that he did understand that something was wrong—unable to fight back and control himself because of lack of spiritual strength, to becoming an enlightened subject. Dwelling at a point of arrival (being saved) and being in possession of a superior knowledge, he now exercises a definitional or categorical control over his past and present condition. He has, in other words, become in charge of his own life and narrative.

For Manuel, being a converted, saved, and transformed person was facilitated by a new community of significant others. He explained that he had very little contact with his 'worldly' friends with whom he used to drink, party, smoke marihuana, do drugs, and womanise. When he ran into some of them they would usually talk for a while and get along well but he did not participate in their sinful activities. He now spent most of his time at home or in the church where he had made new friends.

André

I first interviewed André in July 2000. He was a university student in his early twenties (he has now graduated) and had moved to Valparaíso from Los Andes, a large provincial town in central Chile, to study six months after becoming saved. He was currently living alone in a rented room. His mother was a highly committed member of the EPC in Los Andes, and for years she had persistently yet unsuccessfully tried to introduce André, his father, and his brothers and sisters to the church. After finishing high school and failing in his first attempt to enter the university, André was feeling dejected. Besides his academic trouble, he had serious emotional love-related problems. He spent most of his time partying and smoking marihuana. Sometimes he felt that his conscience was trying to tell him that he needed to change his life (only after being saved did he realise that God had been working with his conscience). Eventually he was feeling so miserable that he was crying all the time and even considering suicide. In a moment of absolute desperation he decided to ask God for help. He started attending church meetings, talking with other congregants, and reading the Bible and Christian literature:

> André: So I started going to the church, I started to seek the Lord, little by little. I talked to some brothers. And I had a book about spiritual matters

which I started to read. And through this book the Lord made me understand many things. I would stay up and read until 3 a.m. in the morning. The book was precious, and it helped me understand the things that the Lord had done for me. The more I read and understood, the more I realised how bad I was. Before that I didn't think that I was all that bad, I thought that I was a good guy doing a few bad things. I thought that someone bad is an assassin, someone who kills and steals from others, and I didn't do these things. But as I got closer to the Lord I came to look at myself as very bad, miserable, worthless. Until one day in the church, a Sunday in the evening, I experienced a manifestation of the power of the Lord…. You know the greatest sins that you commit, like the drugs, the vices, sins that the flesh obliges you to commit, you can't control yourself, and you do it by nature. But afterwards, when you are closer to the Lord, you realise that these things are bad. But you also realise that it is not easy, because the flesh is powerful. And I realised that I could not stop sinning; I tried really hard, until I read the word of God, and I realised that I couldn't, so I said to the Lord: 'I cannot do it, please do it for me.' And so he did.

Like Manuel, André conceives of his pre-conversion condition as characterised by ignorance and lack of clarity ('I didn't think that I was all that bad'). The process leading to conversion is described as a process of radical self-searching and enlightenment. André gradually began to reflect upon himself in new ways, and in the process he realised that he was unable to control himself. A Christian understanding of the flesh (as opposed to the spirit) as having its own sinful will provides a conceptual tool for thematising this lack of control. Diabolic forces are not mentioned in this excerpt, but a little later in the interview, André explained that he was convinced that the Devil had been controlling and guiding him before salvation. Thus the movement from being a controlled object to an enlightened self-controlling subject—or a subject who wittingly lets himself be controlled by the Holy Spirit—is also a salient feature of this testimony. Like Manuel, André only had minimal contact with his old friends from the 'world', whereas his most significant others all belonged to the church. He had good relationships with his fellow university students, but he never participated in any social activities with them in his free time.

Converted Selves

In the case of André, as of Manuel, conversion can be seen as comprising processes where new or former peripheral knowledge, for example, of demonic causality and the power of the flesh, and cultural–linguistic typifications, for example, 'belonging to the "world"', become central for self-objectification and narrative reconstruction. Acquiring such knowledge and typifications is an inherently social process. Thus Manuel told me that it was his father who first became aware that a suicidal spirit was a work. For André, getting closer to God provided him with new perspectives, enabling him to look at himself as 'very bad, miserable, worthless.' He described how this process was preceded by his mother's yearlong attempts to introduce him to the truth of the gospel and facilitated by conversations with other congregants and by a book he was reading. In a similar vein, Ingrid, who was quoted at the beginning of this chapter, described how being situated in a particular social situation resulted in new ways of reflecting upon herself. At some point during the church meeting she was attending, an intersection occurred between a story of a sermon, namely about Mary Magdalene, and Ingrid's own story, as she felt that God was trying to tell her something. In these examples we can see how conversion, resulting in new self-objectifications and new narrative identities, occur through a dynamic interplay between public and private worlds.[6]

The role of significant Pentecostal others in the development and sustentation of a new narrative identity deserves a few more comments. For converts, a new religious community is more than a point of reference when evaluating people, situations, and life projects (Hefner 1993: 25) and more than a source of conceptual, linguistic resources for individual autobiographic reconstruction. The community also serves as a source of social recognition of new religious identities. In an intriguing and persuasive attempt to construct a synthesis between Ricoeur's notion of narrative identity and Mead's theory of the human self (Mead 1962), Douglas Ezzy argues that narrative identity is integrally social. Not only is shared language the means by use of which single events can be organised into a coherent narrative but narrative identity and the sense of self-sameness are also dependant upon the recognition of others of the individual as the same person (Ezzy 1998: 241). This point is certainly valid in the case of Pentecostals for whom self-identification as former sinners who are now born-again

---

[6] These points find consonance with George Herbert Mead's understanding of the human self as emerging through the interplay between inter- and intra-subjective processes and depending upon the appropriation of a shared language (1962: 147; see chapter 2 of this book).

self-controlling subjects depends upon Pentecostal significant others recognising a person in this way. Apart from expressing a commitment to the values of a religious community, the public narration of testimonies during Pentecostal services can be seen as a particular ritualised act in which social recognition of narratively constructed self-sameness is sought.

As I went by collecting testimonies of salvation from Pentecostals I was struck by another feature, namely that conversion—in addition to implying new ways of reflecting upon oneself—was also frequently described as a process of learning to carry out an inner dialogue with God by identifying or objectifying certain aspects of internal responsiveness as divine presence. In the excerpt in the previous section André describes how he started seeking the Lord in the church and through a book. But as mentioned he also explained to me that it was in fact God who had approached him by working with his conscience, making him feel that he was on a wrong path.

The conscience is in various cultures conceived of as a fundamental part of our humanity, yet at the same time as being external to us and acting with a certain autonomy as it tells us what to do and makes us feel guilty. This is vividly illustrated in comics where a good and an evil conscience are struggling to influence the conduct of a person or an animal with human attributes. Such widespread folk conceptions of the conscience as being both autonomous and internal to us connect well with Christian understandings of the influence of sacred others on the mental activity of a person.[7] Apart from André I spoke to several congregants who described the presence of God within them as a conscience that made them aware of certain things such as their own imperfections and responsibilities to act or behave in a certain way.

Drawing on Robbins's distinction between 'believe in' and 'believe that' I argued earlier in this chapter that conversion should not be seen as a question of coming to believe *that* God exists, but rather as a process through which the belief *in* a powerful God begins to inform reflection upon oneself and the social world. The notion of a caring and ever-present God who actively interferes in human affairs and who struggles against the 'world' or the devil not only provides an interpretative framework or attribution scheme by use of which lived

---

[7] In cartoons with Tom and Jerry or Disney cartoons with Pluto, the good conscience looks like an angel, whereas the evil, green (the colour of envy) conscience has diabolic features.

experience is charged with meaning and direction; it further provides a cognitive model for relating to one's own mental activity and especially for interpreting apparent discontinuities in one's everyday flow of thoughts (see Luhrmann 2006: 4).

André recalled how God would sometimes speak to him when he was partying with his friends. In these situations he felt that something internal, a mind or a conscience, was trying to tell him that he was in an inappropriate place. At the time he was unable to identify that 'something' as the voice of God. He gave me one particular example of an instance when God had approached him:

> I arrived at this party. And it was like someone was saying to me, 'What are you doing here?' Well, at the time I thought that it was just my own mind talking to me. But later I realised that it was actually God who was approaching me.

Later in the interview André told me that he was now having internal conversations with God all the time. In these conversations God guided him and told him what to do. He mostly received divine messages in the form of sudden thoughts or intuitions. In chapter 2 I described how Mead conceives of reflective thought as an internal conversation. As conversation requires at least two participants, reflective thought must in this view always imply the presence of an internal other. The self in the work of Mead is defined as a site of symbolic awareness and internal responsiveness between the 'I' and the 'me'. The latter is the immediate experience of the self whereas the former is the subjective attitude of response to and reflection upon this experience. Applying Mead's perspective of the self, we can see conversion to Pentecostalism as a process through which people learn to objectify the other, the 'me' to whom the 'I' responds in internal conversation, in a culturally specific way, namely as the voice of God. Conversion, in other words, takes place as reflective thought is framed as a conversation with God. Through conversations with his mother and other congregants and through the book he was reading, André not only learnt to reflect upon himself in new ways but also eventually became engaged in a new meta-reflection upon his own reflective activity.

In the present chapter attention has been focused on narrative processes. However, to a large extent experiences of divine presence and the development of a personal relationship between individual believers and God occur through bodily engagement in Pentecostal ritual.

I have chosen to address narratives and ritual separately, ritual being the topic of the next chapter. For now it suffices to point out that learning to talk with God by identifying him as an internal other and possible partner of conversation is facilitated and in most cases preceded by some ritual, bodily experience, which is interpreted as an encounter with divine power.

Post-Conversion Life Stories

Pentecostal narrative practice is not confined to the construction of testimonies but includes the narrating of numerous everyday anecdotes as well as longer post-conversion life stories. And while their time span varies from a few minutes to several years, anecdotes, testimonies, and life stories are constructed through similar processes of emplotment and informed by a similar Pentecostal politics of storytelling, a main principle being crediting divine rather than human agency and planning for positive achievements. Thus anecdotes and life stories can be seen as important ways of continuously re-narrating the engagement of the Pentecostal subject with divine others. It follows that Pentecostal identity construction through the narrative practice of emplotment is better seen as a work-in-progress than a once-and-for-all completed project. The narrating of anecdotes in both and ritual and informal everyday contexts is a topic that I will address in chapter 8. In the following I will give an example of a story about divine planning of a post-conversion life course.

I interviewed Marcelo in the living room of his home, the lower part of a two-storey house in a lower middle-class neighbourhood. His wife Erna was present the whole time and joined in on our conversation on several occasions. She was twenty-eight and had been a congregant since she was eight. Her mother had been the first family member to convert from Catholicism after being left by her father and going through serious emotional and financial crisis. Erna had originally come to the EPC in order to accompany her mother, but at fourteen she had made a personal decision to receive Christ as her saviour. Marcelo was twenty-nine years and originally came from a small town in Southern Chile. He had been born and raised within a Pentecostal family and made a personal decision to receive Christ at thirteen. He started the interview by explaining to me that his testimony was somehow atypical. As he had become a Christian very early in life, there would be no standard accounts of a miserable life in the 'world'. At seventeen he finished high school and decided to join the marines:

> Marcelo: I finished high school, and then I applied to join the marines. And when I was told that I had been accepted, well I had actually already sensed it because I had been praying to the Lord and my family had been praying too. And now I was thinking about what it would mean to leave my home; I had never been away from my home before, so I said to the Lord, 'Look, if this is your will, you will open all doors for me so that there won't be any problems and everything will work out fine for me.' And everything worked out just fine. From the whole region only seven of the applicants entered the armed forces, so I felt confident that God had arranged things to permit me to enter the armed forces.

During his first five years in the armed forces Marcelo lived in different parts of Chile where he attended various Pentecostal churches whenever he had the chance. He was then transferred to Valparaíso where he joined the EPC and met Erna.

> I had the future ahead of me in the armed forces; I was doing well, and I was good at everything, swimming, shooting, running. And then suddenly it was as if everything fell apart. I found out that I was sick; I had a heart disease. So the armed forces decided to pension me off, as if I had finished my military career. And now I analyse all this, and I reach the conclusion that God permitted that I should enter the armed forces and spend ten years there; well, I think that somehow God wanted to form my character, my life, and maybe prepare me for something else, something more than that, maybe to serve him. Now I have time to devote my whole life to serve the church and serve God without having to worry about work and money.

> ML: So you receive a pension now?

> Marcello: Yes, like if I had worked for twenty years. So for me this is a blessing, because it is difficult to leave the armed forces like that. Some people leave after nineteen years, and they leave without this pension, and they have to work. In my case, I was doing really well, I had specialised in mechanics, and I had the best grades among more than one thousand students. And I said, 'How is this possible?' And I asked him, 'Why is this happening; you are giving me all these benefits, and then at the same time you are taking it all away from me?' But today I think, and I was talking with her [Erna] about it the other day, imagine, if all this had not happened, maybe we would never have married, I would have had to leave Valparaíso, my period here would have finished in December, and then they would have sent me somewhere else, maybe to Iquique [in

Northern Chile] for five years. And many of the things I am able to do here in the church, I couldn't have done them. Well, maybe there would have been someone else instead of me. But God gave me this opportunity, so that I can be here, so you start looking at all these things and you start realising that God never leaves you alone. I had to make a lot of decisions. My family lives in the south, and they want me to come back and stay with them. But I say no! If the Lord took me out the armed forces and gave me freedom, why is that? To go home and live with my parents without doing anything? That is not logical. Logic says that he gave me freedom to serve him. He said to me, 'I give you your salary every month.' We both have free medical care. So in order not to understand, well you would have to have a brain like this [makes a gesture with his thumb and forefinger indicating 'tiny'] to say, 'This is not the work of the Lord.' And the fact is that all this has been the will of God, this is what God wants for me now that I am prepared, if the Lord needs me. For example, if the pastor needs help, I cannot say that I am not able to help him.

ML: So you don't work now?

Marcello: No, I am not working, I could work in mechanics, I have been offered jobs in Viña, and I could look for work in other parts.

Erna: But he also says to me that that would be to limit himself, if the Lord gave him freedom, what is that freedom for?

Marcello: If the pastor says to me that I should help him, how could I say no, because I have to work? I think that the Lord put me in this situation so that, when the pastor says, 'Let's go and do this,' I can say, 'Amen, let's go!' Because the pastor needs a person to help him with all kinds of things!

Here a divine plan for salvation, and more particularly the role that God has for Marcelo within it seems to be the master attribution scheme that informs casual interferences and interpretations of details. The confusion that Marcello expressed in a conversation with God after first getting sick was caused by events, which, at the time, did not seem to fit or make sense within the overall narrative structure of his life story. But after engaging in interpretive processes of emplotment, partly in interaction with Erna, the pieces were put together, coherence recreated, and confusion and the sense of ambiguity replaced by clarity and a renewed sense of direction. Rather than being experienced as a mere succession, lived time becomes structured, meaningful, and coherent by being enrolled within biblical time and thus liberated from elements of ambiguity, chance, and bad luck.

Narratives are models of and for reality (Geertz 1973: 93), interpretative reconstructions of the past and 'sketches of possibilities, prophecies, or scenarios for things that might be' (Peel 1995: 584). According to Ricoeur the narrative construction of plots mediates between two levels of time, namely succession and configuration, the latter being characterised by movement from a given origin and towards a certain end (1984: 85, see also Carr 1991: 167). By articulating a sense of direction, narrative imagination provides a symbolic structure and a temporal schema for present and future action. In the last part of the excerpt it becomes evident that Marcelo's decisions to stay in Valparaíso instead of going back to his hometown and to be available for the pastor instead of looking for a job are informed by the same narrative structure that informs his interpretation of the past. Marcelo's life becomes meaningful by being narratively reviewed in the light of Pentecostal religious knowledge or master attribution schemes *and* by being lived according to a narrative script.

Testimonies as Social Interaction

I have so far conceived of testimonies and post-conversion life stories as cultural, rhetorical strategies by use of which converts reconstruct their autobiographic past while at the same time provide themselves with scenarios for future action. Though testimonies are individual stories they are also deeply embedded in the social fabric of the religious community. And while they can be rehearsed and modified in soliloquy—or in an internal dialogue with God—learning to construct them is never a solitary process.

One important way of learning to construct a personal testimony of salvation is by listening to the testimonies of others. Though the construction of testimonies can be seen as a socially informed introspective process, we should not lose sight of the fact that testimonies are also told to other people. The narrating of testimonies to others is a way of socially positioning oneself as a born-again Pentecostal and of seeking social recognition of narratively constructed self-sameness. But the narrating of testimonies also opens up a religious world to be explored by listeners. The study of testimonies should therefore not be confined to a concern with the autobiographic reconstructions of narrators but include a focus on the intersection between the world of the story and the world of the listener. No text is closed upon itself, and as Ricoeur puts it, the analysis of a text should not try to restore the intentions of the author, but rather

> make explicit the movement by which the text unfolds a world in front of itself. What is interpreted in the text is the proposing of a world that I might inhabit and into which project my own most powers. (1984: 81)

A few scholars of conversion have argued that the social power of testimonies lies in their practicality. Testimonies are often told in a way that enables the listener to identify with the 'I' of the story and to participate in and live out its exampled world, which is always described as superior to the everyday world (Susumu 1986; Booth 1995; Lindhardt 2011; Pfeil 2011). Arguing along similar lines Susan Harding suggests that the study of religious conversion will benefit from a focus on undramatic rhetorical recruiting techniques. One such technique is witnessing, defined by Harding as a conversation between a saved witness, who determines the terms and the direction of the conversation, and an unsaved listener. The purpose of witnessing, she argues, is to separate the listener from a prior given reality by linguistically constituting a new compelling religious reality or truth (1987: 169). In the following I will highlight a few narrative as well as non-linguistic strategies by use of which listeners of testimonies are invited to project themselves into the religious world of the story.

Many testimonies are partly told in the second ('you' or in Spanish *tu*) or third ('one'/*uno*) person. And though they are accounts of past events, the narrator sometimes shifts between the past and the present tense. Such rhetorical strategies serve to elevate the story from a strictly personal biography to a more general level. A few pages back I cited André, whose testimony illustrates processes of self-reflection and autobiographic reconstruction. But his testimony can be explored a bit further, as it also exemplifies strategies of embracing the listener and suggesting that he might identify with the story. I will save the reader the trouble of going back and forth by citing him once more, though in a slightly reduced version:

> Before I didn't think that I was all that bad. I thought that I was a good guy doing a few bad things. I thought that someone bad is an assassin, someone who kills and steals from others, and I didn't do these things. But as I got closer to the Lord I came to look at myself as very bad, miserable, worthless. You know the greatest sins that you commit, like the drugs, the vices, sins that the flesh obliges you to commit, you can't control these things yourself, and you do it by nature. But afterwards, when

you are closer to the Lord, you realise that these things are bad. But you also realise that it is not easy, because the flesh is powerful. And I realised that I could not stop sinning; I tried really hard, until I read the word of God, and I realised that I couldn't, so I said to the Lord, 'I cannot do it, please do it for me.' And so he did.

By changing between past and present tense and between the first and the second person André indirectly implies that his personal story could also be relevant for the listener, in this case the anthropologist. Through such shifts the biographic past of the narrator invades and merges with the present of the listener. The two are further united with the eternal, timeless truth of the gospel to which the story also testifies. The invitation to the listener to adopt the perspective of the narrator is reinforced by the use of direct speech at the end of the excerpt. The words: 'I cannot do it, please do it for me' are parts of André's unique and personal story about finding God. But their repetition in a conversation with an anthropologist is more than a representation of what took place in the past. By being spoken once more, the words are also placed into an intersubjective presence, where they become available for re-appropriation by listeners as a recipe for approaching God (as with other Pentecostal friends and informants, André was quite concerned with introducing me to my saviour).

One day my wife and I were walking through a local vegetable and fruit market in Valparaíso, where we met an older woman from the EPC who was selling potatoes. She instantly asked my wife why she never joined me in the church. When my wife replied that she was a Catholic and pretty content with her religion, the woman responded by telling us her own testimony of salvation. She had once been a young and misguided Catholic, wrongfully believing that Catholic doctrines were true. At that point she had been ignorant of the existence of a living God who is actually able to interfere in human affairs and make a difference. I remember her saying to my wife: 'I was just like you, very Catholic; I didn't want to have anything to do with the Evangelicals, I thought that they were all wrong and crazy.' She was finally persuaded to come to the EPC where she received Christ as a personal saviour and found true happiness. After telling us about this experience the old woman looked intensely into the eyes of my wife and explained that she originally and reluctantly came to the church because of problems and sufferings 'that only the Lord knew.' Though guessing about possible unspoken intentions of informants is not a standard social-scientific procedure, I will nevertheless share an untested assumption I made with the reader: I think that the old woman *could* have been meaning to imply that whatever secret problems my wife might have, the Lord was already well aware of them and that such intimidating intimacy with the Lord was an unavoidable fact of life, better to be accepted sooner than later. But more importantly—and whether or not my assumption is correct—that was how the listeners, my wife and I, *perceived* the situation, or how the world of the story unfolded. However, no new convert was gained from this encounter.

In July 2001, a choir from a local branch of the EPC in Santiago made a weekend trip to visit their spiritual brothers and sisters in Valparaíso. Congregants in Valparaíso saw this visit as a great spiritual blessing, which they had been preparing for weeks with practical arrangements, praying, and fasting. On Saturday evening an extraordinary vigil (late-night meeting) was organised in the main church in downtown Valparaíso. The church was more full than usual. As the visit from Santiago was considered a special occasion several congregants had persuaded non-saved relatives to come to church on this Saturday. One of the visitors from Santiago, a man in his fifties, was invited to address to the congregation. He introduced himself by telling us his personal testimony of salvation. He described himself as having been a man with many vices, wandering around in the 'world', directed straight towards hell. At one point he had come to the EPC:

> I came to a church much like this one. It was a vigil on a Saturday, just like the vigil we have to day. Christ manifested his glorious power and transformed me. I cannot explain with words what I felt, but I can tell you that the power that transformed me is also present here, tonight [...] God is here tonight ... maybe there is someone here who has come for the first time. I came to a meeting just like this one, and in that opportunity I said, 'God, let your spirit descend in this church to transform my life and make me a new creature because I don't like my life the way it is right now.' And it is certain, like we sing: though everyone says it is not true, I feel it now in my life. [...] That night God transformed me; this man so full of vices and sin, God took away the sin from me, that Saturday. I had been invited to the vigil, but I know now that he was the one who invited me, not my wife or my mother-in-law.

After finishing his testimony he went on to talk about other subjects. But at the end of his speech he made an explicit invitation to all non-saved persons to come forward to the pulpit and pray for salvation. As usual, when such an invitation is made, a number of the already converted/saved congregants went forward to pray, but I could not spot any new converts (and despite intimate gazes from a couple of congregants, suggesting that this was my opportunity, I remained seated on my spot).

In these examples the invitation to the listener to enter the world of the narrative and live out its plot is evident. The older woman at the vegetable market explicitly identified her own past with my wife's present condition ('I was just like you'), misguided by false Catholic doctrines and popular prejudices about Pentecostals, and unaware of the existence of a living God. The testimony from the vigil is told in general terms and without specific references to time and place, thus making it easy for listeners to project themselves into the world of the story, identify with the narrator, and live out the plots themselves. Terms and phrases like 'vices', 'wandering around in the "world"', and 'directed straight towards hell' are used by the preacher to describe his own pre-converted past, but are at the same time implicitly offered to potential converts as rhetorical, conceptual resources for self-reflection as well as to already converted/saved congregants as a means of continuous elaboration and modification of their own narrative identity.

In the first part of the excerpt, the similarity between the original context of the speaker's own conversion and the present context of potential conversion is established ('I came to a church much like this one. It was a vigil on a Saturday, just like the vigil we have to day'). As the testimony continues the similarity of contexts is explicitly confirmed ('the power that transformed me is also present here, tonight [...] maybe there is someone here who has come for the first time. I came to meeting just like this one'). Eventually the narrator guides potential converts in praying for salvation by citing his own prayer from the night he was saved ('God, let your spirit descend in this church to transform my life and make me a new creature because I don't like my life the way it is right now'). Here, he is not just speaking for himself but on behalf of anyone who can identify with the story. Once uttered, his words become detached from the speech situation and gain a life of their own so that potential converts may expropriate them in order to describe their own life and articulate a personal request for salvation. And already converted/saved congregants may take this opportunity to relive and confirm their own salvation and identity as born-again Pentecostals. The identification of many listeners with the story was reflected in their responses to it: many were truly excited and started screaming, 'Amen', 'Alleluia', or 'Glory to God'.[8]

---

[8] Peter Stromberg uses the term 'impression point' to refer to a point in which a religious story connects with a personal aspect of a person's life and hence becomes meaningful at an individual level (1985, see also Rambo 1993: 83).

Finally, the narrator asserts that it was really God—rather than wife or mother-in-law—who had invited him to the vigil where he was saved. This assertion could be seen (once more I am guessing) as an implicit suggestion to non-converted/saved listeners, who had been invited to this special event (a visit from Santiago) by their converted/ saved family members, to reconsider their presence in the church as a result of a divine plan.

Through the stories that are told a verbal context of divine presence and interference is established, and the listeners are invited to reinterpret their own experience within this context. In addition to being a reconstructive representation of a lived past, the narrating of a testimony can also be seen as a certain ritual action, tailored to the here and now of listeners (see also Pfeil 2011). The religious world of testimonies is pregnant with meaning and potentiality. Like a horizon it does not have a definite ending to be reached once and for all but can always be explored further by both narrator and listener.

The effects of spoken words or the extent to which listeners may become prone to accept invitations to enter the world of the story are influenced by a number of factors. The reader will probably agree that the experience of watching a movie is highly dependant upon the context of viewing (the most intense experiences occurring in cinemas where attention towards the movie is focused and there are no distractions). In a similar vein the ability of spoken words to touch, move, or absorb the listener depends upon the social, physical context of speech. One factor influencing the effects of words is a sensation of intimacy, existential immediacy, and social enclosure in the speech situation. Intimacy between narrator and listener may result from intense eye contact. My wife confessed to me that she had felt uncomfortable and a little intimidated when the old woman at the vegetable market looked intensely into her eyes. The eye contact between the two women was a powerful strategy of momentarily pushing the surrounding world into the background and establishing that the story being told (which in this case was about intimacy between a woman and God and about lack of secrecy in this relation) took place within a shared and present world, equally accessible and relevant to both narrator and listener. In my own experience intense eye contact with Pentecostals during attempts to convert me can indeed produce sensations of powerful immediacy, intimidating intimacy, and of being cut off from the surroundings, which in turn makes it difficult not to be absorbed by the religious world that is being unfolded during a conversation.

While such intimacy mostly made me feel uncomfortable, I can easily imagine that it can have the opposite effect on others. Another strategy of creating intimacy and enclosure is direct physical contact. For example a narrator may touch the arm of a listener when the former is about to say something considered particularly important or relevant for the latter.

When testimonies are narrated in church meetings an atmosphere of intimacy and sensual immediacy has usually been constituted through a number of ritual bodily practices such as initial singing and praying (see chapter 7). In some church meetings rather dramatic spiritual manifestations occur, mostly during singing, when participants start crying, screaming, dancing, and jumping, all of which are character-ised by an apparent absence of inhibitions. Direct physical and intimate contact take place in praying with the imposition of hands or when participants feel touched by the power of God and start embracing each other.

Finally, the very content, structure, and performance of testimonies may contribute to sensations of intimacy. Narrating a testimony is sometimes a quite emotional performance with tears and trembling voices. Not only do testimonies show a willingness to expose oneself emotionally and admit how weak, ignorant, sinful, and even stupid one used to be; they also very often include personal details such as accounts of suffering, emotional distress, physical, and even sexual abuse, etc. As noted by Gretchen Pfeil, narratives of conversion can structure them-selves as personally, intimately, and dynamically addressed, and the narrated suffering is an important part of an addressee stance of inti-macy (2011: 285).

Conclusion

In this chapter I have highlighted the central and multifaceted role of narrative practice in the conversion and religious life of Pentecostals. More than a question of gaining profound understandings of theologi-cal doctrines and biblical truths, conversion is foremost a process of acquiring a new identity by learning to apply a certain narrative model in self-reflection and autobiographic reconstruction. It is in large part through the narrating of stories about themselves, their pre-conversion troubles, and post-conversion life with God that converts constitute and elaborate their own self-identities as born-again Pentecostals and provide themselves with schemes for future action.

I have further emphasised the importance of narrative practice for Pentecostal sociality and solidarity. Through the construction of testimonies and other stories, shared religious knowledge becomes self-knowledge. And by being structured in accordance with a standard narrative model, individual stories become episodes or variants of a shared religious story about a tension between the 'world' and a God who plans and controls the lives of his children. The public narration of a testimony of conversion is a way of socially positioning oneself within a religious community while at the same time confirming and committing oneself to its basic values and world views.

Finally I demonstrated how the narrating of testimonies—and this point can very well be extended to include other kinds of stories (see chapter 8)—opens up a religious world, pregnant with meaning and potentiality. Thus I argued that the study of religious conversion and continuing growth in faith over time can benefit from a focus on testimonies and other kinds of narrative practice as social interaction that unites narrator and listener in the world of the story. Pentecostals conceive of conversion and salvation as a movement away from the 'world' or the domain of the Devil and towards intimacy with God. This movement is not, however, made once and for all, but rather it forms part of an ongoing Pentecostal identity project (cf. Cortén & Marshall-Fratani 2001: 11; Robbins 2004b: 128). Testimonies and other stories are crucial means of narrating and re-narrating the engagement of Pentecostals with God and simultaneously of (re)constituting and continuously unfolding a shared religious life world to be inhabited and explored by narrator and listener alike.

CHAPTER SEVEN

WHEN GOD INTERFERES: RITUAL, EMPOWERMENT, AND DIVINE PRESENCE

It is common knowledge among members of the EPC in Valparaíso that good things only happen when God makes them happen. A fundamental theological principle, which is to variable extents characteristic of Pentecostalism in many parts of the world but is extremely outspoken in this particular church, is an understanding of human powerlessness and total dependence upon an almighty God as the source of all good things. As described in chapter 5 the theology of impotence informs Pentecostal discourses and understandings of politics and healing. When congregants tell each other about good things that have happened to them, God rather than human effort is given the credit, and terms like 'miracle' or 'blessing' are often used. Thus they may explain how God has given them new jobs, homes, or furniture without making any reference to the human agency and contacts that such acquisitions usually depend upon. When asked how they or a family member are doing the appropriate answer is 'fine, thanks to God' (*bien, gracias a Dios*), and I was often corrected when I answered with a simple 'fine.'

In this chapter I explore how theological notions of human powerlessness and dependence upon God are actualised and unfolded, rather than symbolically represented, through the bodily and rhetoric engagement in Pentecostal ritual. I pursue my analysis by examining different strategies by use of which divine presence becomes manifest as a part of the ritual communicative community, and the active interference of God is established as the only true source of consequential action. I hope to demonstrate that important insights into the cultural micro-dynamics of Latin American Pentecostalism will emerge from an explicit focus on ritual, a topic sadly neglected in most of the existing literature (for an exception see Lehmann 1996). I conceive of Pentecostal ritual as an important arena for symbolic struggle over definitions and categorisations of social reality. I further argue that it is mainly through the engagement in different practices of worship that Pentecostal dispositions for orientation towards and communion with the sacred are acquired and exercised.

Ritual, Power, and Creativity

Members of the EPC commonly evaluate meetings according to whether or not divine presence and power could be felt rather than whether or not new wisdom or biblical insights were gained from a sermon. After meetings I sometimes heard congregants comment that their batteries had been reloaded or they would touch their chests and say that they felt strengthened by the power of God. The term most frequently used to describe subjective experience of divine empowerment is *gozo*, meaning sublime pleasure or enjoyment. Pentecostals describe *gozo* as a sensation of energy, warmth, and extreme happiness that can pervade the whole body but is mostly located in the chest. The most visible manifestations of *gozo* occur when congregants feel overwhelmed by divine power and start dancing, jumping, moving their arms, screaming, weeping, laughing, and speaking in tongues, but *gozo* is also experienced in less manifest ways by congregants who remain standing quietly on the spot.

An increasing number of anthropologists have come to think of ritual as a contested arena for creative social action, resistance, and negotiation of identity (Comaroff & Comaroff 1993; Hughes-Freeland & Crain 1998; Weiss 2004). In her study of South African Zionist churches during apartheid, Comaroff demonstrates how ritual provides actors for whom open political struggle seems like a distant option with an appropriate medium through which the values and structures of a contradictory world can be manipulated and addressed (1985: 196). Pursuing a related analysis in this and the next chapter I explore how Pentecostal ritual practices redefine the social world and not least the position of Pentecostals within it. The privileged access to divine power is an essential part of such defiance and redefinition. Not only is divine empowerment important as a fundamental contrast to the godless 'world' and the theologically important notion of human powerlessness, but by being the ones who activate transformative power through ritual practice congregants indirectly constitute themselves as spiritual subjects with the ability to act upon the world.

Another important trend in recent anthropological literature is a move away from earlier views on ritual as a symbolic expression and performative enactment of prior patterns of belief, thought, and social organisation. Csordas argues that ritual is better seen as structurally prior to the generation of such patterns (1997: 155) and similar arguments are made by Talal Asad and Catherine Bell, who, like Csordas, mainly see ritual as creative social and bodily practice. Inspired by Marcel Mauss's classical essay 'Techniques of the Body' (1973) Asad pleads for a phenomenological approach to ritual as performance where certain embodied and linguistic skills are presupposed and acquired (1993). In a study of disciplinary rites in medieval monasteries, he argues that embodied practice, including the language in use, is a precondition for religious experiences and that the ability to enter into communion with God is the ability of an experienced or taught body (ibid.: 76). In a similar way, Bell argues that the main purpose of ritualisation is not social solidarity or conflict resolution but the production of ritualised agents with an embodied cultural sense or practical knowledge of ritual. Such practical knowledge

> is not an inflexible set of assumptions, beliefs or body postures; rather it is the ability to deploy, play, and manipulate basic schemes in ways that appropriate and condition experience effectively. *It is a mastery that experiences itself as relatively empowered, not as conditioned or moulded.* (1992: 221, emphasis added)

The term 'ritualisation' is proposed by Bell as an alternative to ritual. She defines 'ritualisation' as 'a way of acting that is designed and orchestrated to distinguish and privilege what is being done in comparison to other, usually more quotidian activities' (1992: 74). Instead of trying to impose analytical categories of what is or is not ritual on different activities, we are better served by paying attention to specific cultural strategies for creating a distinction between categories of activity as sacred and profane (ibid.). What distinguishes Pentecostal ritual life from more mundane activities is the perceived presence and active interference of God. This, however, is not a clear cut distinction. An advantage of Bell's perspective is that it allows us to measure the extent to which a given situation or act should be classified as ritual (sacred) or non-ritual (profane) across a continuum. The presence of God is frequently perceived and deduced by congregants outside of strictly ritual contexts, for example, during informal conversations or simply as a pleasant accompanying presence in everyday life. Nevertheless, I think that it does make sense to regard church meetings as distinguished, that is more ritualised, activities, where certain strategies that work better in a structured (ritual) environment within a delimited church space are deployed in order establish a context of divine presence and interference.

The Informality of Pentecostal Ritual Life

Congregants from the EPC and of most other Chilean Pentecostal churches do not use the word 'ritual' to refer to their own communal worship activities. Commonly associated with rigid, man-made liturgies and structures, characteristic of Catholic services, ritual provides a marked contrast to the spontaneous, informal, and experiential forms of worship in Pentecostals churches, where the Holy Spirit is free to move and manifest itself. In baptisms, weddings, and funerals, clear prescriptions are followed, but otherwise, most formal ritual practices that can be associated with Catholicism are avoided or minimised. In baptism, no godfathers or godmothers are appointed, and the practice of confimation of teenagers is absent in the EPC as in most other Pentecostal churches. The Holy Communion is only given once a year, usually around Easter. Prescribed prayers such as the Lord's Prayer or confessions are not parts of church meetings. In the EPC the words 'glory to God, glory to God, glory to God' (*gloria a Dios, gloria a Dios, gloria a Dios*) are uttered in different situations: after singing, praying, and witnessing, when visitors are welcomed and greeted, as an expression of gratitude to God for the money that is collected during meetings, or as a way of welcoming and celebrating the perceived presence of the Holy Spirit. Besides this phrase, sermons, testimonies, and sharing often end with the words: 'All honour, glory and praise be to the Lord' (*para el Señor es toda honra, gloria y alabanza*), but otherwise there are no standard ritual utterances in this church.

According to Bell ritualisation may maximise or minimise its distinction from other practices. The degree of differentiation should itself be seen as strategic and part of the logic of the act (ibid.: 93). One important effect of the minimisation of strictly formal practices in Pentecostal church meetings is that the distance between ritual experts and lay people, who are mainly receivers or targets of ritual action, is reduced. Another and equally important effect is a blurring of boundaries between ritual and everyday practice. This point, to which I will return in the next chapter, has been forcefully established by Csordas, who argues that the transformative effects of Catholic charismatic ritual genres 'transcend the boundaries of ritual events like prayer meeting, blending over into the sphere of everyday life and contributing to the transformation of the habitus' (1997: 198–9).

Scholarly analysis should not necessarily be guided by emic use of terms, and I concur with scholars such as Robbins (2001, 2011) and

Albrecht (1999) who argue that it does indeed make sense to regard many Pentecostal-charismatic cooperative and spiritually oriented church activities as rituals. But my own use of the term leans more towards Bell's notion of ritualisation than Pentecostal understandings of ritual as strictly formal, prescribed behaviour with no scope for spontaneous expression. Drawing on the work of Bell, Asad, and not least Csordas, I hope to demonstrate how Pentecostal forms of worship collapse classical analytical dichotomies, for instance between spontaneity and control, informality and formality, immediacy and structure, as even the most informal, spontaneous behaviours and sudden experiences of spiritual flow are in fact culturally taught, prescribed, and coordinated within a controlled and structured ritual environment. Further, I suggest that maintaining an analytical distinction between ritual and everyday practice, while keeping in mind (with Bell) that the difference between the two should be measured across a continuum will be helpful in analyzing how certain ritual elements penetrate into the sphere of every day life while others do not.

In the sections that follow I will first provide a brief description of a typical church meeting in the EPC. I will then examine different strategies of ritualisation, namely, positional practices, singing and different rhetorical techniques. The latter include spontaneous shifts between addressing human listeners and God, interruptions, emotional display and shifts in tonality, and finally the constitution of speech acts where the uttered words appear to originate from God.

The Structure of Church Meetings

Church meetings, lasting between one and a half to three hours, are held each night from Sunday to Friday at 7 or 7.30 p.m., and one or two times each month, vigils (late-night meetings) are held on Saturday, lasting up to five hours. Other church-related activities such as preaching on the street, meetings of the *dorcas* (married women and widows), and choir practice take place on late afternoons and during weekends.

Despite the absence of formal prescribed liturgy, most church meetings do have a clear structure. Meetings start with a hymn, announced by the leader of the day (always a man who has been a congregant for some time and has a certain status in the church). Then all congregants kneel and pray for a few minutes. Nobody screams but many members speak so that it can be heard. After another hymn, money is collected and the leader then reads a passage from the Bible. When he finishes, congregants rise and shout, 'Glory to God,' three times with their arms stretched upwards in order to thank God for his message. More praying and singing then follows. During initial hymns the first spiritual manifestations may occur. A few members may start dancing, screaming, or jumping on the spot or moving their arms, but the atmosphere hardly ever becomes truly dramatic at this point. On Sundays the choir performs a few hymns after the initial singing and praying.

After a few practical announcements, the sermon follows, usually lasting no less than one hour except on Mondays, when the sermon is brief so that time is left for witnessing. The preachers usually speak without a script and only make very few if any references to the Bible. The most common themes are the difference between the life with God and the godless 'world', the privilege of being a child of God, human impotence and divine omnipotence, and not least divine and diabolic interference in human life. This interference is illustrated by numerous anecdotes, both from the preacher's personal life and the lives of other Pentecostals.

When the sermon has finished, it is again time to pray, and afterwards a few hymns are sung. During the last hymns, afflicted persons may come forward so that other congregants can pray for their healing. It is especially during the last hymns that the most dramatic spiritual manifestations—dancing, screaming, jumping, and glossolalia—occur. What might at first seem as uncontrolled behaviour is actually subject to some control. When dancing around with their eyes closed congregants always avoid hitting or bumping into each other, and they only move forward, whereas I never saw anyone dancing towards the back of church. If some congregants are still dancing, screaming, jumping, and speaking in tongues when a hymn has finished, the last bars are repeated two or three times in order to allow the Holy Spirit to work. Spiritual manifestations should never be interrupted abruptly but are allowed to die out little by little, and the singing continues until most people are calm.

The meetings end with one person saying a closing prayer on behalf of all the other congregants who are now quiet (a few may be sobbing or murmuring a little). In that way, spiritual manifestations, which take a form that *resembles* uncontrolled individual hysteria, are always encompassed by the protective order of the church community. After the final prayer, the meeting ends and congregants greet each other and leave.

Positional Practices

Despite the importance of the written word, the Bible, Pentecostalism is foremost a religion of oral and bodily practices. According to Quentin Schultze the primacy of oral over literate culture among poor Latin Americans explains in large part the appeal of Pentecostalism. Whereas the printed word objectifies and rationalises life, orality is character-ised by powerful immediacy, commonality, playfulness, performance, and presentness (1994: 71). But the effects of spoken language are dependant upon extra-linguistic factors such as an implicit consensus between speaker and listeners concerning the basic premises upon which utterances are made. Another important factor is the organisa-tion and positioning of human bodies in church space.

When the choir of the EPC performs on Sundays its members stand in front of the pulpit (turning their backs against it) and face the audience, who are sitting on benches. When the singing has finished, it is time to give thanks to God for the performances of the choir. The choir members turn around and face the pulpit while turning their backs against the audience. The choir and the audience then raise their hands and shout, 'Glory to God,' three times. After a theatre play or a concert, the performers usually face the audience and receive their applause. But after choir singing both performers and audience partici-pate in the applause and do not look at each other's faces (the audience can see the backs and necks of the choir members), and the choir does not receive the applause. In this way attention is directed away from the interaction between human performers and audience and towards another dimension. And by thanking God rather than the performers, human creativity is strategically neglected and church members are reminded that only God can make good things such as beautiful sing-ing happen.

During communal prayers all church members kneel and pray for themselves while facing the pulpit. The preacher also kneels at the pulpit, but he usually turns his body ninety degrees and faces the side wall of the church. Similar positional practices can be observed during collective singing, where spiritual manifestations most often occur. Church members stand up and face the pulpit while singing, and if someone in the back of the church starts screaming, dancing, jumping, those standing in front do not turn their heads to watch him or her. Through such positional practices, divine power is experienced as having multiple origins. As the loudness of the singing and screaming increase, the church may at some point appear to have a life of its own, which can contribute to sensations of divine power being present in the church room (see Csordas 1997: 110). If the church members were standing in a circle, divine power could be perceived as originating from within an introverted and enclosed human community. But this is avoided by the fixation of gazes, as church members do not look at each other's faces but only at the backs and necks of the persons in front. At times, it seems that divine power comes from behind, especially for participants who are standing in front and who can hear but not see other singing, screaming, and dancing brothers and sisters in Christ in the back, or from the sides (when a neighbour is touched by the spirit), an effect which is supported by the acoustics of the church building. When the choir and all church members face the pulpit and they give their applause to God, it is indicated that he is present in the front of the church. And the fixation of bodies and gazes during praise and prayers indicate that God is present in the front or the side of the church. Through such positional practices, the church space is constituted as a site that is pervaded by divine presence and empowerment.

A similar positioning of bodies can be observed on Monday meetings, which take place in small local church buildings in different parts of the city. On Mondays, the main activity is sharing. After a little singing, praying, and a brief sermon the participants take turns in standing up and thanking God for being with them. They more often than not take the opportunity to share an anecdote about how God has manifested himself in their lives during the past week. Or they may retell their personal testimony of salvation in a summarized version. Through such storytelling, experience is structured and ultimately altered by being articulated within the terms of the religious community and in accordance with a certain politics of storytelling dictating that God rather than humans should be held responsible for all good achievements. At the same time singular events and personal biographies become inscribed as episodes within a shared biblical metanarrative about the divine plan of salvation and the eternal tension between the church and the 'world'. Thus sharing also becomes a public through an implicit statement of commitment to the Pentecostal community as well as a confirmation of its basic theological and ontological premises.

During sharing the person who is speaking stands up on the spot while the listeners remain seated. Everybody is facing the pulpit except the leader who is standing at the pulpit facing the other participants.

In other Pentecostal churches in Chile and elsewhere different spatial practices can be observed during sharing, as the speaker comes forward and faces the audience, a positioning that emphasises the human community between them. But in the EPC, speaker and listeners do not look at each other. If someone who is sitting in the back of the church stands up to thank God, the church members sitting in front do not turn around and watch him or her but remain seated in the same position, looking forwards. The leader of the day, who stands at the pulpit, is sometimes looking directly at the speaker. But it is common for the latter to be looking forwards without searching for any eye contact with the leader, the only person whose face is available to sight. As speaker and listeners avoid looking at each other, the ritual community is extended beyond the human participants and a context of divine presence is produced.

Singing

Singing is a central part of ritual life in most Chilean Pentecostal churches, including the EPC. Not only does the church have a choir that performs on Sundays, but church meetings always start and end with collective singing. Besides these scheduled performances, hymns are sung spontaneously during meetings to praise God and welcome his presence. In the EPC, no musical instruments are played apart from the occasional use of a small electric organ. Most hymns are slow and do not have very lively rhythms (a marked contrast to Latin American popular or 'worldly' music) and the dancing that can be observed when someone feels touched by the Holy Spirit does not follow the rhythm of the music.

Spiritual manifestations such as dancing, jumping, screaming, and weeping most commonly occur during singing. As Albrecht has argued, music can embrace worshippers and usher them into the presence of God (1999: 143). Singing is a discursive practice, in that hymns have semantically meaningful contents.[1] And it is a form of worship that

---

[1] Common themes of Pentecostal songs are the privilege of being saved, spiritual compensation for social miseries, spiritual warfare, and not least divine presence. When sermons and testimonies are interrupted because of perceived divine presence and interference (see below) church members commonly react by standing up and singing hymns that confirm the presence of God among them. One such hymn has the following words: *La presencia de Dios está aquí, yo la siento en mi* (The presence of God

engages the body. Congregants sit down during sermons and witnessing, but they stand up while singing and many of them start swaying
their upper bodies. Sitting down facilitates concentrated appropriation
of intellectual truths, whereas standing and oscillatory movements
facilitate engagement and encounters with experiential truths.

The atmosphere that is produced during singing resembles Victor
Turner's notion of a spontaneous communitas, defined as 'a feeling of
endless power ... a flash of lucid mutual understanding on the existential level,' where it is felt that 'all problems ... could be resolved, whether
emotional or cognitive, if only the group that is felt (in the first person)
as "essentially us" could sustain its intersubjective illumination' (1982:
47–8). Unlike structure, which is institutionalised and exclusive, communitas is immediate, inclusive, and tends to reduce the relevance of
role and status. In the EPC the importance of status in 'worldly' terms
is repeatedly downplayed in sermons, witnessing, and the narrating of
testimonies. But the ritual cultivation of spontaneous communitas,
characterised by absence of structural differentiation may be as important as explicit statements for the constitution of a religious community
where 'worldly' hierarchies are rejected in favour of spiritual equality.

Whereas communitas is an intrinsically social experience it may
have qualities of flow, a term Turner borrows from Mihaly Csiskzen-
mihalyi (Turner 1982: 56). Flow is an individual experience that occurs
in certain kinds of actions (such as rock climbing or playing music)
where consciousness and attention are limited and extremely focused.
In flow experiences, action and awareness seem to merge and distinctions between self and environment, between stimulus and response
are blurred (Neitz & Spickard 1990: 20). Such absorption can follow
from the engagement of the standing and swaying body in the act of
singing, where divine power is experienced as immediate and intimate
rather than discursively meaningful. Rhythm and song can lead to fixation of attention and suspension of breath, which in turn lower the
efficiency of the brain (Williams 1981: 141), and certain oscillatory
motions with the upper body can influence the equilibrium sense and
the operation of the vestibular system (Humphrey & Laidlaw 1994:
234). Besides these effects, the emotional excitement that can be
produced by rhythm, song, and dance-like movements reduce the

---

is here, I feel it). Another one goes like this: *Él está aqui. Que hermoso es. El lo prometió,
donde hay dos o tres.* (He [the Lord] is here. Oh, so beautiful he is. He promised that
wherever two or three are gathered [he will be there].)

range of sensory perceptions while at the same time strengthen the central dominant response (Williams 1981: 142). When I asked congregants, who in their own words had been 'taken by the Lord' and started dancing, jumping, or screaming during singing, how they experienced it, what they mostly remembered were sensations of extreme happiness, warmth, energy, invincibility, and *gozo*. They generally claimed to have had little or no reflective awareness of what was happening around them. Little or no awareness of the surroundings was also frequently reported by congregants who do not start screaming, dancing, or speaking in tongues during singing, but remain standing quietly on their spot and experience *gozo* and empowerment in less manifest ways.

As argued by Bourdieu bodily language is more vague and ambiguous than ordinary language. Words tend to limit the range of choice, which is why ritual roots are broader than linguistic roots and the gymnastics of ritual always seems richer than verbal translations that can be given of it (1977: 120). In a similar vein Michael Jackson argues that movements of the body can do more than words can say. Activities such as dance and music can move people to participate in a world beyond accustomed roles and to recognise themselves as members of a community, a common body:

> It is because action speaks louder and more ambiguously than words that they are more likely to lead us to common truths; not semantic truths, established by others at other times, but experiential truths which seem to issue from within our own Being when we break the momentum of the discursive mind or throw ourselves into some collective activity in which we each find our own meaning yet sustain the impression of having a common cause. (1983: 339)

It seems that a lot would be missed by regarding ritual acts as mere expressions of prior ideas and thoughts. Much of the richness and potentiality of ritual action are irreducible and remain beyond the discursive. Pentecostal ritualised practice can be seen as constituting and nourishing a particular relationship between humans and God through an unmediated bodily engagement with divine power—rather than merely representing this relationship. Human powerlessness and dependence upon an almighty God are salient during singing and spiritual manifestations, as it is only by suspending intellectual, rational control and allowing God to be in charge that the individual may experience his power. What takes place in ritual life is not a performative symbolic enactment of prior theological understandings of powerlessness and dependence, but an actual act and experience of surrender.

Addressing God

The integration of God into the ritual community is partly achieved through the use of rhetorical techniques that indicate that he is present as one of the listeners of the spoken word. This can be illustrated by quoting Carmen, a housewife in her early thirties who stood up during a Monday meeting and thanked God for being with her:

> The Lord is great and wonderful. I wish to glorify him because of how beautiful, perfect, and wonderful he is. He is the best. I used to be so sad, and now I am so happy. So many bad things happen in the 'world', but nothing happens to me, because you come to the church, and the Lord protects you, and you feel that the enemy [Satan] respects you, you feel you're not alone, you're with the Lord, so the bad things don't happen to you.... Thanks to him, my husband has a job; my health is fine. All I want to do is to thank the Lord, because he is so nice, and he is present in my life; his divine protection is with us; he is so great. Now I'm so happy that I feel my heart is falling out of my body. He is here now, and all I want to do is to glorify him; I think that it is the most wonderful thing that has happened to any of us. If it hadn't been for him, I don't know what my life would be like; my soul would have been lost, if it hadn't been for the Lord. There are so many persons in the 'world' who have it all; they have a house, a car, but how are their hearts? Sad! They don't have any reward! They don't have anyone who blesses them. We, the children of God are short of many material things, but what does it matter? We have something greater—the Lord! And for me the Lord is the best there is; my Lord is so beautiful, and I want to say to you, Lord, I love you, I love you, and I don't ever want you to leave me Lord; protect me; if it weren't for you, I don't know what I would do, Lord. I have no life without you Lord, and I want to glorify you.

Unfortunately a written reproduction of this declaration of love to God does not give the reader an impression of the passion with which it was made nor of the atmosphere in the church. At times Carmen was screaming, at times almost crying with joy. The other participants were truly excited and constantly interfered, shouting 'Amen', 'Alleluia', and 'Glory to God'. When she finished, we all had to stand up and shout, 'Glory to God', three times and then sing a hymn.

At the end of Carmen's speech, an interesting shift can be observed. She suddenly changes from addressing the other church members to addressing God directly, telling him how much she loves him. Shifts between addressing human co-participants and addressing a divine other are common in many religious rituals, but they are often more clearly announced, for example, with the words, 'Let us pray,' or 'Let us give thanks to the Lord,' and with a different bodily attitude, such as the introverted and folded position of prayer, closed eyes, or looking upwards with raised arms instead of looking at the human audience, all of which indicates that the receiver of the spoken message is now another. The sudden, spontaneous and unannounced shift reinforces the sensation that God has actually been present as part of the audience the whole time. Neither the bodily attitude and position of Carmen nor the tone of voice, which was already loud and emotional, nor the informal and improvised nature of her speech changed when she addressed God directly. In this way, the different receivers of the speech, the human participants and God, become more integrated, and divine presence in the ritual community is presented as such a natural and common thing that it can (almost) be taken for granted.

Spontaneous shifts from addressing other church members to addressing God directly are common in sermons and sharing, though they are sometimes accompanied by an altered tone of voice, weeping, and movements with the arms, which indicate that the speaker has been touched by the Holy Spirit. On Mondays when church members stand up and speak about divine interference in their lives, they frequently include God among their listeners as they shift between telling others how he has helped them and thanking him directly. The position of the body is hardly ever changed during such shifts. While God is obviously very different from the human listeners, the informal and spontaneous ways of addressing him serve to include him as an intimate and natural part of the ritual community.

Tonality, Interruptions, and Emotional Display

Congregants from the EPC frequently and proudly emphasise that prescribed liturgy is absent from their church activities. Too much manmade liturgy and formalisation, so they believe, will inhibit the interference of the Holy Spirit. While such interference is certainly intended by human participants and must to a large extent be facilitated and conditioned by their wilful surrender, it can never be planned or programmed by humans but must ultimately occur when and where

God wishes it to occur. And though it is certainly disappointing when God does not interfere, the possibility that he *might* not is essential for the understanding of the nature of divine interference. Apparent unpredictability and spontaneity, the sensation that some aspects of actions occur independently of human preparation and planning, are fundamental phenomenological criterions for manifestations and experiences of the sacred (see Csordas 1997).

Sudden bodily movements, shifts in tonality, emotional display, and different outbursts are all characterised by an apparent independence of the intentions and plans of the actor, who seems to be overwhelmed rather than in total control. Such behaviour is seen as an index of divine presence and inspiration. I often heard Pentecostal preachers preach for up to an hour in an altered voice at the point of crying but without breaking into uncontrolled tears, though I was expecting this to happen any minute. But it is also common that the tone of voice of the preacher or of witnessing lay members during Monday meetings changes between screaming, crying, whispering, and laughing.

A frequently used rhetorical technique in preaching and witnessing is a gradual alteration of the voice towards a climax. On one occasion a preacher explained how divine healing is far superior to the healing that can be found in hospitals.

> Here in Valparaíso, we have Christian doctors. God has cured people here, in Valparaíso, in the church, in Evangelical Pentecostal Chuuuuuurch.

During these sentences the tone of voice was gradually altered and the last words 'Pentecostal Chuuuuuurch' were shouted and accompanied by raised arms. Such changes in the tone and the constitution of a climax usually evoke responses among members of the audience, who start shouting, 'Amen,' 'Alleluia,' 'Glory to God,' or even dancing and jumping. Bodily movements and changes in tonality are important non-semantic techniques for creating an atmosphere of divine presence. However, it should the added that the utterances that most frequently evoke dramatic responses among the audience do have specific contents, namely that God is present in the church or that the congregants enjoy spiritual privileges that the people from the 'world', who may be materially richer, do not have.

Different kinds of interruptive outbursts are important and indeed welcomed parts of ritual life. A whole regime of emotional display is at work as both preacher and members of the audience frequently start weeping, screaming and crying, and moving their bodies during sermons and witnessing. In all fairness, I must emphasise that members of the EPC are actually very careful not to confuse human emotions with spiritual interferences. When I once referred to a recent church meeting as *emocionante* (touching, emotional), I was immediately asked by a Pentecostal friend if I really meant that or if I did not rather mean that the presence of the Holy Spirit could be felt during the meeting. But the display of behaviour that to a non-Pentecostal observer like myself seems like very emotional outbursts (and despite possible objections from my Pentecostal friends, I will stick to this term, since I believe that it will work better than other terms in enabling non-Pentecostal readers to imagine the kind of behaviour that can be observed in church meetings), is an important strategy of ritualisation by use of which divine presence becomes manifest.[2]

It is common for preachers to interrupt themselves during sermons because they feel overwhelmed with the divine power and love that they are talking about. Such interruptions may be more or less dramatic. The pastor in the EPC frequently starts weeping and screaming, 'Alleluia,' or 'Glory to God,' in the middle of a sermon. He then wipes away the tears on his face with a handkerchief and says, 'Alleluia,' or 'Glory to God,' or 'Blessed be the Lord,' in a mild tone of voice, half weeping, half laughing before he continues preaching. On one occasion he was telling a story about woman who had a vision, where the hills of Valparaíso were filled with the light of the Holy Spirit. At the end of the story he suddenly said, 'Days of glory are coming,' three times, gradually altering his voice until he shouted the third 'days of glory are coming' with his arms raised, and at this point several congregants started screaming. Such interruptions also occur during Monday meetings when congregants testify and witness about divine interference in their lives. They may suddenly feel so overwhelmed that they start weeping or screaming, 'Glory to God,' 'Alleluia,' or 'Praise the sweet name of the saviour.' The listeners usually react to such outbursts by standing up and singing a hymn in order to welcome the interference of the Holy Spirit and encourage it to continue. Attempts to inhibit spiritual interference by encouraging the congregants who make

---

[2] According to Pentecostals it does occur that a strong desire to experience divine presence leads someone to be fooled by his or her own emotions so that he or she may start acting *as if* God had manifested himself. But it is important to be able to distinguish such human emotional outburst from true divine manifestations.

outburst to sit down and keep quiet and by insisting on proceeding with the sermon before the Holy Spirit has finished its manifestation are considered a very serious sin. With such interruptions, sermons, witnessing, and testifying can be prolonged by several minutes.

Spontaneous outbursts made by the preacher or the audience during sermons and witnessing often take a less dramatic form than screaming, crying, jumping, and dancing. The preacher may interrupt himself continuously with outbursts that are not part of the story that is being told or the explanation that is being given, as in the following excerpt from a sermon:

> The Lord is always worried about us brothers and sisters. Blessed be the Lord. I have a lot of experience, praise the Lord. I have seen how merciful our God is. I work as a carpenter, and sometimes there is no work. But the Lord has always helped us, brothers. When I did not serve the Lord, sometimes I did not have enough food or clothing. Oh blessed be the Lord, that is why I say that God is always worried about us, brothers, oh praise the Lord. Because God loves us. Let us praise the Lord. [All congregants stand up with raised hands and shout, 'Glory to God,' three times.]

Such outbursts ('Oh blessed be the Lord.... oh praise the Lord') are not particularly disturbing and do not represent major ruptures in the sermon except at the end of the excerpt when all members stand up and shout, 'Glory to God,' three times. In a similar way, listeners often start saying or murmuring, 'Amen,' 'Glory to God,' 'There is power in your blood, oh Lamb of God,' 'Oh yes, Lord,' or 'That is right Lord,' during sermons. While not programmed or formally prescribed, the constant outbursts from listeners and the regular interruptions of the sermons because of the perceived presence of the Holy Spirit requires that all members stand up and praise God are expected and very much welcomed in church meetings. The outbursts do not only indicate that God is present; they also address him directly and hence establish and confirm a social relationship with him. And by making such outbursts the audience becomes active participants rather than passive listeners in a communicative process that involves God.

The rhetorical constitution of divine presence during church meetings can be further illustrated by an example. In August 2000, the choir members of the church made a weekend trip to Santiago to visit a sister church and participate in a few meetings. On the following Monday, the program was changed. Instead of the usual meetings in local church buildings, a big meeting in the central church building was organised so that all congregants would immediately be able to share the great blessing that God had given the congregation, namely the trip of the choir to Santiago. One of the choir members, a man in his late twenties, spoke for about one hour about the trip. The choir members had travelled to Santiago in an old bus, and on the way out of Valparaíso, they were stopped by the police who wanted to check if the driver had all the necessary documents. No doubt this was a satanic attack, an attempt to sabotage the *gozo* that the choir members were about to experience in Santiago, so all the passengers immediately kneeled and prayed for God to help them and after a while the police allowed them to continue. After this anecdote a description of a church meeting in Santiago followed:

> The pastor said, 'These brothers and sisters from Valparaíso, they have come a long way, but God has accompanied them, and they will bring *gozo* back to their church. [Several congregants shout, 'Amen,' 'Alleluia,' 'Glory to God.'] ... The meeting was supposed to end at 10 p.m., but we make our program, and the Lord makes his own program. [Again congregants shout, 'Amen,' 'Glory to God.'] The Lord manifested himself, he started to move his church, and we started to sing and sing and sing ... [At this point the preacher seems to be entering some kind of mild ecstasy. He is speaking in a soft and mild tone of voice, laughing gently and joyfully] ... And then a sister prophesied. She said, "The Lord will return very soon, very soon! The windows of heaven shall be opened for the brothers [congregants scream: 'Amen'] and blessed be the youth of the church; it is soon time to enjoy the great second revival that the Lord has promised us." [A few congregants start dancing, jumping, weeping, and screaming.] This is the promise of God. [The preacher first starts weeping mildly. He then screams:] Oh Lord receive the tears of your people, oh Holy Spirit of God.' [Several congregants now start dancing, weeping, jumping, screaming, and moving their arms. The remaining congregants all stand up and shout, 'Glory to God,' three times with their hands raised and then begin singing a hymn. It takes several minutes before the preacher can continue.]

After the speech another choir member, a boy in his early teens, came forward to thank God for giving him this incredible blessing, a trip to Santiago with the choir. He was so overwhelmed that he spoke with a trembling voice and had to interrupt himself several times as he started weeping. The rest of the congregants reacted by standing up and shouting, 'Glory to God,' three times and then sang a hymn.

In ritual rhetorical processes, a trip to Santiago, organised and paid by the congregants themselves, and participation in a church meeting, which according to the descriptions did not differ radically from many church meetings in Valparaíso, are constituted as tremendous divine blessings. Through shifts in tonality, shifts between addressing the human audience and God directly, emotional display, and frequent interruptive outbursts from speaker and listeners, divine presence becomes manifest in Pentecostal ritual life, both as a perceived and overwhelming presence in the church room, imposing itself on the communication between preacher and audience, and as an interfering factor in the stories that are being told. Representation and presence become intertwined as congregants simultaneously communicate *about* and are overwhelmed *by* divine presence and power. The fact that the church meeting in Santiago did not end according to man-made plans at 10 p.m. but had to be prolonged was seen as a clear and much welcomed result of divine interference, as were the frequent interruptions of the story about the trip to Santiago.

Like positional practices, the different rhetorical techniques are important strategies of ritualising communication and distinguishing it from other and more mundane forms of communication. Unlike church services in the Catholic Church and mainline Protestant churches where prescribed liturgy is followed and unlike many 'traditional' rituals, studied by anthropologists (for example, Bloch 1998), Pentecostal ritualised communication is not distinguished from other kinds of communication by a prevalence of highly formalised speech where choice of intonation and scope for improvisation are limited. On the contrary, divine interference becomes manifest in the aspects of communication that seem to be beyond human planning, such as spontaneous shifts in tonality, emotional outbursts, and interruptions.

Theoretical perspectives on ritual as conventionalised and formal-ised behaviour that expresses public morality but is unfit for the spontaneous expression of emotions (Bloch 1998; Tambiah 1979; Rappaport 1999) face some obvious limits in the case of Pentecostalism, where spontaneity and emotional display are essential ingredients of ritual life.[3] But that does not mean that Pentecostal church meetings should be seen as occasions where prior and natural emotions are allowed to be articulated. While sermons, testimonies, and witnessing can be prepared, shifts in tonality, outbursts, and sudden urges to glorify God are all aspects of communicative action that seem to work independently of human intentions and preparations. But spontaneous outbursts are

---

[3] For a critique of such views, see Asad 1993.

intentionally co-ordinated (Csordas 1997: 113) and occur in a restricted community of believers within an enclosed church space, where a context of intimate divine presence and power is established through positional and other practices. The most dramatic divine manifestations such as glossolalia, prophesying, laughing, screaming, weeping, dancing, and jumping very rarely occur at the beginning of church meetings but only after an intimate and intense atmosphere has been produced by initial praying and singing. The love of God, the urge to glorify him, and the spontaneous inclinations to make outbursts are emotions that are organised and evoked through embodied ritualised practice including language in use.

I fully agree with Csordas that ritual language should be seen as technique of the body, 'a tool for reordering the behavioural environment, cultivating the dispositions of the habitus, and creating the sacred self' (ibid.: 262). The abilities to use language in certain ways, to make sudden shifts in tonality, to talk for a long time in an altered tone of voice at the point of crying but without breaking into tears, or to start screaming, weeping mildly, and laughing during a speech are all acquired abilities of a ritually taught body with dispositions for being in communion with divine power.

Look Who's Talking

Sensations of divine presence and empowerment in Pentecostal ritual life are reinforced by perceptions of spoken language as originating from God rather than human speakers. In the EPC the constitution of speech acts where the uttered words seem to have certain autonomy in relation to the speaker is an important strategy of ritualization through which different kinds of language use can be distinguished from each other.

Glossolalia and prophesy are the types of ritualized speech where divine presence and inspiration is most salient. As prophecies are seen as a direct message from God, they must be given spontaneously as a result of sudden divine inspiration rather than human planning (see Csordas 1997: 125). And the perception of the autonomy of spoken words is reinforced, as persons who are prophesying often seem to be in a state of trance, as if they were not being themselves. After having prophesied, they may not even remember what they said. Glossolalia, the utterance of meaningless sounds, is seen as a direct communication with the Holy Spirit. People speaking in tongues usually have full awareness, and while they are able to stop if they wish, they cannot control what comes out of their mouth during glossolalia. As the uttered sounds have no semantic (human) meaning, language appears as an autonomous non-human force.

However, only very few members of the EPC and mostly elderly women possess the gift of prophecy and sometimes weeks or months may pass without any prophecies in the church. And many church members have never spoken in tongues. Nevertheless the experience of divine inspiration during speech is shared by all active church members with a testimony of salvation. Preaching in the church or on the street, witnessing, testifying, praying, or simply informal conversations are all linguistic activities, where divine authorship of spoken words can be perceived. In these speech acts, the divine 'I' does not impose itself as compellingly upon the human speaking 'I' as in glossolalia and prophesying but is nevertheless still felt as an alien, though pleasant and intimate, presence. Several church members explained to me how the Holy Spirit imposed itself upon them during witnessing and street preaching or during conversations with non-Pentecostals whom they tried to convert. They would simply open their mouths and the words would flow by themselves. And sometimes they would even be surprised when listening to the words that came out of their own mouths.

Church members frequently mention how God has spoken to them through instruments or how they have themselves been used as instruments. By this is meant that God uses one Pentecostal to speak to another about a personal matter concerning the listener and of which the speaker could not have known beforehand, except through a divine revelation. One person may talk about something another person has been thinking but not told anyone. In such cases the presence of God in the speaking subject is less compelling than in prophesies and glossolalia but stronger than during inspired preaching, witnessing, and testifying. Some, mostly younger, church members told me that they felt that God had only inspired them during street preaching, witnessing, and personal conversations with other Pentecostals and non-Pentecostals, but that they were longing and praying for a stronger experience of being taken and used by God, for example, prophesying, speaking in tongues, or being used as instruments. The experiences that they were longing for consisted in moments of speech, during which the spoken words would appear as more external to them, the speakers, than ever before.

It is generally assumed that preachers in the church are under divine influence, and this assumption is reinforced by the reactions of listeners. Thus it is quite uncommon to congratulate a preacher with an inspiring sermon. Church members often say that the presence of God can be felt in a sermon and that God often uses a given preacher in beautiful ways, but the rhetorical skills of a preacher are rarely praised. Church members who feel touched or inspired during a sermon frequently react by making outbursts such as 'that's right Lord' or 'yes Lord' (rather than 'that's right preacher' or 'yes preacher'). Rhetorical creativity is not ascribed to human speakers, since all consequential language use originates from God.

The perceptions of divine authorship of language may at times lead to experiences of words as having thing-like qualities. Edgardo, an unskilled worker in his forties, once described to me how he would feel touched by the words that were preached in the church.

> Sometimes the words that you hear in the church come upon you, and they fill your whole life; it is like an ecstasy. The words come and they reach your soul. And you know, sometimes we speak in tongues, but that it is not something of our own, it is so great, we are just like the cups that are filled, this excellent power of God comes upon us.

We can see how glossolalia is characterised by an intense experience of a divine other imposing himself upon the speaking subject as if he was a cup waiting to be filled. But in Edgardo's description, the semantically meaningful words that he hears preached in the church also appear as manifestations of divine power. Words are not just signs, consisting of arbitrary phonetic signifiers referring to a signified, namely divine presence and power. And the powerful and dramatic utterance of words is more than an icon of divine power and more than an index, indicating that the speaker is under divine influence. Certainly, spoken words contain all these qualities as signs, indexes, and icons of divine presence and power. But words also take on the virtual status of things in a kind of language fetishism. At some point during ritual, distinctions between the symbolic and the real are collapsed (Coleman 2000a: 131), and it appears that the words *are* themselves the very power of God imposing itself upon speaking and listening subjects, filling their lives and reaching their souls.

When spoken language appears to originate from God rather than the speaker, linguistic, acoustic forms may themselves be perceived as sources of power. But perceptions of divine authorship also serve to invest the message with extra authority. Evoking God as the ultimate author of spoken word is an important way of encouraging obedience and commitment. On one occasion a preacher scolded his audience for not coming to church every day and for sometimes arriving late. He then added that someone might argue that he was in no position to tell others how they should behave, which would indeed be true, but the reprimand did not come from him but from the Holy Spirit. Church members also regularly remind each other that they should not come to church in order to listen to the sermon of a particular brother—and if they did, they might start focusing on all his imperfections, his physical appearance, etc.—but only to hear what God has to say.

The divine authorship of preaching was made quite explicit during a church meeting when a preacher, at the end of a sermon, made the following statement:

> It is important to remember what the Lord has told us today, Sunday, 9 September. Remember that I told you that it is important always to have a good conduct, at home and in all other places. And I told you that my things are more important than anything else, more important than your homes or your guests.[4]

Here the preacher suddenly makes a shift from speaking about the Lord in the third person to speaking in the first person. This shift was not accompanied by an altered tone of voice or by bodily movements. The 'I' in the excerpt does not belong to the human speaker but to God. The smooth, spontaneous, and apparently very unproblematic and uncontroversial shift from speaking about God to speaking as God (no eyebrows were raised among the listeners, for whom such a shift seemed like a perfectly natural thing) indicates that the latter did not suddenly, dramatically, and out of the blue impose himself upon the speaker but that he had been an integral part of the communicative process the whole time. The shift does not announce a fundamental change in the authorship of the speech but mainly states explicitly what is already known and most of the time taken for granted.

Divine authorship of spoken words is frequently manifested more dramatically. The exact extent to which words originate from God or from the animator is often unclear, but the rhetorical techniques described in the previous section, emotional display, shifts in tonality,

---

[4] It had been said earlier that a church member who receives a guest in his home should not skip a meeting on that account but instead bring the guest to the church.

and bodily movements all serve as indexes that the balance between human and divine contributions to the speaking process has shifted and that the speaker is now mainly an instrument of God. On another occasion a preacher ended his sermon by encouraging all church members to pray:

> Dear brothers and sisters come forward and pray [speaking in a slightly altered tone of voice]. The Lord asks you to come forward and pray [shouting, weeping, and moving his arms].

In the first part of the excerpt the preacher addresses the audience as 'brothers and sisters', that is, as fellow human children of the same heavenly father. In the second part, God is still being referred to in the third person, but at the same time he is now the one who really invites church members to come forward and pray. By uttering words in a more dramatic and emotional way, it is indicated that the human speaker is now foremost a channel through which God addresses his children.

Through the use of different rhetorical strategies of ritualization, divine inspiration can be experienced and manifested in more or less dramatic ways. God manifests himself, sometimes as an extraordinary and overwhelming presence, producing intense reactions and sensations of *gozo* and sometimes as a taken-for-granted, intimate, and almost ordinary part of the ritual communicative community of speakers and listeners.

Praying

Veronica, a rather shy woman in her forties once told me that she never participated in street preaching or in Monday meetings, because she always became extremely nervous when she had to speak in public. She was now asking God to help her with this problem and had already experienced some progress:

> Now I pray a lot, and I fast frequently so that the Lord will give me the words. I am a coward; I really don't like to stand up and speak in public. But you know, today, I went to the meeting with the *dorcas* [a women's group], and when the meeting finished the leader asked me to stand up and say the final prayer. And I did not want to do it, but I stood up anyway, and then the words just came out of my mouth. Afterwards I was shaking because the Holy Spirit had come upon me.

Spoken, prayed words in a ritual contexts are here not presented as originating from the creativity and intentions of the speaking subject but as an external power, a gift that may or may not be given by God.

Though praying is commonly conceived of as a communicative situation, where humans speak and God listens and sometimes answers, several Pentecostals explained to me how God enabled them to pray by letting the words come to them. The ease with which church members can pray for up to an hour or more without running out of words was repeatedly emphasised as a marked contrast to pre-conversion experience with praying. Rather than a monologue, praying takes the form of a dialogue or an intimate communion with God who is also the source of the words that are uttered by the human participant. This is particularly salient when someone starts praying in Spanish and ends up speaking in tongues, which is, however, not seen as the end of one activity and the beginning of a new, but merely as a continuation and climax of praying.

The complexity of praying as a communicative situation where a person talks to and with God, senses his answers and attention, but where it is at the same time really God who talks through the praying person is also salient at the end of church meetings when afflicted participants come forward and are prayed for. In such cases the power of healing must pass through the person who prays with his or her hands imposed on the head of the afflicted. Rather than the praying person asking God to send his power directly to the afflicted—a situation where physical contact between the two human participants in the triad would be of minor importance—the one who prays becomes a necessary instrument or channel for the transmission of divine power. The praying consists in asking God for help and in demanding the problem and sometimes the demonic forces that may have caused it to leave. This demand is made by a praying human being with the authority that is given by God, but it is also, to an extent which is often not quite clear, made by God himself through the person who prays. It is worth noticing that experiences of divine presence, empowerment, and *gozo*, of pleasant streams of energy and warmth running through the body during praying for healing, are more frequently reported by the ones who pray than by the afflicted.

The Otherness of Language

In his seminal study of ritual language in a North American Catholic Charismatic community, Csordas argues that it is the otherness of language that makes certain kinds of linguistic action apt for cultural objectifications as divine presence and that the mystification of this otherness is a rhetorical condition for the efficacy of prophecy (1997: 241). Csordas proposes an interesting view on the existential otherness of language as grounded in the otherness that it shares as a feature of embodiment. He presents his argument through a discussion with Stanley Tambiah who sees language as being both outside us, in that it is part of a cultural heritage and within us, since we generate it as agents (1968: 184, quoted in Csordas 1997: 237). In this view language has a certain objectivity and independence as a cultural system that pre-exists the speaking individual who must appropriate it. But according to Csordas the textualized approach of Tambiah leads him to see language as a representation rather than an instance of force. Drawing on Merleau-Ponty (1962), Csordas argues that the otherness, which makes language apt for certain mystifications, is better ascribed to language being part of our embodied existence. At its root language is incarnate, a phonetic gesture with immanent meaning. While our bodies are compellingly ours, they are also alien presences, imposing limits on our being (for example, by aging and tiring) and 'to the extent that our experience of language is also experience of our bodies, it partakes of this ambiguous embodied otherness (1997: 238).

I find the perspective of Csordas both original and persuasive, but I think there may be a little more to be said about the autonomy of language as experienced by members of the EPC. In addition to the views of the otherness of language as grounded in processes of externalisation and objectification and as grounded in the concrete otherness that it shares as a feature of embodiment, I propose that the perceived autonomy of spoken language may *also* be the result of subjects being enrolled in a Pentecostal discursive formation with strict rules and doctrines for enunciation.

While Csordas sees glossolalia as the clearest example of speech as a phonetic gesture in which the speaker takes up an existential position in the world, in that glossolalia takes the form of nonsense, he argues that all language is incarnate and has a gestural, existential meaning (ibid.: 238). Thus it is implied that his argument about the mystification of the embodied otherness of language also applies to other, less dramatic ritual genres. But apart from glossolalia Csordas's main focus in the discussion on the otherness of language is prophecy. Glossolalia and prophesy are the ritualised speech acts where divine inspiration is felt most compellingly. The argument that I am about to make may not enrich our understanding of glossolalia, but I think it may help us grasp how language can be experienced as speaking itself during less dramatic forms of divinely inspired speech, such as preaching, witnessing, testifying, praying, and evangelising.

In chapter 2 I introduced the work of Boone, who—drawing on Foucault—proposes a view of Protestant Fundamentalism as a discourse in which both objects and fundamentalist subjects are constituted. According to Boone the rules of fundamentalist discourse operate according to a uniform anonymity on all individuals who speak in its field (1989: 82, see also Foucault 1972: 63). Such rules govern not only what may be said and by whom, but also how possible themes or objects of discourse should be conceptually elaborated. As illustrated in several chapters (earlier and subsequent chapters, as well as the present one), the theological notions of human powerlessness and dependence upon an almighty God as the source of good things and the contrast between the 'world' of sin and the life with God are pervasive Pentecostal conceptual principles. These principles provide a framework for the construction of personal narratives (chapter 6), for the narrating of anecdotes about good things that have happened to congregants (chapter 8), for talking about politics and healing (chapter 5), and for the evaluation of consequential ritual action (this chapter). A discursive formation also consists of rules for non-semantic aspects of speech. Foucault uses the concept of ritual to refer to, amongst other things, the 'gestures, behaviour, circumstances, and the whole set of signs which must accompany discourse' (ibid.: 62). Finally, there are rules for enunciative modalities (Foucault 1972: 73), that is, types of discursive activity, such as (in the case of Pentecostalism) preaching, testifying, sharing, praying, and prophesying. Each of these modalities is tied to certain situations, locations, and positions. The latter may be more or less restricted. Most congregants are allowed to participate in street preaching, but only long-term and faithful male congregants can preach in the church on Sundays. Inspired by Foucault, Boone argues that fundamentalist discourse exercises more power over the speaking subject than the other way around:

> No single individual is smart enough or powerful enough to manipulate fundamentalist discourse fully, and in certain ways, the discourse manipulates him. To enjoy credibility, one must ensure that one's own discourse is following the explicit and implicit rules of the general discourse.... The personal power of the preacher pales in comparison with the impersonal power of fundamentalist discourse. (Boone 1989: 15)

In order to produce valid 'true' statements, congregants are bound to follow the explicit and implicit rules of general discourse. And many enunciative situations are fairly standardised. When preaching on the street, members of the EPC walk from street corner to street corner, and only a few minutes are spent on each spot. The message is mostly limited to a brief explanation of how Christ died on the cross to offer the rest of us eternal salvation and how release from present frustrations can be found by turning to him. I never observed emotional outbursts like the ones described earlier during street preaching.

This is not to say that Pentecostal enunciative modalities demand highly formalised, liturgical speech and repetition of standard utterances. And I am by no means arguing that discourse should be seen as a negative social constraint that is imposed upon otherwise naturally free and creative communication (and nothing would be further from Foucault's position). As Sherry Ortner points out (1990: 6), there is no freedom to narrate outside of a discourse, though alternative discourses may be sought. The power of Pentecostal discourse does not work by coercion but as a structure of action that incites, induces, and guides the possibility of linguistic conduct. A partial synthesis of a Foucauldian analysis of discourse with a more phenomenological approach may help us understand how congregants who follow the rules of discourse come to experience their own ritual linguistic mastery as empowered rather than conditioned. Being enrolled within a Pentecostal discursive formation, having internalised its rules (for example, of conceptual elaborations) as part of one's linguistic dispositions, and having developed bodily dispositions for being in communion with divine power, congregants frequently find themselves in enunciative situations where it would simply not or at least very rarely occur to them to make certain statements and gestures, while others, while not learnt and rehearsed beforehand, are made with an ease and apparent naturalness so that it seems that all one has to do is to open the mouth and allow God to let the words flow.

When congregants tell each other stories during church meetings on Mondays about good things that have happened to them, they do not feel constrained and obliged to include God in a story where he does not really belong and which would be much easier to tell if he could be left out. On the contrary, it would feel unnatural for them not to make God the main character in a story about human fortune. Human impotence and divine interference are fundamental ontological principles, inscribed, partly through ritual practice, as parts of the dispositions that spontaneously inform interpretation and narrative articulation of events.

Pentecostal discourse manipulates its subjects, not by enforcing social constraints upon otherwise naturally free speech, but by modulating improvisation and spontaneity through the creation of enunciative modalities, where certain kinds of utterances, gestures, and outbursts seem to flow in an unforced way. Language appears autonomous as specific (more or less ritualised) enunciative situations and positions, combined with certain acquired embodied and linguistic dispositions, enable statements to be made spontaneously and with little effort, and this apparent autonomy can be objectified as divine inspiration.

Ritual beyond Ritual

In this chapter I have conceived of Pentecostal ritual as a set of practices through which certain dispositions or practical skills for orientation towards the sacred are acquired and exercised. In ritual God becomes manifest as an interfering force in the lives of congregants. But divine presence and interference are also experienced outside of strictly ritual contexts. Congregants do not 'take off' the ritually cultivated embodied and linguistic dispositions for experiencing the sacred and reordering the behavioural environment, as one might take off a particular ritual garment at the end of a service. On the contrary, these dispositions form part of what Simon Coleman and Peter Collins refer to as an all-pervading aesthetic consistency, or a habitus, which is always a potential arena for inspired action (2000: 318, 320, 324–5).

The partial penetration of Pentecostal ritual language and rhetorical techniques into everyday conversation is a topic that I address in the next chapter. What I wish to point out here is that sensations of divine companionship and empowerment are quite pervasive features of Pentecostal daily life. Several ritualised practices, such as praying, singing, and speaking in tongues in order to build up oneself spiritually and take control of the immediate environment, can take place in various social settings. 'Wherever I go, I say. "Jesus, you are with me, you will protect me, and I feel confident that things will work out well," ' a woman from the EPC once told me. Marcelo (who also made an appearance in chapter 6) offered me a more elaborate description of how interaction with God, sometimes resulting in high levels of arousal, pervaded his everyday existence:

> I feel the *gozo* of God; many times I feel the presence of the Holy Spirit, when I am in the bus, in the supermarket, walking on the street, and I feel like shouting, 'Glory to God, alleluia!' It is like a necessity of the heart, a necessity from the inside to say, 'Thank you Lord; I praise you; I glorify your name.' ... Now you two are leaving [referring his wife who was about to leave for a women's meeting in the church and to the visiting anthropologist], but his presence will remain here in this home.... Often, I don't just kneel to pray, but also, like you and I are talking now, I talk with him; I go around in my home, and for me it is like a person who is present here. I do not see him, but he is very real for me; I know he is here, that he hears me and he sees me. So it is not that I just go to church to find God; wherever God wants me to be, I look for him.

Francisco, a young man from the EPC recalled how his first powerful encounter God had taken place during a church meeting. This experience turned out to be the beginning of a long and beautiful friendship:

> Francisco: Suddenly something great came upon me, a power like fire, like when you are in the sun or near a fireplace, and I was burning; I was really burning. One has so much power, and when the power is inside you, you start shaking.
>
> ML: [a little confused over his choice of words] Did it hurt?
>
> Francisco: Nooo, it was an inexplicable happiness; I was happy, such a big happiness. And afterwards one starts having more faith. One starts believing more in the Lord. And since that moment the Lord has never left me. And it became so easy for me to preach on the street. Once we went to preach, and I felt embarrassed; I was worried; it was one month later. But I liked preaching, and the Lord loosened my tongue, he gave me more abilities to speak to people.

In this description, the sensation of being allied with and accompanied by God enabled Francisco to overcome the obstacle of embarrassment and engage with the social world in new ways. A little later in the interview he explained to me how his relationship with the Lord had now developed and matured:

> Most of the time, I am thinking about the Lord, about feeling good with the Lord. I talk with the Lord all the time; he guides me. He tells me what to do.... It is not like before when I was alone; now I am always with the Lord (*siempre ando con el Señor*). I talk with him on the street, in the bus, at home.

In the previous chapter, I drew on Mead's definition of the self as a site of internal responsiveness between the 'I' and the 'me', the latter being constituted by the generalised social response of human others. I argued that conversion can, in part, be seen as a process of learning to identify the internal other, the 'me' to whom the 'I' responds in internal conversation as a divine voice and hence of framing reflective thought as a conversation with God. However, I also noted that the identification of God as an intimate internal other and partner of conversation more often than not follows some ritual bodily experience of divine presence. In the present chapter I have focused on the ways in which such experiences are produced from the kinaesthetic and rhetorical engagement in worship. As noted by Tanya Luhrmann, the processes of learning to have certain religious experiences cannot be easily disentangled from learning the words to describe them (2004: 525). Writing on the Horizon Christian Fellowship in Southern California, Luhrmann argues that congregants become intimate with God as they learn to use their own bodies to create a sense of the reality of someone external to them. That learning process

> is complex and subtle: It involves developing a cognitive model of who the person is in the relationship; a metakinethic responsiveness that can be interpreted as the presence of another being; and many repetitions of apparent dialogue through which a person develops an imagined sense of participation and exchange. (ibid.: 527)

Recalling the arguments I made in chapter 6, I now propose that the extension of a personal relationship between Pentecostals and God beyond ritual contexts and into everyday quiet thought activity (talking with God on the street, in the bus, etc.) can be fruitfully grasped by supplementing the work of scholars such as Luhrmann and Csordas with Mead's understanding of the self and reflective thought as an internal conversation. What I argue is that having developed an embodied, cognitive sensibility to the sacred, that is, having learnt to use one's body in a certain way, having acquired dispositions for certain kinds of spontaneous behaviour, and having learnt to identify or objectify certain bodily and emotional states and spontaneous inclinations as divine presence, an increased consciousness of and focus upon possible communication with God is generated. A similar cultural identification or objectification of the socially constituted 'me' to which the 'I' responds in internal conversation can then easily follow. In other words, the identification of God as a partner of internal conversation is facilitated and prepared by physical experiences of his presence.

Conclusion

This chapter has highlighted the constitutive role of ritual in Pentecostal religious life. It is in large part through the bodily and rhetorical participation in ritual life that congregants learn the faith, become tied together in a human–divine community, and develop new ways of relating to themselves and the world. In Pentecostal discourses and ritual practice, secular notions of power as embedded in political, economic, and scientific institutions and exercised by their agents are disqualified in favour of a notion of divine power that is accessible to and activated by worshipping congregants. By accepting and even idealising human powerlessness and total dependence on God but at the same time establishing an intimate and embodied relationship with his transformative power members of the EPC defy the logic of secular social and cultural hierarchies and constitute an alternate theological and ontological position for themselves in the social world. In ritual life, the sensations of powerlessness and insufficiency that many congregants experience in secular social fields become revaluated as fundamental criterions for the efficiency of spoken language. Like other kinds of transformative action, consequential ritual speech is not produced by independent and creative subjects but by subjects who surrender their individuality and autonomy to God. Through the strategic neglect of human creativity and agency, Pentecostal ritual practice constitutes an inversion of a modernist individualist ethos.

My intention has been to portray Pentecostal ritual practice as more than a symbolic representation of theological notions of divine power, human powerlessness, and dependency. In church meetings the power of God is experienced, not as an intellectual construct, but as an active force that moves among human participants, works on and through their bodies, and frequently interrupts their communication. It is only when God interferes that otherwise powerless humans are able to produce beautiful singing and consequential speech. And it is by planning church meetings, sermons, and testimonies, only to let those plans be undermined by divine interruptions, that empowerment is found.

The positioning of bodies, the bodily engagement in worship and the different ways in which words are uttered should not be seen as arbitrary forms through which the real stuff, the meaningful content or the biblical message, of ritual life is presented. On the contrary, the endlessly repeated theological message that humans are powerless in themselves but that God is powerful and present in the lives of his children is inseparably intertwined with the communicative forms or strategies of ritualisation through which divine presence, power, and interference become manifest in church meetings. A focus on ritual practice as an empowering bodily and communicative engagement with perceived divine presence can pave the way for better understandings of Pentecostal subjectivity and world constructions in Chile and elsewhere.

CHAPTER EIGHT

BANAL RE-ENCHANTMENT

Shortly after arriving in Chile in November 2008, I spoke on the phone with Eloiza, a woman in her early forties from the EPC. She told me that her family was presently very short of money because her husband, Edgardo, also a congregant and a good friend of mine, had been unemployed for some months. 'But we know why, don't we Martin?' she asked me. 'Eeeh, yeah,' I replied, without being absolutely certain what she was referring to. But Eloiza helped me out as she continued, 'He is probably testing Edgardo.'

Had the last statement been made in a conversation between Eloiza and a Chilean Catholic, unfamiliar with Pentecostal terminology and interpretive schemes, one can imagine that the latter would have reacted by asking, 'Who is he?' In this private conversation Eloiza was applying a highly restricted or condensed code (Bernstein 1971), taking for granted that the listener would know that the *he* responsible for the present situation could only be God! Further she was obviously assuming that the listener was familiar with the Pentecostal concept of a 'test' (*prueba*).[1]

The idea that religious fundamentalism can be understood only in relation to its others, namely secularisation, disenchantment, and modernism, has been voiced repeatedly in the literature (Shupe & Hadden 1992; Mardsen 1991; Marty 1992; Marty & Appleby 1992; Riesebrodt 1993; Hawley & Proudfoot 1994). Secularisation or disenchantment can be defined as processes through which several spheres of life become subject to human control. Secularisation does not necessarily lead to atheism, but it does imply a compartmentalisation of religion in modern society, separating it from public policy and from the spheres of factual and authoritative (for example, scientific) knowledge about the world. Modernism, on the other hand, is the holistic

---

[1] Members of the EPC believe that God sometimes tests his children by letting them go through periods of hardship, but that some kind of reward such as strengthening of faith will eventually follow. Thus Pentecostals cope with hardship by placing it within a narrative of divine plans and spiritual growth.

ideological framework of secular modernity with deep roots in enlightenment ideas of rationality, reason, and progress (see Lawrence 1989: 2).
Puzzled by the persistence, creative innovation, and partial radicalisa-
tion of religious beliefs, practices, and institutions in the contemporary
(modern) world, scholars have for some time been arguing that religious fundamentalists react to processes of secularisation by trying to
re-sacralise the world in what is better seen as a cyclical than a linear
process (Shupe & Hadden 1992: 113).

There are a number of ways in which religious fundamentalists may
do that. The goal of many Islamic fundamentalist movements is the
establishment of an Islamic state, where sharia is fully implanted and
applied to all citizens, voluntary or by force (Haynes 1995: 9). Within
Hinduism, Buddhism, and Jewish Zionism, fundamentalism has
been inextricably linked to nationalist goals, sometimes pursued
through violent actions (ibid.: 24; Tambiah 1996; Peste 2006). Some
North American New Christian Right organisations like the Moral
Majority Coalition support conservative candidates and try to sensitise
Christians to political issues and bring Christian values and principles
into the heart of public policy. The political goals of the Moral Majority
Coalition include public prayer in public schools, new tax laws making
it easier for parents to send their children to private Christian schools,
the teaching of the Genesis story of the Old Testament as a plausible
alternative to evolutionism, and a general revision of school books so
that they do not promote secular humanism. Besides these goals, the
Moral Majority Coalition actively opposes legal abortion (Bruce 1987:
183–5). North American Fundamentalists have also founded creationist science institutes, trying to make contemporary biology and geol-
ogy fit within the framework of Old Testament teachings (Harrold, Eve
& Taylor 2004).

Unlike Islamic, Buddhist, Jewish Zionist, and Hindu fundamentalists, and the North American Religious Right, the EPC has no
overt political agenda.[2] But what I intend to demonstrate in the present

---

[2] I acknowledge that the inclusion of Pentecostalism with a broader category of
Protestant Fundamentalism is not uncontroversial. Historically Protestant Fundamentalism and Pentecostalism are two distinct movements, both of which originated
in the United States in the early twentieth century (see Spittler 1994), and many scholars find it necessary to make clear distinctions between them (Ammerman 1994a;
Robbins 2004, 2011), partly because many Fundamentalists believe that the gifts of the
Holy Spirit were only available to believers during the time of the Apostles. Yet several
others have argued that North and Latin American Pentecostalism is in many ways

chapter is that Pentecostal/fundamentalist struggles to re-sacralise, de-secularise, or re-enchant the social world can also be fought in other and more 'banal' or trivial ways. The title of the chapter is inspired by an influential book by Michael Billig, *Banal Nationalism* (1995). Writing mainly on England, Billig introduces the term 'banal national-ism' in order to cover a number of everyday ideological habits through which a sense of nationhood and national identity is reproduced in the lives of citizens. Instead of restricting the concept of nationalism to exotic exemplars, characterised by the use of explicit, passionate rheto-ric and ensigns, Billig suggests that careful attention should be focused on more routine, familiar forms of nationalism through which citizens are continuously reminded of their national identity. These forms, or 'banal flagging', are not confined to politics but include taken-for-granted uses of indexical terms such as 'we', 'here', and 'this' in numer-ous contexts such as weather reports and news about sport events. Billig describes national identity as a 'routine way of talking and listen-ing: It is a form of life which habitually closes the front door, and seals the borders' (ibid.: 109).

In this chapter I shed light on different 'banal' ritual and habitual everyday practices through which members of the EPC challenge secular modernist ideologies and repeatedly remind themselves and each other that their lives and social world are pervaded by divine pres-ence, company, and transformative intervention. While such practices

---

a fundamentalistic religion that embraces fundamentalist asceticism and the beliefs in biblical inerrancy (Spittler 1994; Cleary & Steigenga 2007; Freston 2006). The British anthropologist David Lehmann has further pointed to anti-cosmopolitanism, the obsession with the control of women's sexuality, and a deep distrust of intellectuals and academic institutions as distinguishing features that Latin American Pentecostal-ism shares with other fundamentalist movements (1996). The German sociologist Martin Riesebrodt has made a distinction between book-centred rational and experience-centred charismatic fundamentalisms. Both wish to rationalise conduct according to absolute moral principles, but experience-centred fundamentalism adds the ability to experience gifts of grace as confirmation of salvation (1993: 18). Elsewhere Riesebrodt and Kelly Chong include Latin American Pentecostalism within the category of charismatic fundamentalism (1999). Here I do not wish to dwell too much at definitional controversies. Suffice it to say that I find Riesebrodt's distinction helpful, as it allows us acknowledge the fundamentalistic character of Pentecostalism, or at least of some of its variants, while at the same time being sensitive to important histori-cal and doctrinal differences between conservative Evangelical Protestant (fundamen-talistic) groups. (Spittler, 1994, has made a similar point with regards to North American Pentecostalism.) In my view, a traditional Chilean Pentecostal church, like the EPC is certainly fundamentalistic enough to be compared with other religious fundamentalisms.

downplay the importance of human agency, mere coincidence, and good and bad luck in the interpretation of events, they simultaneously serve as reminders of the authority and responsibility of congregants to act upon the world by accessing and activating divine power. The practices to be considered in the following are preaching on the street, sharing and thanksgiving during church meetings, informal conversation, joking, praying, and internal conversation with God. Drawing on some of the theoretical perspectives introduced in the previous chapter, especially the work of Csordas (1997) and Bell (1992), I argue that the Pentecostal re-enchantment of the world occurs when boundaries between ritual and non-ritual spheres of activities become blurred, and divine presence, company, and intervention are established as pervasive features of everyday life.

Making Authoritative Statements

In a thought-provoking study of how language and the status of statements have been affected by secularisation processes, Richard Fenn argues that human speech acts in modern industrial society are haunted by slipperiness, ambiguity, and uncertainty. Making a statement with a status beyond mere opinion becomes increasingly difficult, and as ordinary discourse is caught up in the process of negotiating praise and blame, speakers and listeners rarely get the sense that all has been said and done. According to Fenn, the secularisation of language has created a demand for the kind of speech acts that in modern society are reserved to the elites, and the growth of Pentecostalism can, in part, be seen as a response to this demand:

> Some religious groups ... flourish precisely because they provide the unauthorised and untrained, the laity, with opportunities to declare, pronounce and direct.... Religious groups with Pentecostal fervour and authority in their acts of speech may indeed flourish precisely because of the successful secularisation of educational, economic or political institutions in modern societies. (Fenn 1981: 119)

Bourdieu pursues a related analysis of language and the status of statements in *Language and Symbolic Power* (1991). Drawing on the speech act theory of John Austin (1975) he points out that the power of words and statements, or the ability to do things with words, cannot be aptly captured by focusing solely on inherent principles of language and discourse. Rather it is the 'social position of the speaker, access to legitimate instruments of expression, participation in the authority of the institution [that] make all the difference, irreducible to discourse as such' (Bourdieu 1991: 109).

In a (post-)modern world, where knowledge is constantly being revisited, and the privilege of making authoritative statements is confined to experts, Pentecostalism reasserts a structure of authority, providing its members with an unshakeable fundament from which they can speak about the world. In the EPC as in other Pentecostal churches, the expertise and spiritual authority of individual lay members are asserted and continuously reconfirmed through lay leadership, active lay participation in ritual life, the prevalence of narrative theology, and not least preaching on the street.

Street Preaching

Street preaching has been a characteristic feature of Chilean Pentecostalism since the very beginning, and to many other Chileans, Pentecostals are foremost known as the ones who preach and sing on the streets and the *plazas* (public squares). On weekdays, street preaching mainly takes place between 6 and 7.30 p.m. On Sundays street preachers can be observed early in the morning and during the afternoon. When preaching on the street, members of the EPC gather in groups of five to twenty people on a street corner. They then divide themselves into smaller groups of two to four people, who follow the same route but stop at different corners and preach the necessity of salvation and sing a few hymns. When the groups reunite, they may stay together for a while and sing a hymn, after which new groups are formed. A normal session of street preaching takes around thirty to forty minutes but only a few minutes are spent at each spot. Before reaching the church, the whole group is reunited, and they then walk together to the church in two lines. On Sundays, when Pentecostals preach in the *plazas*, they usually remain on the same spot and in larger groups for a longer period. Members of other Pentecostal denominations such as the Methodist Pentecostal Church and the United Methodist Pentecostal Church use guitars, microphones, and loudspeakers when preaching and singing on the *plazas*.

As a strategy of evangelisation, street preaching must be considered a failure. On Sunday mornings, enthusiastic Pentecostals start preaching in almost empty streets and *plazas* between 8.30 and 9.30 a.m.

They then go to the church to assist the Sunday school at 10 a.m., that is, at about the same time as other people, potential listeners, start gathering in the *plazas*, and as sellers, buyers, and spectators of the various street markets arrive. On weekdays and Sunday afternoons, numerous audiences are sometimes found, especially on the *plazas*, but often empty streets are also chosen for preaching. I attended street preaching several times as an observer and on no occasion did any pedestrian stop to listen. Since the same streets are used for preaching week after week and the same message of salvation in Christ is preached over and over, most people have become used to the preaching as a permanent and hardly significant part of street life. I have only met one woman who claimed that she was inspired to visit a Pentecostal church after listening to street preaching.

There are several reasons why street preaching is not efficient as a strategy of conversion. The effects of language are influenced by a number of extra-linguistic factors. In chapter 6 on conversion I argued that sensations of intimacy between speaker and listener can influence the effects of language. In street preaching a number of factors impede the creation of such intimacy. Unlike preaching in the church, street preachers have no means of monopolising the available physical space, which is not closed upon the audience but open and filled with alternative projects. The attention of the audience is not nearly as focused on the street as in the church, and even if someone does stop to listen he or she is likely to be distracted by what goes on elsewhere in the physical space. When sitting on benches between other congregants during a church meeting and obeying church norms, according to which it is not appropriate to look backwards but only forwards, listeners have little freedom of movement, experience few distractions, and are caught in a situation of communicative openness and vulnerability. By contrast the potential audience in street preaching is mostly standing and walking, and they enjoy a freedom of movement, which enables a quick shift of attention.

However, I think it would be a mistake to evaluate street preaching according to the number of converts it produces. Preaching the necessity of salvation on the streets may have little effect on the audience, but what it does to the preachers is by no means insignificant. It is quite common for members of the EPC to talk about how they feel empowered, blessed, and touched by the Holy Spirit during and after street preaching, whereas accounts of the reactions of listeners are rarer. Preaching on the street is one of the occasions where the priesthood of all believers is most clearly practised. Whereas women and young members are only occasionally given the opportunity to speak in the church from the pulpit, they can preach on the street three to four times a week. In street preaching all participants are granted an important enunciative position as active ritual experts and ambassadors of God in a corrupted 'world'. Pentecostals do not just turn their back on the 'world' by adopting a position of empty and passive avoidance. Street preaching is a ritual form of confronting and reaching out for the 'world' from a position of authority. Thus it becomes a crucial activity through which congregants are constituted and constitute themselves as active Pentecostal subjects with a mission in a world, and 'world', of misguided sinners and with the ability, the commitment, and the duty to make important authoritative statements.

Sharing and Thanksgiving

On Mondays, sharing and individual thanksgiving to God take up a good part of church meetings in the EPC. Monday meetings are held in local church buildings all over Valparaíso. After a few hymns, practical announcements, and a short speech or sermon by a leader, participants stand up, one at the time, and thank God for being with them and providing them with basic necessities. They sometimes take the opportunity to re-narrate their personal testimony of salvation, though in a reduced version. Or they relate an anecdote about divine and sometimes satanic intervention in their life during the past week or at some earlier occasion. Like Carmen, who was quoted in chapter 7 (page 134), congregants may also make quite passionate declarations of love to the Lord during sharing and thanksgiving.

In a ritualised context, that is a church meeting with a clear structure, fixed sequence of events, and spatial positioning of human bodies (see also the section on positional practices in chapter 7): congregants stand up, one at the time, while the rest remain seated and do not look at the one who stands. Congregants start their expression of gratitude in similar ways: 'In this night I thank the Lord' or 'In this night I praise the Lord' or 'In this night I praise and glorify the sweet name of my saviour.' They usually end with the words 'to the Lord are all the honour, glory, and praise.' But in between standard beginnings and endings, personal anecdotes about sacred intervention in everyday life are told, often at some length.

The individual narrating of anecdotes in a ritual context is informed by the same Pentecostal politics of storytelling as preaching and the narrating of personal testimonies and post-conversion life stories (see chapter 6). Notions of human powerlessness and dependence upon God as the source of all good things and the theologically fundamental dualism between the 'world' and the privileged life with God provide a framework for the construction of anecdotes. Like the public narrating of a personal testimony of salvation, the sharing of anecdotes becomes an implicit statement of commitment to a religious community and a reaffirmation of its basic values and world views. The sharing of anecdotes can, in other words, be seen as a rhetorical process through which a shared religious life world is constructed, unfolded, reproduced, and modified.

The time has now come to introduce a few examples of the anecdotes that are shared by congregants on Mondays. Liz, a nineteen–year-old unemployed girl, once stood up during a Monday meeting and recalled how both God and the Devil had intervened in her life on the previous day:

> Yesterday I was very sad, so I prayed to the Lord. I said to him, 'Lord I'm not asking for gold or silver, but I want to feel your presence.' And I felt it so I became very happy. I was very happy. Then the enemy [Satan] attacked me. I was cutting some vegetables, and I cut three of my fingers. But I didn't get angry; I cried for the Lord, because I was bleeding a lot, but I didn't get angry. He [Satan] wanted me to get angry, but nevertheless I was still happy with the Lord.

Through the narrating of such anecdotes, a communion is created between the contemporary life of congregants and the eternal truth of the Gospel (see also Pfeil 2011). A quite trivial everyday event, cutting one's fingers, is interpreted as a minor part or episode within a biblical metanarrative of cosmic warfare between God and the Devil. This metanarrative is simultaneously a model of and for reality (Geertz 1973: 93). Apart from providing a framework or attribution scheme for the interpretation of experiences, it also provides Liz with a scheme or script for present and future action. In this case action consisted in praying or crying for the Lord so that she could be happy and later continue to be happy despite her bleeding fingers. In this, as in several other anecdotes, it becomes evident that divine intervention in human affairs is anticipated and actively sought rather than just retrospectively ascribed to a given situation or event. Lived experience is charged with the significance it derives from both retentions and pretensions.

José André, an unskilled worker in his fifties, once stood up on a Monday and related another anecdote about anticipated divine intervention in a particular situation:

> I thank the Lord in this night, dear brothers [and sisters], for giving me this great opportunity to be here in his house. I praise the name of Jesus, because one day he saved me and forgave me and cured me. The Lord has done such wonderful things for us, and we should always remember that because it is too marvellous. The Lord helps me to be faithful, brothers [and sisters], so that I never forget how he has changed my heart. Because sometimes you talk with people from the 'world' who do not know God, and they talk about television and pain and suffering. When the Lord saved me, it was the most beautiful day in my life. And the other day I had been asked to preach the word in Placeres [a local church building in outer Valparaíso]. And it was raining hard, and when I had to leave my home I said to him: 'Lord, I don't have adequate clothes for the rain. I want to serve you; you have given me this responsibility; please stop the rain, so that I can get there.' And God is so great, his love and his mercy are so great that he stopped the rain, and I could go to Placeres. And then the meeting started, and it started to rain again. But inside there was a rain of grace. And when the meeting stopped, I asked the Lord to stop the rain again, because I did not want to come home wet. And he did it again, brothers [and sisters], so we could all go home without getting wet.

Recalling some of the theoretical perspectives that were introduced in chapter 2, the excerpt can be seen as a ritual action in which José André creatively uses available religious knowledge, rhetorical resources, and persuasive means in order to make sense of events, articulate a vision, and convince himself and others that the world is constituted in a certain way (Csordas 1997: 139). But, adopting a Foucauldian perspective, it could also be argued that the rules of the Pentecostal discursive formation make it extremely unlikely that someone in this specific enunciative position and situation would narrate such an anecdote about avoiding the rain without placing God at the centre stage. In other words, the creative construction of meaning and the production of meaning-creating subjects only occur within discursive formations, governing how statements can be made and distributed.

On another occasion Monica, a woman in her sixties who had been living alone since her husband left her twenty years earlier and was making a modest living as a domestic servant, stood up during a Monday meeting and expressed her gratitude to the Lord for providing her with all basic necessities. She then related an anecdote about how God had helped her the previous week when she had been appointed to cook lunch for the workers in the construction of the new church building:

> The other day I was in the kitchen in the construction, preparing the lunch for the workers. And I could see that I would not be able to finish in time. And I was embarrassed to ask the working brothers to help me, so I said to the Lord, 'Lord, why don't you send me someone to help me?' And suddenly brother Mauricio came and asked if I needed help. So you can see that the Lord is always with you; he is always worried about you.

Again we can see how divine intervention is on the one hand antici-pated and sought and, on the other, retrospectively inferred. What is also worth noticing is how Monica refers to her interaction with Lord in a way which is quite similar to the way in which many people—Pentecostals and others—refer to past conversations with human oth-ers. It is not difficult to imagine Monica narrating a similar anecdote about a conversation with a human being. Such an anecdote could include a sentence like the following: 'So I said to the pastor, "Pastor, why don't you send someone to help me?"' Through the acts of thanks-giving and sharing on Mondays, lay Pentecostals continuously re-nar-rate their engagement with sacred others, presenting and constituting divine presence, company, and consequential intervention in human affairs as fundamental parts of everyday life.

From Ritual to Everyday Speech

Thanksgiving and sharing on Mondays are important rhetorical/narrative exercises through which lay Pentecostals develop a practi-cal sense of discursive–theological reality construction. By ritually talking about the world in particular ways, people become active co-constructors of the specific re-enchanted social reality they are part of. But talking about the world in particular ways is not limited to church meetings. As argued by Csordas, ritual genres such as sharing can find their way into everyday conversation and become part of the organisa-tion of a linguistic habitus (1997: 200). In private informal conversa-tions, congregants frequently relate anecdotes, similar to or almost identical with the ones related during church meetings, about divine presence and intervention in their lives.

In chapter 7 I introduced Catherine Bell's concept of ritualisation. As this concept allows us to conceive of the relationship between ritual and non-ritual practices and situations as one of graduation rather than absolute division, it is particularly relevant in a study of Pentecostal forms of worship and not least of the blurring of boundaries between ritual and everyday speech. However, I also argued that maintaining an analytical boundary between ritual and non-ritual practices will be helpful in analysing how certain elements of ritual penetrate the sphere of everyday life, while others do not. It is such an analysis that I pursue in the following.

Several specific ritual features of Monday meetings do not blend into everyday informal conversation. These features include fixed bodily positioning, the avoidance of eye contact between speaker and listeners, standing up when talking, waiting for permission to speak by a ritual leader, standardised verbal beginnings (for example, 'in this night I thank the Lord for giving me the opportunity to be here in his house of worship') and closings ('All honour, glory and praise be to the Lord'), dramatic shifts in tonality and the making of loud emotional outbursts because of a sudden urge to glorify God. All these practices mark a distinction between different communicative situations. They would seem odd during informal private conversations, whereas they make perfect sense within a particular ritual situation. When sharing anecdotes about divine intervention in everyday contexts, congregants usually look at each other, and whether they stand or sit depends on the context and practical requirements of a given situation. During private storytelling congregants do occasionally start weeping a little or interrupt their stories with a 'glory to God' but such outbursts are rarer, quieter, and less dramatic than during Monday meetings.

Nevertheless, the construction and narrating of anecdotes constitute important points of convergence between ritualised and everyday speech acts. The same Pentecostal politics of storytelling informs different kinds of linguistic interaction, a main principle being strategically downplaying or neglecting transformative human agency or the power of mere coincidence and instead crediting divine agency for positive achievements. A few excerpts from my numerous informal conversations with congregants can illustrate this point. Rosa, a housewife and mother in her late thirties, once told me how she and her family had moved to Valparaíso from a smaller nearby town, Quilpue:

> After the Lord had taken my grandmother, we lived for a while in a small house that the Lord had given us in Quilpue. But then the Lord gave us an apartment in Valparaíso. Here in Valparaíso, my mother was very sick until the Lord cured her.

Any account of the human efforts and contacts which are usually implied in finding and buying or renting a place to live is left out of this description. Further the healing of the mother is simply ascribed to divine agency. Apparently Rosa found it unnecessary to explain whether the mother had been healed by praying alone or whether God had in this case chosen to use human doctors as his instruments (as he sometimes does, see also chapter 5). The negligence of human agency was also salient in the following exchange between myself and Enrique, a retired unskilled worker in his seventies, whose only son was working as a taxi driver:

> ML: So, how is your son doing?
> Enrique: He is fine; he is not working because his car is out of order, but the Lord gave him a pension, two hundred thousand pesos each month, so he can put food on the table.
> ML: But how was he able to get a pension, if he has not even turned forty and has no physical disability?
> Enrique: I prayed to the Lord and asked for help, and the Lord gave him a pension!

A year later Enrique had forgotten about this conversation, and he told me once more that his son was receiving a monthly pension of two hundred thousand pesos. Instead of reminding him that he had already told me that, I once again expressed my surprise that a young and seemingly fit man could get a pension, but this time Enrique just responded by pointing his forefinger upwards, indicating that the pension came from above.

Assuming that the two hundred thousand pesos are not dropping from heaven each month, some layers are obviously missing from the story about the son's early pension. Explanations of human agency, personal conditions, disabilities, or political, bureaucratic rules and procedures on the basis of which the son was given a pension are left out of this account, as Enrique goes straight to what he considers to be the ultimate source of the pension, divine intervention. In fact, the only human agency in this story is that of Enrique himself, who prayed to the Lord for help. Only several years later did I learn (from another family member) that the son received the pension because of a minor physical disability due to a work accident.

Jaime, a man in his late fifties told me how he and his wife were saved and she was healed from a disease at a big open-air revival meeting with a foreign preacher in the late 1970s. After being saved they had to find themselves a church:

Jaime: The preacher said, 'Everyone who has accepted Christ in his heart in this afternoon, go and find a church as soon as possible.' He didn't say, 'Go to this or that specific church,' he gave us freedom to find a church. So after that day we started praying to God that he would help us find a good church. We put our lives in his hand, and we got many invitations, but the Lord brought us here [to the EPC].
ML: And how did you know that this was the right church?
Jaime: Because my mother-in-law had joined this church; she had accepted Christ on that same occasion, and she started to attend meetings in this church.

This story differs from Enrique's story about the son's early pension and Rosa's story about finding a place to live and the healing of her mother, in that a more mundane explanation how Jaime and his wife ended up in the EPC was offered. But the mother-in-law only appeared in the story when the anthropologist asked directly for more specific details. She is by no means presented as a main character but rather as an instrument of God, a detail that may but needs not be included, in the story about how and why Jaime and wife joined the EPC and not some other church.

The shading of ritualised rhetoric and discursive principles of story-telling into everyday conversation is prevalent in the many anecdotes that congregants narrate to one another or to anthropologists but can also be observed in other kinds of linguistic interaction. I have mentioned that congregants usually reply, 'Fine, thanks to the Lord,' whenever someone asks them how they or their family members are doing. And if they are facing some difficult task or challenge in life such as an exam in school, a job interview, a period of illness, financial problems, etc., they commonly remark that they hope that things will work out well 'con la ayuda del Señor' (with the help of the Lord).

In August 2000, some of the men in the EPC were involved in the construction of the new church building. On one occasion all the construction workers were asked to stay behind in the church after a meeting in order to plan the work of coming months and make individual schedules. This extra meeting was held for purely practical reasons. The ritual activities of the day had finished, and the majority of the congregants had gone home. The extra meeting did not start with a prayer, a hymn, or readings from the Bible. Nevertheless, the borderline between ritual and practical (secular) activities was by no means as clear as might have been expected. When the congregant in charge of the construction work addressed the rest of the workers, hardly a sentence was uttered where the words 'God' or 'the Lord' did not appear.

The necessity of making a work schedule for each of the workers and
the ambition of finishing the work soon were expressed as follows:

> Thanks to the Lord, a great part of the church construction has been fin-
> ished. Now each of us has to make a commitment to the Lord to work in
> the church a certain amount of days. With the help of the Lord we can
> finish the construction soon, if the Lord keeps helping us.

Another congregant then stepped forwards in order to inform the others about a meeting he and a few others had had with some local political authorities concerning construction permits:

> The Lord was with us during that meeting. We knew that one of the per-
> sons would be a little difficult to convince, but the Lord touched the heart
> of that person, and he turned out to be very helpful; I think that the Lord
> helped us. In the moment when we really needed help, the Lord helped
> us. Now each of us has to help so that we can finish the construction. The
> Lord has helped us; we should be happy! And if the Lord keeps helping
> us we can finish the construction in January. May God help us all, my
> brothers.

Pentecostal rhetoric and conceptual elaborations penetrate what could
be considered mundane levels of discourse. The schedule of the workers is conceptualised as a commitment to God. In this situation it was
difficult to avoid mentioning the fact that the construction of the
church building was indeed dependant upon the human effort of each
worker. We can see how both of the speakers tried to cope with this
challenge by letting individual responsibility be overshadowed by the
emphasis on the dependence on God. Theological notions of human
impotence and total dependence on an almighty God as the source of
all good things are woven through every thread of planning, practical
arrangements, and accounts of bureaucratic processes. In the second
excerpt, the speaker explains that a non-Pentecostal person turned out
to be helpful because the 'Lord touched the heart of that person.' This
expression is frequently used by congregants in stories, told in both
ritual and non-ritual contexts, about non-Pentecostals who have done
good deeds and helped others in an unselfish way.

The Lord also appears in humorous comments like the following:
'Brother Ivan has quite a bad temper. Maybe the Lord needs to cut him
with a spiritual axe!' Or: 'That brother is very flirtatious with the girls.
It seems as if the Lord is enlightening his eyes, whenever he talks
to them!' On one occasion a young woman from the EPC tried to
frighten one of the young men by sneaking up behind him and
shouting, 'Buuuh!' while suddenly touching his back. She was a little

disappointed when she saw that he was not frightened, but he gave her the following explanation: 'I wasn't frightened, because the Lord revealed to me that a spirit of the 'world' [a demon] was trying to attack me from behind!' Ritually cultivated rhetoric dispositions blend into everyday linguistic practice, and even jokes are often informed by Pentecostal understandings of an ever- and omnipresent God who frequently interferes in human affairs.

Similar to how a sense of national identity and belonging is mainly constituted and nurtured in 'homely discourse' where familiar habits of language act as reminders of nationhood (Billig 1995: 93, 127) and a widely shared frame of reference can be taken for granted, the importance of banal linguistic, ritual, and everyday practice for the construction of a re-enchanted social reality can hardly be overrated. By sharing anecdotes about sacred intervention in ritual and everyday life and by including the Lord in mundane levels of discourse such as planning, practical arrangements, and joking, congregants continuously partake in the unfolding of an enchanted life world while at the same time inviting each other to inhabit it. Such banal linguistic practices constitute an important 'weapon of the weak' (Scott 1990) in symbolic struggles over categorisations and definitions of social reality.

Praying and Talking with the Lord

Praying takes up a good part of church meetings. Some congregants like to arrive before a meeting starts in order to pray for themselves, and during meetings there are several moments of collective praying, both at the beginning and towards the end. Besides these times of communal prayer, most congregants pray at home every day. Some congregants told me that they prayed for at least half an hour every morning and that they would sometimes wake up in the middle of the night and pray for up to an hour. Praying at home or in the church mostly takes place in a folded, introverted position.

Writing on North American Protestant Fundamentalists, Nancy Ammerman (1994b: 61) sees praying as a rhetorical exercise in speaking about the world in God's terms and in standing outside of everyday reality, experiencing the sacred in a way that relativises the mundane. Praying is also an important activity in which Pentecostals develop and nourish a relationship with God through dialogue or, in the words of Lurhmann, 'through an actual conversation between two intentional consciousnesses' (2006: 4) Congregants from the EPC tend to describe praying as an intimate and pleasant conversation with God, quite comparable to conversations between friends or between a husband and a wife.

Learning to carry out such a dialogue is foremost a question of learning to seek for and interpret God's presence and responses, for example, in sensations of internal peace, relief, and happiness or *gozo* sometimes resulting in outward manifestations such as tears. Congregants from the EPC further discern divine communication in spontaneous thoughts or intuitions. Luhrmann argues that the experiential emphasis that characterises much of contemporary North American religiosity encourages people to attend to their own consciousness and seek for moments of discontinuity (2005: 141). In a similar vein, Jon Bialecki, writing on a Californian Vineyard Church, notes that a sudden thought or an odd idea that does not seem to arise from one's previous chain of thoughts can be taken as indication of divine will (2011: 267). These points also apply in the case of congregants from the EPC for whom a divine message during praying often takes the form of sudden thoughts or intuitions, informing them of a state of affairs or indicating appropriate courses action. During praying, congregants may suddenly feel inspired to pray for someone else, to read the Bible, or to visit someone. Or they may feel that something is informing them that a given problem will be solved. Such intuitive inspiration is sometimes accompanied by a strong affective sensation.

God may also appear as an audible internal voice, telling Pentecostals what to do or informing them about a present state of affairs or future developments. Fernando, an unemployed man in his thirties recalled how God had recently talked to him:

> Sometimes you even hear a voice. When my mother was sick, I was praying and praying to the Lord, but nothing happened. 'Lord, help my mother, she is still young.' I was in the church, talking with the Lord for three hours. Then I got up and went out to do some shopping. I was walking across *Plaza Italia*, and I was talking with God, and I said to him, 'My mother is going to die,' and suddenly I heard someone saying to me with a voice like ours: 'Don't worry, she will not die.' And a great happiness came upon me, and I started to weep on the street, and a woman said to me, 'Are you all right?' And I said: 'Yes, I am happy!' [Woman:] 'Then how come you are weeping?' [Fernando:] 'I am weeping of happiness!' [Woman:] 'How can you weep of happiness? You are crazy!' she said, and then she left.

Apart from exemplifying how Pentecostals sometimes experience being misunderstood and regarded as crazy by people from the 'world' this excerpt also illustrates how talking with God takes place in various settings. Praying is a ritual practice that is very easily extended beyond strictly ritual or domestic contexts. Through praying people learn to think and reflect in terms of an internal conversation with a divine other (see chapter 6 and 7; see also Neitz 1987: 119–20; Csordas 1997: 199). In Fernando's description there seems to be no clear-cut distinction between praying and simply talking with God. Fernando uses the two expressions interchangeably when describing what he was doing for three hours in the church. When he was later walking across *Plaza Italia* he was still talking with God, and this was when he had a powerful religious experience as he heard the voice of the latter.

At times congregants do distinguish between praying and talking with God, important marks of distinction being different bodily positions and the extent to which their attention and focus are divided. But it is clear from their descriptions that they perceive the relationship between the two as one of graduation. Andrea, a thirty-five-year-old woman from the EPC, gave me the following explanation:

> I am in contact with the Lord all the time. I talk with him all day long. I also have my intimate moments of prayer, where I kneel down or read the Word. But I do not need to say, 'Now I will talk with the Lord.' Because I am really talking with him all the time! For instance, I start peeling the potatoes and I say, 'Lord, I am going to make mashed potatoes, because Valentina [her daughter] likes to eat that.' So I talk with him all the time; when I am in the bus or sometimes when I am talking with people, in my mind I am communicating with him.

Everyday Conversations with and about the Lord

It should have become clear by now that God and Jesus, both of whom are referred to as 'the Lord' are very important figures in the lives of Pentecostals. Besides being given the credit for all positive achievements (healing, getting pensions, avoiding the rain, finding housing, meeting basic necessities, etc.) the Lord is also present in the lives of Pentecostals as an intimate partner of interaction; as someone whose physical presence they sometimes experience, most notably but by no means exclusively in ritual life; and as someone with whom they have dialogues on an everyday basis.

In a fascinating study of the human cognitive architecture and its role in the generation, spread, and stabilisation of religious ideas and customs, Pascal Boyer makes an interesting observation, namely that interaction with supernatural others is to a large extent informed by the same inference and other cognitive systems that regulate interaction between humans (2001). On the one hand, what makes supernatural agents supernatural is that they are believed to be invested with certain counter-intuitive or counter-ontological properties (ibid.: 64). In the case of the Christian God and Jesus (after the resurrection) these properties include the ability to be in several places at the same time, immortality, immateriality, not being limited by the autonomous functioning of a body (for example, by aging, tiring, being hungry), having access to strategic information (for example, about people's inner thoughts and desires), and not least the ability to influence a course of events in ways that are impossible for ordinary humans (for example, making the rain start and stop at a particular time). On the other hand, the reason why interaction with supernatural beings feels natural for religious people is that the former are also understood to possess a number of humanlike qualities (ibid.: 163). God and Jesus are believed to have a mind, memory, intentions, motivations, a will, linguistic mastery, and the ability to see, hear, and understand what a human being communicates to them, even when communication consists of indirect hints. They are further believed to be concerned with human decisions, actions, and their consequences. As noted by Boyer, religious conceptualisations of supernatural beings are organised around intuitive notions of agency in general while at the same time violating a few deep ontological assumptions (ibid.: 144).

For members of the EPC, as for many other Pentecostal-charismatic Christians in Chile and elsewhere, the Lord is a sacred other, believed to be invested with tremendous supernatural powers to act upon the world. But he is also an intimate and familiar other, possessing a lot of ideal human qualities. He is emphatic, loving, caring, sensitive, and a good listener who is never indifferent but always deeply concerned with the problems and well-being of his people. For Pentecostals, the Lord is a daily companion, a husband, a best friend, a father, and provider of basic necessities. Paola, a twenty-five-year-old university student from the EPC once explained to me what she saw as the main benefits of being a Christian:

> The best thing about being a Christian is having the certainty that the Lord loves me; knowing that you are free in the Lord, free to live for him

and serve him. Knowing that he is with you, that he takes care of you, that you can talk with him and that he responds you. Really, I find a tremendous happiness in knowing him. Knowing that he is not the God of some religion, not someone who is far away. Knowing that he is nearby, that he loves you, that he is worried about you, that he meets all your necessities.

At this point, a short note concerning the dilemmas of translation that anthropologists are frequently faced with should be made. The English words 'the Lord' are actually not a totally adequate translation of the Spanish 'el Señor.' Whereas 'Lord' has an aristocratic sound to it, Señor is a standard respectful way of addressing men in Chile. The way in which many Chileans use the term Señor in everyday life is similar to the way many English speakers use the term 'sir', for example, as a way of respectfully addressing a policeman, a superior, or just any senior male. And when talking about another man in the third person, Chileans will also sometimes refer to him as a Señor. Within Pentecostal churches confusion concerning whom el Señor may refer to is to large extent avoided, as Pentecostal men consequently address each other and are addressed by women as 'brothers' (hermanos). By referring to God/Jesus with a term that is also commonly used to refer to male human others, the sensation that the former is a familiar other with human attributes is reinforced.[3]

Apart from talking with the Lord as they talk with other humans, congregants from the EPC also talk about him in ways that reaffirm his status and qualities as an intimate, familiar, and humanlike other. Claudia, a housewife in her late thirties, once told me how she and her family (husband and son) had to move from their small apartment to a little house in a different part of Valparaíso, because the pastor of the EPC had asked her husband to be the caretaker of a small local church building. A few days earlier I had overheard her telling the same story to a couple of women from the church. She was not too happy about having to move but nevertheless agreed to do so after the Lord presented himself to her in a dream and informed her that she would have to leave her home. Though this revelation was a source of considerable

---

[3] Like Danish, French, German, and many other languages, the Spanish language has a formal and an informal version of the English term 'you' (second-person singular). When Chileans address a man as Señor they will usually also address him with the formal usted rather than the informal tu (you). But when speaking to God, Pentecostals almost always use tu despite referring to him as Señor.

comfort, she still felt quite stressed and frustrated because of all the practical things she had to take care of:

> Claudia: I had to quit my job at the factory, because it is too far away from here, I would not have time to send my son to school, and I would have to take two different busses and spend too much money on bus fare. And I only had one week to take care of all those things, so I said to the Lord, 'Look, Lord, if it is your will that we should move to that other house, I have one week to take care of all these things; I don't know how I can do it; I have to quit my job and all that; you will have to do it for me.' I told him, 'If you want to take me there to that new house, Lord, you will have to take care of everything for me, my job, the money, and all those things.' And you know, three days later, I had no job; they told me in the factory that they had to let me go, because there was no more work.

> ML: Ooh, what a … [I was just about to say 'coincidence' but interrupted myself, when I saw Claudia pointing her forefinger upwards.]

> Claudia: The Lord arranged things so that I could leave my job. And he gave me one week to take care of things. And we did not have any furniture, but the Lord gave me furniture. And I said to the Lord, 'Lord you have brought me here because you need me here to work.' My relationship with the Lord is like that; I tell him things. You know, if we can't rely on the Lord, then on whom else can we rely? No one! So I said to the Lord, 'Lord, you are my guide, you are my eyes.'

Claudia is a long-term and very committed congregant who was saved and baptised with the Holy Spirit as a young teenager. It became evident in this and in my numerous other conversations with her that she had developed an intimate and confident relationship with the Lord. She clearly feels that she is able to speak with him openly and freely about her problems and about his responsibility to help her solve them ('If you want to take me there to that new house, Lord, you will have to take care of everything for me.' … 'My relationship with the Lord is like that, I tell him things').

Claudia's story about her conversation with the Lord is in some ways similar to the stories that Pentecostals, as well as many other people all over the world—religious and non-religious—frequently tell each other about conversations with human others. As in the example with Monica (page 163–164) it is not difficult to imagine Claudia narrating a similar story about a conversation with an other person (for example, 'So I said to my husband, "Look, Pedro, if it is your will … "'). Like human others, the Lord becomes a significant social other, with whom Pentecostals have conversations and to whom they refer in the third person when they tell each other stories. In the church construction I often overheard conversations between male workers or the women in the kitchen, where they would refer to the Lord as a common friend, much in the same way that they would refer to non-present congregants.

Conclusion

'We will arrive around noon, and then the Lord will give us a nice lunch.'
(*Preacher from the EPC, informing the congregation about an excursion to the country site the following Saturday*)

In this chapter I have argued for an acknowledgement of the importance of banal habitual practices (mostly linguistic but also a few non-linguistic ones such as pointing a forefinger upwards as an index of God) in the study of the religious re-enchantment of social reality. Through a number of routine ritual and everyday practices, the powerful and extraordinary, yet also intimate and familiar presence of a divine other is continuously constituted and reconstituted as a pervasive feature of Pentecostal life. Such practices do not aim at the remaking of social, political structures or at inserting Christian values and principles into the heart of public policy. They do, however, represent a defiance of secular modernism by articulating an alternative and re-enchanted version of the social world.

I have argued that Pentecostalism reasserts a structure of authority, providing adherents with a power base from which they can reach out to the world and make authoritative statements. Exploring the blurring of boundaries between ritual and non-ritual spheres of activity I further demonstrated how the Pentecostal re-enchantment of life occurs as notions of transformative sacred agency are continuously placed at the very foundation of knowledge about the social world. For members of the EPC, the Lord is not a distant figure, whose presence they might feel during worship but who is otherwise largely irrelevant in daily life. On the contrary a number of banal practices serve as constant and implicit reminders that the Lord is omnipresent and frequently intervening in human affairs. The Lord is a security provider who helps people get pensions and find housing. He was in charge of the construction of the new church building, where he took care of bureaucratic issues and helped the workers finishing the work in time. He is the one who provides congregants with lunch when they make excursions. He gives his children (like Claudia) furniture when they need it, and he takes care of different work-related problems. He is also an efficient doctor, and he is believed to be responsible for the relatively good Chilean economy (see chapter 5). The Lord symbolically replaces the state, civil society, politicians, and the health system. Finally he is present in the everyday life of Pentecostals as a significant social other and partner of internal conversation, and as someone to whom they refer in the third person—much in the same way as they refer to other humans—when they narrate anecdotes to one another.

CHAPTER NINE

PENTECOSTALISM AND GENDER

I met my husband in La Serena [in Northern Chile], because I was working there, but he was a drug addict and an alcoholic. But he was a discrete
drug addict and alcoholic; he went to parties, but he did not go around
drunk or high on the streets, so I never suspected anything. So we got
married in 1993.... Well, then I started suspecting, and I found injections
at home and some drugs. It was terrible for me. The first time I suspected
that something was wrong, he came home, and he talked pure nonsense.
Then he started coming home drunk. It was horrible; I was shocked. So I
started praying to the Lord, asking him to be merciful. And he did something really beautiful for my husband. And you know, before that, he had
long hair, he was a hippie. And he was irresponsible. He worked, but he
always lost his jobs after a while. He used to go out and get drunk with his
friends and come home late. But God changes things! He transformed
my husband totally; he changed it all—the way he talks, his hair cut—and
my husband threw all his records away, all his old clothes, all of it. And
before that, my husband thought that he was a superhero. You know, the
'world' that does not know the Lord thinks that we Christians are like the
opium, the lowest of the lowest, but we live with the Lord, and we know
where we come from. (*Silvia, housewife in her mid-thirties*)

Arguably the most significant contribution of Pentecostalism to
processes of cultural change in Latin America lies in the movement's
potential to bring about transformations in the private domestic
spheres by redefining gender relationships and economic priorities.
Whereas much of the literature dealing with Pentecostalism's potential
as a democratizing force is either inconclusive (Freston 2001, 2004,
2006) or offers speculative arguments (Willems 1967; Sepúlveda 1988;
David Martin 1990; Ossa 1991; Christian Smith 1994; Fediakova
2004), a substantial amount of ethnographic studies point to restored
marriages, an increase in the self-confidence and autonomy of women
and a decrease in male alcoholism, drug abuse, aggressiveness, and
infidelity as consequences of conversion (Brusco 1995; Hurtado 1993;
Mariz & Campos Machado 1997; Mariz 1994; Burdick 1993; Slootweg
1991; Bernice Martin 1995; Chesnut 2003; Lesley Gill 1990; Montecino
& Obach 2002; Smilde 2007). Furthermore existing studies have almost
unanimously emphasised the ability of Pentecostalism to improve the

position of lower class Latin American women in a way that is non-threatening to men, something that liberal middle-class feminism has been less successful in achieving (Freston 2006: 259).

The present chapter sheds light on different aspects of Pentecostal gender politics. In line with the existing literature I demonstrate how conversion very often results in a re-socialisation of men. And I argue that participation in the Pentecostal church life provides women with a new sense of power and autonomy. This occurs, partly because male and female priorities tend to coincide within Pentecostal households, and partly because women are given new public positions in Pentecostal religious life.

The most original contribution to the existing literature on Latin American Pentecostalism and gender comes in the second part of the chapter. I explore how a sense of female autonomy and self-sufficiency is constituted through a personal love relationship with Jesus, sometimes described by women as a spiritual husband. Finally I argue that the control of the sexuality and physical appearance of women is an important strategy for recreating a profound sense of security and establishing a sense of sacred order in an otherwise messy 'world'.

Domesticated Men

In chapter 6 I noted that a higher number of women than men convert to Pentecostalism because of social problems such as broken relationships or illness in the family. The conversion of men, on the other hand, tends to be motivated by individualistic problems. Thus male testimonies often include accounts of pre-conversion alcoholism, drug abuse, and violent behaviour and of changed habits of consumption and an increased orientation towards the domestic sphere after conversion.

Elizabeth Brusco's study of the conversion of men to Evangelical religion in Columbia has in many ways set the stage for the study of Latin American Pentecostalism and gender. Brusco's main argument, practically undisputed by later scholars, is that conversion of men results in a transformation of *machismo* personalities. She defines *machismo* as a public male role, characterised by alienation from the domestic sphere, exaggerated aggressiveness and intransigence in male-to-male relations, and arrogance and sexual aggression in male-to-female relationships (1995: 78; see also Mansilla 2008: 73). The *machismo* man tends to see himself as a free agent in the public sphere rather than a representative of a nuclear family. Whereas female identity in Colombian (and Latin American) lower classes is mainly related to motherhood and domestic activities, men tend to have individualistic patterns of consumption and spend more money in the public sphere, for example, on drinking, gambling, and womanising. For economically dependant women, such differences in priorities can be a source of problems and stress.

According to Brusco, conversion results in the domestication of men, as participation in Evangelical communities fosters a 'feminist ethos ... that sets a definite tone of appropriate behaviour and a standardised system of emotional attitudes' (1995: 129–30). As Evangelical belief becomes the main determinant of husband–wife relations, traditional boundaries between male–public and female–private spheres are redefined. In the Evangelical community, a man mainly gains social prestige by being a faithful and responsible father and husband. As alcohol, tobacco, gambling, and extramarital sexual liaisons are banned, conversion very often results in new and less individualistic patterns of consumption (ibid.: 124–35).

While the position of women is improved by the domestication and feminization of a converted husband, the authority of the latter within the household is not challenged. On the contrary patriarchal subordination of women is maintained but becomes justified in biblical terms (see also Montecino & Obach 2002; Freston 2006). According to Evangelical standards a wife is supposed to be obedient to the head of the household, her husband, while he on the other hand must treat her and the children with love and respect. As male and female aspirations and priorities are more likely to coincide in an Evangelical family, male authority becomes consensual rather than contested.

Scholars working in different Latin American countries have found patterns quite similar to the ones described above (Sjørup 1995; Montecino & Obach 2002; Mariz 1994; Lesley Gill 1990).[1] My own findings in the EPC and other Chilean Pentecostal churches do not distort the general picture of Latin American Pentecostalism as a religious movement that has been remarkably successful in redefining gender relationships and not least in changing male behavior. In addition to new patterns of consumption, very frequently reported in male testimonies, conversion often results in new ways of speaking. In chapter 5

---

[1] Brusco's book was published in 1995 but several scholars refer to her PhD dissertation from 1986.

I mentioned that Pentecostals do not swear and that they avoid using the *double sentido* (double sense). And I noticed that non-Pentecostal men, in all social classes, generally swear a little more than women. It should therefore come as no surprise that accounts of transformed language use figure more prominently in male than female testimonies of salvation.[2] Luis, a retired worker from the EPC explained to me how his conversion from Catholicism changed his way of speaking, his economic priorities, and not least his relationship with his wife:

> When I met the Lord, before that I used to swear a lot, I was really good at swearing. That changed immediately, I never swore again. And it wasn't because I decided never to swear again. I didn't even say to myself, 'I will never swear again,' but those words just didn't come out of my mouth anymore. And with my wife things changed completely. Completely! I started to be more affectionate with her, more responsible. Before I was irresponsible, because first comes your friends, the drinks, and the women. Those are the three things that the people of the 'world' are never short of. I used to go out all night. So that changed totally. Now there's peace, there's calmness, there's conversation. If we need anything, we talk about how to do it: 'I would like to do this or that'; 'ok fine, let's do it,' but before it wasn't like that. There's more harmony, more communication. Communication is important, so now things have changed. Before we used to have arguments; she would throw the plates at me, or sometimes a tomato, and I would leave the house and slam the door. But not anymore! Now everything is very different. I help her doing the laundry, the dishes. I help her doing all kind of things. A total transformation! Now I don't look at the woman as a woman for my satisfaction, I look at her as a companion that God has given me. The Bible says that God gave Adam a companion. It wasn't a woman for his personal satisfaction, and it wasn't his domestic servant either. The Bible says that the man is the head of the home, but one cannot be a male chauvinist (*machista*). I don't say, 'It has to be like that!' There must be harmony in the home. And besides, the children can also see their parents and the way they behave.

In this account, conversion is in large part described of as a process of domestication, reorientation, and redefinition of values. While considering himself the boss of his household, Luis also makes an explicit distinction between biblically grounded male authority and male chauvinism. The former is based on mutual respect, communication, and the ability to maintain a harmonious, peaceful domestic environment. Luis took great pride in being a responsible family man. At the time of

---

[2] The Chilean scholars Sonia Montecino and Alexandra Obach have made a similar observation with regards to Pentecostal men in the neighbourhood of La Pintana in Santiago (2002: 81).

the interview he was the leader of a local church building. When preaching he frequently talked about his warm and loving relationship to his wife, children, and grandchildren.

Another remarkable feature of Pentecostal men, which clearly contrasts with general *macho* standards, is that they weep a lot and are quite comfortable with telling others about how they have wept on different occasions. Weeping during church meetings is quite normal and is seen as an index of the presence of the Holy Spirit rather than emotional weakness. Juan, a man in his forties, told me how he had converted from Catholicism, when his already converted wife had persuaded him to come and pick her up after a church meeting. His arrived early, and though his initial intention was to wait for her outside, he eventually decided to enter the church and see what was going on. To his own surprise he suddenly felt overwhelmed by the presence of the Holy Spirit and started weeping. In his own words: 'And when I was inside, during the meeting, I suddenly started to weep. I thought, "Why am I weeping? Men don't weep; men don't weep!"' During my fieldwork, Juan often wept during church meetings and felt quite comfortable about it. Pentecostal men also confess having wept when praying alone. And when they tell each other anecdotes about divine blessings and intervention in everyday affairs, a few tears sometimes stream from their eyes. Such display and accounts of emotions, which could easily associated with weakness and lack of macho toughness (see Montecino & Obach 2002: 82), pose no threat to the social status of a man within the church. The pastor of the EPC always has a handkerchief at hand when preaching, and he frequently uses it.

The Pentecostal rejection of the 'world' of sin is foremost a rejection of a public sphere where macho values predominate. A majority of women in the EPC do not have an active past in Chilean public life, for example, as professionals, as politically active citizens, or as particularly bohemian and sexually liberal women.[3] It follows that conversion to a Pentecostal church that denounces the 'world' does not necessarily

---

[3] Obviously women's pre-conversion "sexual sins' may be under-reported in a testimony told in the church or in a conversation with a foreign male anthropologist. Yet several other studies, conducted by female researchers, confirm that a majority of Pentecostal women in Latin America had austere lifestyles prior to conversion. Brusco argues that conversion to Evangelical churches means a new asceticism for Colombian men, whereas Colombian women, Evangelical and Catholic, are already ascetic (1995: 124). The Brazilian sociologists Cecilia Mariz and Maria Campos Machado found that Brazilian Pentecostal women drank little or no alcohol and restricted their sexual activity to partners or spouses before converting (1997: 50)

imply a drastic change of lifestyle in the case of women. To be sure, Pentecostal women conceive of salvation as a radical and empowering transformation, which they narrate in terms of a dualism between living in the 'world' and being close to God. But in female testimonies this dualism mostly takes the form of a contrast between security and insecurity, illness and healing, and not least between the presence and absence of a loving and protecting saviour and to a much lesser extent between and sinful and a sanctified life. The theme of self-control (that is, having achieved it after conversion), on the other hand, is much more dominant in the testimonies of men (such as Manuel and André whom we met in chapter 6) than of women (see also Montecino & Obach 2002: 80).

Gender Roles and Positions in the EPC

Despite the feminisation and domestication of men, 'patriarchy' does not seem like an unfitting term for describing both the internal structure of the EPC and the values and norms organizing domestic life and divisions of labour. The pastor and the leaders of the choir, the youth group, and local church buildings are all men. Women are not allowed to preach or lead meetings, and the practical divisions of labour in the church follow traditional gender patterns. Men construct and maintain church buildings, install electricity, etc., whereas women cook meals for male workers and wash the dishes. Women are also in charge of cleaning the church and for buying and watering flowers that are sometimes placed in front of the church during meetings. Some church activities such as vigils on Saturdays are followed or preceded by a meal, which is always prepared and served by the women.

Among elder and to some extent among younger congregants the ideal that the man alone should work and provide for his family while the wife should stay at home prevails, though economic circumstances often result in gaps between ideals and practice. For many unskilled Pentecostal women who can only aspire for low-status jobs with low salaries and long working hours, working is more a question of necessity than of self-realisation. In the case of younger Pentecostal women, some of whom are pursuing higher education or have become professionals, such traditional norms concerning work are on the decrease. In these aspects Pentecostals do not differ from other Chileans.

Gendered identities are not given by nature but constituted through everyday performative action, where certain embodied, gendered modes of comportment or hexis are developed and exercised (see Butler 1990: 25; Bourdieu 1977: 93). Such everyday performance includes particular gendered ways of inhabiting and orienting oneself in domestic space. When I had tea or meals in the homes of members of the EPC, the women would always sit closer to the kitchen than the men. While the women would eventually sit down and take part in the conversations, their attention and bodily focus were most of the time divided between the conversation and some other task, for example, the kitchen or the children, and much of the talking was done standing or sitting in a leaned forward position, facilitating a quick change of focus. For women and especially non-working and lower class house-wives, the home is the workplace and requires constant alertness. For men, on the other hand, the home is mainly a place of relaxation, which is reflected in their bodily comportment and undivided focus during meals and conversations.[4]

Most married women, widows, or de facto divorced women belong to the *dorcas*, a women's group that gathers once a week in the after-noon. The topics that are discussed during the meetings of the *dorcas* are not international politics, but rather how to be a good and faithful wife and mother, and how to behave in a strategic non-confrontational way towards a non-converted husband.

There are, in other words, several aspects of Pentecostal life and practice that reaffirm traditional patriarchal ideals of female subordi-nation and commitment to the domestic spheres (see Orellana Rojas 2009). However, the improved position of Pentecostal women is not only achieved when the reformation of macho men results in domestic consensus concerning feminine priorities. Approximately two-thirds of active congregants in EPC are women, and many of them do not really benefit from the domestication of men, as they are either unmar-ried, widows, or separated from their husbands. Besides, some married women live as devoted congregants for decades even though their hus-bands never convert.

In addition to the domestication of men, participation in Pentecostal church life empowers women by providing them with new public

---

[4] Such gendered differences in domestic bodily behaviour and orientation are not a Pentecostal peculiarity. I have observed similar patterns in non-Pentecostal lower-class households.

positions (Drogus 1997; Cleary & Sepúlveda 1997; Freston 2006; Montecino & Obach 2002). Though women do not preach in the church and do not occupy leadership positions—except as leaders of female groups—they regularly practice the priesthood of all believers. Vigils are held in local church buildings on Saturdays once or twice a month. The hosts will usually invite a specific group of guests to a vigil, for example, the members of another local church building, the members of the choir, or the cyclists. At such occasions, the guests, including the women, are invited to come forward, one at the time, and address the congregation. They often introduce themselves by narrating their own testimony of salvation. On church meetings on Mondays, all congregants, including women, are allowed and indeed expected to stand up, one by one, and express their gratitude to the Lord for being with them. Such thanksgiving is mostly accompanied by anecdotes about divine intervention in everyday affairs (see chapter 8). Prophesies can be given by both women and men, but are in fact almost always given by the former. Praying for healing with the imposition of hands during church meeting is done by men, but women often visit sick people in their homes and pray for healing. Street preaching is an activity in which women may participate two to three times a week. In practice, the formal, patriarchal church structure is counterweighted by a number of occasions where women become religious subjects, rather than passive receivers of a message, acting with the same spiritual authority as men (see Anrade Cardemil 2008). The empowerment and autonomy of Pentecostal women is further cultivated through a personal relationship with Jesus, a theme I will address in the next section.

Hooking Up with Jesus

Dora is a widow in her late sixties, whose marriage to an abusive, violent, and heavy-drinking husband had been anything but harmonious. She owns an old house and is able to make a modest living by renting a couple of rooms to some other congregants. During my conversations with her, she frequently emphasised how she was now married to Jesus, who took care of her, and that they loved each other very much. In her own words:

> You know, I tell him: you are my husband now; you must take care of me. And he does. Sometimes I don't have food and money, but it always works out somehow.

Dora further told me that she had actually been unfaithful to the Lord a few times. She did not specify if this infidelity was of a sexual nature, and though I was, admittedly, quite curious, I decided that it would be inappropriate to ask. Infidelity may simply mean that she had sinned in some way or failed to devote enough time to church meetings and praying. After admitting to her own infidelity Dora went on to emphasise that the Lord had always been faithful to her.

In addition to new networks of mutual support (see Lesley Gill 1990; Slootweg 1991; Orellana Rojas 2009), Pentecostal women also find much comfort, emotional support, and a certain moral, spiritual autonomy in their personal relationship with their heavenly saviour. This relationship is mainly nourished through praying, daily internal conversation, and different experiences of divine presence in ritual as well as everyday life (see chapter 6, 7, and 8). Like Dora, several other Pentecostal women, most of whom were widows, unmarried, or de facto divorced, tend to describe their relationship with the Lord as a love relationship between husband and wife. Clara, a single mother in her mid-thirties who had left a violent husband some years ago, explained how the Lord was now the only man in her life:

> I have a man—the Lord! He is the man of the house. I talk with him all day long. The Lord showed me that I do not need a man, because he is with me. Why would I need a man to protect me, if the greatest protector of all is living with me? Sure, as a woman I have felt the need to be with someone, but the Lord said to me: I meet all your necessities! You do not need the physical presence of man. If I need affection, the Lord gives me affection. He gives me all the love that I need. If I need protection, he protects me.

Ana Maria is another widow from the EPC who spends most of her time on church activities. She receives a tiny pension and lives alone, as all her children and grandchildren have moved to other cities. During church meetings she frequently feels that she is being visited by the Holy Spirit and starts dancing and jumping. On Mondays where a substantial part of church meetings are spent on individual witnessing and thanksgiving to the Lord, she usually speaks with great passion and devotion about her heavenly husband. When I once suggested an interview, she said I could visit her at home on the condition that my wife accompanied me. Since she was now married to Jesus she had decided it would be inappropriate to receive male visitors alone. She described her relationship to the Lord as follows:

Ana Maria: When walking in the street, I'm always singing, so I don't even have time to see the things of the 'world'. I'm always talking with the Lord—I sing; I pray. Early in the morning I pray; then I prepare my breakfast; I lay the table for him too; he eats with me, my Lord; I put a cup for him, just a cup, without anything in it, and I start to ask for the blessing, and the Holy Spirit comes, and there he is. And I start talking to Jehovah. At lunch as well, it is wonderful, that is something really beautiful.

ML: Do you live alone?

Ana Maria: Alone with the Lord, but I never ever feel lonely. I'm with the Holy Spirit all the time. I am not alone. I love him, and he loves me. Well, he loves all of us. It is pure love. Sometimes the only thing I want to do is to go up to be with my Lord. But well, I'll have to wait until he wants me to go. The Lord is my husband. He is my friend, my doctor. I don't like the doctors of the 'world' very much.

In previous chapters I have explored how a personal relationship with the Lord is constituted and nourished through a number of ritual and everyday practices. In the case of Ana Maria as of many other Pentecostal women I spoke to, internal dialogues with the Lord are described as a pervasive feature of everyday existence. In Ana Maria's description we can further see how orientation toward the sacred is accompanied by a demonstrative indifference to what goes on in the 'world'.

When I first met Ana Maria, I asked her if she was married. She replied that her husband '*está con el Señor*' (is with the Lord) and then added that she had been a widow for five years now. Unfortunately her husband had only been saved three months before dying. Before that he had been '*muy porfiado y muy metido en el "mundo"*' (very stubborn and very involved with the 'world'). Though grateful that he had ultimately been saved, Ana Maria mostly spoke of her late husband with bitterness and resentment. At no point did I get the impression that she was missing his company very much. For Ana Maria as for many other Pentecostal women, a loving and fulfilling relationship with a human man is, at best, a rather distant memory. In the excerpt above she explains that she is longing 'to go up to be with [her] Lord', but I never heard her express any desire of being reunited with her human husband in heaven.

Whether or not the relation of some Pentecostal women to Jesus contains imagined erotic elements was an issue about which I did not dare to ask questions. It would, in any case, probably have been pointless to do so. If women from the EPC or other Pentecostal churches have erotic fantasies about Jesus, I seriously doubt that they would be willing to tell me about them. According to typical *macho* norms, the man is expected to be sexually aggressive and the woman more passive. But Pentecostal marriages, both between human spouses and imagined marriages between women and Jesus, are based on more female premises, such as communication, tenderness, and mutual understanding, and I do not think that imagined sexuality is a core feature of the female communion with Jesus. The obligation to satisfy male sexual needs even if a woman takes no pleasure in the act is certainly not a part of this relationship.[5] But intimacy, intense love, tenderness, fascination by the beauty of the other person, confidence, company, responsibility, the ideal of faithfulness, care taking, protection, and the providing of basic necessities are crucial features of the relationship between Pentecostal women and Jesus. And throughout my fieldwork I was repeatedly struck by the way analogies to human love relationships were used, especially by women in all ages, to describe this relationship. Like Dora, many of them regretted having been unfaithful to their Lord. And women sometimes remarked that they missed the initial period of being intensely in love after recently having met the Lord. After some time the relationship had become a little less passionate and intense. Such accounts parallel typical accounts of how love relationships between human partners tend to become pervaded by daily routines and therefore less intense over time, which is why many people in long-term relationships sometimes think nostalgically about the initial period with their partner and miss the sensation of being very passionately in love. Given the passionate declarations of love that Pentecostal women sometimes make to Jesus, and considering all the similarities and parallels between human–human and human–divine love relationships, my guess is that imagined erotic elements could very well be part of the latter. But I can present no empirical data to support this view. While a few men in the EPC also sometimes remark that they miss the first period of intense love to the Lord after being saved, they mostly describe their relationship to the Lord in terms of very intimate friendship or of an unconditional and protective love of a father to his children.

The image of Jesus as an ideal spiritual husband represents a clear and quite explicit alternative to less ideal 'worldly' human *macho*

---

[5] A few Pentecostal men told me that their sexual behaviour had changed after being saved. Not only had they stopped being unfaithful, but they had also become more considerate lovers and started to focus more on the sexual pleasure and satisfaction of their wives.

husbands. I never heard any typical *machismo* features included in descriptions of Jesus, neither by men nor woman. By turning to a spiritual husband who is perfect, gentle, faithful (I never experienced that the belief that Jesus loves all his human children equally was problematised or conceptualised in terms of polygamy), and always present when needed, and by being the ones who occasionally 'cheat a little' but are forgiven and can feel in control as long as they can keep their 'infidelity' in check, Pentecostal women enact a symbolic reversal of human marriages with *macho* men. But while the spiritual marriage gives Pentecostal women a certain autonomy, female behaviour and sexuality are also subject to severe control, a subject to which I will now turn.

The Control of Women

Strict standards for clothing and physical appearance prevail in the EPC. Men are expected to dress decently and modestly and have short hair. In the case of women, long skirts that cover the knees and blouses that cover the shoulders and are not too tight or low necked are compulsory. The use of cosmetics is not allowed, or at least strongly discouraged, and all women must have long hair.

Sexual activities are also subject to severe regulation and control. From time to time congregants must fast and pray intensely if extra spiritual empowerment is required for some reason. The illness of the pastor in 1999, the coming of the new millennium, or the preparation for some extraordinary event, such as the visit of a choir from Santiago (see chapter 7, page 138–140) were all occasions for intensifying the search for divine power and blessings. Besides, congregants often make individual decisions to fast for twelve or eighteen hours. During fasting, married couples are supposed to abstain from sexual activity in order to seek spiritual purity.

Pre- or extra-marital sex is sanctioned, mostly by exclusion from different church activities such as street preaching or excursions with the choir or the youth groups of the church. Non-sexual love relationships between young unmarried men and women are tolerated in the EPC, but not unconditionally. One couple that fell in love had to talk about their relationship with the pastor, the girl's father (also an active congregant), and other congregants. Also, they both prayed to God and asked him to confirm that it was indeed his intention that they should be together. After four months, their relationship was given official approval in the church. But they did not have sex (the man told me and I believe him) before they got married (they now have two children). The man, who originally came from Santiago and had no relatives in Valparaíso, rented a room in the house of an older congregant. The woman would never visit him alone but only in the presence of other congregants. He would mostly visit her, as she lived with her parents and younger brothers. In that way, they could, to some extent, avoid suspicions of immoral sexual conduct.

Male sexuality, though regarded as sinful except within the marriage, is considered less polluting and threatening to the spiritual purity of the Christian community than its female counterpart. Relationships between Pentecostal men and women from the 'world' are strongly discouraged. But incompatibility of different values and the possibility that a 'worldly' woman might oppose Pentecostal man's commitment to his church are more feared than the risk of immoral sexual practice. Female sexuality is a more sensitive issue in the church, where ideals of purity and virginity until marriage are much stronger than among Chilean lay Catholics.

In an intriguing study of fundamentalism and gender Karen M. Brown sees the obsession of religious fundamentalist groups with the control of women as grounded in basic psychological processes (1994). In the early formative period of human development, the child possesses no language and no conceptualisations of time and space. Consequently, emotions like joy, fear, and hunger have an engulfing quality. The child's most profound security is found in the presence of the mother. Brown further points out that fundamentalist movements attempt to control emotions as well as the body with its appetites and sexuality, all of which are both associated with women and perceived as threatening to human life and order (ibid.: 187–9). Combined with deep memories of security with the mother, the fear of these female features produces a powerful ambivalence towards women. This fear results in a strong need to control women and their sexuality, especially in situations of stress and alienation (ibid.: 181).

Binary gender oppositions are basic building blocks of social organisation. Together with the child–adult distinction that is learnt early in life such oppositions serve as raw material for constructions of symbolic order (Hawley & Proudfoot 1994: 27). As with other fundamentalist religious groups, Pentecostals often put a good deal of effort into defining and maintaining boundaries between insiders and outsiders (see Marty 1992). Such boundaries can be constituted and manifested through distinctive semantic practices, many of which are related to ideals of gendered appearances and comportment. For members of the EPC, female sexual liberation and vanity are signs of a 'worldly' apocalyptic corruption and disorder, in opposition to which they define themselves. Controlling the sexuality and physical appearance of women represents a powerful way of recreating the security and manageability of the child's world (Brown 1994: 189) while at the same time producing a sense of sacred order.

Conclusion: Religion, Gender, and Power

Processes of social–cultural transformation or orthodox preservation are often manifested in and closely intertwined with perpetuation and negotiations of gender relationships. As has been shown in this chapter, the difference that being a born-again Christian makes in the lives of congregants is, in fundamental but also complex ways, related to questions of gender. Traditional gender patterns are simultaneously reaffirmed and reworked within the EPC. The personal transformation and change of lifestyle, implied in conversion and narrated in testimonies of salvation, appear to be more radical in the case of men, for whom conversion often results in new patterns of consumption and an increased orientation towards the domestic sphere. But membership in Pentecostal communities also produces a sense of renewal, empowerment, and security among women. Not only does the domestication of men improve the position of women within a household by creating more consensus concerning existing female priorities, participation in Pentecostal churches also gives women new public positions as active religious subjects. The empowerment of Pentecostal women further derives from their 'spiritual marriage' to Jesus. The love relationship between women and their heavenly saviour can make the absence of a human husband—or the presence of an imperfect one—more bearable. And as this relationship is based on female rather than *macho* patriarchal premises, it fosters a feeling of control and autonomy in the lives of women.

Finally I explored how Pentecostal gender politics aims at establishing a sense of sacred order. Like other fundamentalists, members of the EPC conceive of gender roles and relationships and not least female sexuality as some of the areas where the threat of immoral 'worldly' disorder is most likely to manifest itself. The material presented in this chapter illustrates the dual aspects of religious power as a power that has the capacity to liberate, yet also to control and oppress others (Chong 2011). Whether such control is experienced as oppressive is, of course, another question to which no unified and simple answer can be provided. A number of second- (or more) generation teenagers within the EPC have difficulties accommodating themselves to church norms, and some teenage girls have been known to use make-up and wear more provocative clothes in school and other contexts. Some young congregants do leave the church and either join more moderate Pentecostal churches or become churchless believers because they find norms of dress and cosmetics rigid, oppressive, and unnecessary.

For many other Pentecostal women, empowerment and control are not related to sexual liberty and the freedom to drink alcohol, wear cosmetics, and wear whatever clothing they like. And in the case of many Pentecostal men a sense of renewal and self-control derives from deliberately giving up certain liberties and rights. For Pentecostals, freedom and power are foremost freedom and power to exercise self-control; resist temptations; rework social relationships; transform the domestic sphere, often in accordance with existing feminine standards; and— in the case of women—to be married with Jesus but on female terms. A sense of empowerment, autonomy, and self-worth further follows from active, authorised, and outreaching participation in what is perceived as divinely ordained projects and plans and from being able to impose and maintain a little order and clarity in an otherwise messy 'world'.

CHAPTER TEN

WHY THE DEVIL IS SATAN SO IMPORTANT IN CHILEAN PENTECOSTALISM?

In Chile as elsewhere Pentecostalism can be distinguished from mainline Protestantism and Catholicism by the emphasis that is placed on spiritual warfare. A favourite biblical passage in many Pentecostal churches, Ephesians 6: 12, aptly encapsulates Pentecostal understandings of who their true enemies are: 'For we wrestle not against flesh and blood, but against principalities, against powers, against the rulers of the darkness of this world, against spiritual wickedness in high places.' Pentecostals do not see themselves as mere passive spectators of spiritual warfare. As potential targets of demonic attacks and being able to activate and to some extent direct divine power, thereby limiting the activities and influence of the devil in the world, they easily identify themselves with the "we" of this biblical passage (see Lindhardt 2011). The 'world' of sin that for members of the EPC provides a fundamental theological contrast to the sanctified life with God is also commonly conceived of as a state of satanic dominion. In the EPC as in many other Chilean Pentecostal churches, demons are mainly referred to as 'worldly' spirits (*espiritus del mundo*).

Long ago Durkheim noted that Satan, while both impure and inferior to God, is not a profane being. Satan is an anti-god, but nevertheless a god, who is invested with broad powers (1995/1915: 423). Though they are opponents and have contrasting agendas when interfering in human affairs, there are significant similarities between the agency of God and that of Satan. As sacred supernatural others they are both understood (by most people who believe in their existence) to possess humanlike qualities such as a mind, intentions, motivations, memory, linguistic mastery, etc. It follows that interaction with them is to a large extent informed by the same cognitive schemes and intuitive notions of agency that inform interactions between humans. At the same time God and Satan are invested with the same counter-intuitive properties such as immortality, immateriality, the ability to be in several places at the same time, and having access to strategic information, for example, about people's unspoken intentions, motivations, thoughts, and desires (Boyer 2001).

The focus of this chapter is on the role and significance of God's counterpart in Pentecostal life worlds. Given that this role is complex and multifaceted, the chapter is subdivided into different sections, where various aspects of satanic and demonic agency are addressed. After describing their diabologies[1] I argue that congregants from the EPC need the image of a powerful enemy so as to demonstrate the superior power of God and also that their understandings of divine blessings, power, and consequential intervention in human affairs are intrinsically intertwined with notions of diabolic resistance and deceptions. Yet, as will be demonstrated, the powers of darkness also bring elements of ambivalence, doubt, and uncertainty into Pentecostal life. In the subsequent part of the chapter, analytical emphasis is placed on the ways in which diabologies provide Pentecostals with an interpretative framework for understanding and addressing intra-church tensions and conflicts. Drawing on the scholarly literature on African witchcraft I argue that perceived patterns of satanic/demonic strategies for creating disharmony among congregants point towards inherent structural tensions within Pentecostal communities. In other words, what is suggested in the first half of the chapter is that focusing careful attention on discourses on the occult can produce significant insights into other important aspects of Pentecostal life such as intra-church sociality and micro-politics.

A more general argument, which will mainly be pursued in second half of the chapter, is that Satan and his 'worldly' spirits provide Pentecostals with a language for speaking about the difficulty of truly distancing themselves from the 'world' of sin. This difficulty is experienced in different ways: through the sensation that 'worldly' standards, for example, of social status, infiltrate the church community of spiritual equals; in confrontations with non-Pentecostal sceptical others; and, finally, in the form of confusing and sceptical thoughts that challenge Pentecostal doctrines and 'truths'. Drawing on some of the theoretical perspectives on the human self introduced in chapter 2, I devote the last part of the chapter to an analysis of Pentecostal understandings and interpretations of their own mental activity as arenas of spiritual warfare. I look at how Pentecostals develop a specific awareness towards certain aspects of their own thought activity through regular

---

[1] By *diabology* I mean a system (though not necessarily a very fixed, bounded, or coherent one) of beliefs about the Devil and his demons, for instance about their origin, activities, and social organisation.

interaction with fellow congregants. For Pentecostals, maintaining a fundamentalist-Christian identity is continuously being challenged by the culture and structures of plausibility of the Chilean society they live within. What I argue in the last part of the chapter is that their focus on spiritual warfare as fought at an intra-subjective level forms a central part of ongoing efforts to cope with this challenge by cultivating and disciplining a Christian self on an everyday basis.

Pentecostal Diabologies

Like many other Chilean Pentecostals, congregants from the EPC see the biblical story about the angel Lucifer who rebelled against God and was consequently expelled from heaven as a factual historical account.[2] Lucifer, later to be known as Satan or the Devil, was followed by a group of loyal angels who became demons. The Bible does not specify how many (the Book of Revelation merely specifies a third of all angels) but Chilean Pentecostals believe there were billions. Most Chilean Pentecostals I have spoke to about these issues further believe that heaven and hell are the only two places in which a person spends eternity. They sometimes visualise hell as a place of darkness, extreme poverty, deprivation, and suffering, trees without leaves, and eternal fire, often compared with Chile's many volcanoes.

As noted by Birgit Meyer, God's dark counterpart forms a shady side of theology. Because biblical texts detailing the world of demons and Satan are vague and sporadic, consequently there is plenty of room for speculation about their existence, social organisation, and actions in the world (1992: 106). Th e absence of standardised dogmatic discourses on the realm of darkness makes the Pentecostal notion of spiritual warfare a prime example of what Csordas (2007: 261) refers to as a 'transposable message' that can 'find footing across a diversity of linguistic and cultural settings.' As André Corten and Ruth Marshall-Fratani point out, Pentecostal idioms of the occult incite a 'messy exuberance of meaning' (2001: 10) and tend to be 'mobilised much more in response to context than according to any predetermined dogmatic and institutionalised position' (ibid.: 11). The ethnographic literature abundantly illustrates how the realm of darkness provides people in different parts of the world with a set of flexible universal categories for thinking and speaking about a variety of specific local

---

[2] See Ezekiel 28: 14–17, Isaiah 14: 13–14, and Revelation 12: 4, 12: 9.

concerns and problems. Thus African Pentecostals commonly conceive of witchcraft, traditional religion, and Islam as inventions of the Devil (Lindhardt 2009a, 2010; Meyer 1992, 1999a).

Many Chilean Pentecostals (from the EPC and other churches) see Satan as the architect of 'worldly' problems such as political corruption and a decadent mainstream culture, characterised by sexual liberation, drug addiction, alcoholism, popular music with erotic lyrics, etc. Congregants from the EPC further believe that a favourite tactic of Satan is to imitate the work of God in order to create confusion, disorder, and fissions among Christians. Thus they see the emergence of neo-Pentecostal prosperity ministries, many of which are less ascetically focused, as a deceiving satanic imitation of true Pentecostal ministries. Support of this view is found in Matthew 7: 15: 'Beware of false prophets, which come to you in sheep's clothing, but inwardly they are ravening wolves.' Finally, as will be shown a little later, internal conflicts within Pentecostal churches and the lack of Pentecostal unity in Chile (there are several hundred different denominations in the country) are often ascribed to satanic infiltration.

Congregants from the EPC sometimes conceive of the diabolic community in terms of a government with Satan as the president, with a hierarchy of demons who, as ministers or public servants, may secure promotion by making Christians depart from the paths of the Lord. Some of my informants also compared the diabolic community to the structure of Pentecostal churches with a national superintendent (equating with Satan!), pastors, persons with different responsibilities within local congregations (Sunday school teachers, leaders of youth groups, etc.), and ordinary lay people. Demons are mostly classified according to their division of labour, which reflects satanic strategies for influencing and deceiving human beings. A list of well-known demons includes spirits of envy, suicide, depression, schizophrenia, laziness, indifference, and divination.[3]

The Devil and Divine Power: A Symbiosis

Like many other Chilean Pentecostals, congregants from the EPC believe that a main concern of Satan and his demons is sabotaging the

---

[3] This spirit helps people who read tarot cards, a widespread practice in Chile.

work of God.[4] It should therefore come as no surprise that satanic/
demonic intervention is often discerned when congregants experience
that certain obstacles are preventing them from receiving blessings.
The reader may recall the story from chapter 7 about the trip of the
youth choir to Santiago. When driving out of Valparaíso the bus of the
choir was stopped by the police, an incident that was interpreted as a
satanic attempt to sabotage the trip. The anecdote about satanic sabotage that was successfully resisted through immediate praying played a
significant part in the rhetorical constitution of the trip to Santiago as
a great divine blessing.

Congregants from the EPC also explained to me how Satan and his
demons sometimes tried to prevent them from coming to church by
delaying the bus, starting heavy rains, making their children sick, or
creating other kinds of domestic urgencies. An old Pentecostal woman
told me that she was once praying and feeling that the Lord was about
to manifest himself in a very special way. Unfortunately it never happened, as her communion with God was interrupted by a neighbour
who knocked on the door and asked if she could borrow a cup of sugar.
The old woman was convinced that Satan had sent this person to interrupt her prayer and prevent her from receiving the blessing. Another
woman told me that she once left the windows in her kitchen open. But
suddenly they were closed with such power that they were broken,
even though there was no wind on that day. She immediately asked
God to expel the demons that must have broken the window. The EPC
in Valparaíso was going to receive a visit from a sister congregation in
Santiago on the same evening and she felt convinced that the enemy
was trying to sabotage this big blessing.

Pentecostal understandings of spiritual empowerment in ritual (see
chapter 7) are closely linked to notions of struggle and satanic sabotage. A successful church meeting is one where Satan and his demons

---

[4] Though Satan and his demons are held responsible for different kinds of misfortune and hardship, congregants from the EPC also stress that God occasionally tests his
human servants in order to strengthen them spiritually. Temporary unemployment,
economic problems, and other kinds of hardship are often interpreted as *pruebas*, or
'tests', from the Lord. Unlike tests, diabolic attacks cause congregants to depart from
the paths of the Lord. Thus congregants commonly ascribe misfortunes resulting in
self-destruction, depression, suicidal tendencies, sinful 'worldly' behaviour, and lasting
doubt about divine protection and purposes to the influence of the devil. Nevertheless,
several congregants reckon that distinguishing between a test and a satanic attack can
be difficult, especially at the early stages where the results of a misfortune (strengthening or weakening of faith) are not yet clear.

have been defeated, or better, have not even been allowed entrance in the church. In the EPC it was often commented that Satan is standing at the door of the church during meetings, waiting for an occasion to enter and sabotage the work of God. Whether or not Satan manages to enter depends upon the sincerity and enthusiasm with which Pentecostals seek divine presence and power. Openings are provided by sinful thoughts, indifference towards a sermon, too much focus on human co-participants, and a lack of enthusiasm in praying. On one occasion the pastor of the EPC addressed the congregation during the end of a Sunday meeting where another congregant had given the sermon. The pastor explained that he was, at that very moment, receiving a divine power, which he had to pass on to everyone present. He did so by moving his arms as if he was throwing an invisible power towards the congregants, several of whom started screaming, 'Alleluia!' Until that point the atmosphere had been quite dull; no spiritual manifestations had occurred and participants had seemed bored. Afterwards a few congregants commented that they had felt that a satanic force had been blocking the presence and power of God during the service. They were delighted that Satan had finally been defeated at the end. I was also told of a pastor of the EPC church in an unnamed Chilean city who, during a sermon when most members of the congregation were half a sleep, suddenly received a vision of hundreds of demons playing rock music and dancing inside the church. He immediately encouraged the congregants to wake up and pray, and the demons left.

Such stories point to the intrinsically relational nature of divine power. Max Weber's definition of power as 'the probability that one actor within a social relationship will be in a position to carry on his own will despite resistance' (1947: 152) often came to mind during my conversations with Pentecostals about Satan. Power is power over someone or something. The power of God must in large part be activated in order to resist the power of the Satan, but at the same time it is through the relation to—or the symbiosis with—satanic resistance and sabotage that divine power is defined and constituted. Divine protection is only a privilege as long as there is a perceived danger to be protected *from*. Any athlete can testify that competing against a tough opponent makes the taste of victory sweeter in the end. In some of the examples I have given above, the value of divine blessings and empowerment is enhanced by the satanic resistance that must first be overcome. And in a few cases Satan actually succeeds in sabotaging blessings, as in the story of the old woman who did not experience a wonderful divine manifestation because a neighbour interrupted her prayer. However, any tennis player knows that losing a point, a game, or even a set does not necessarily imply losing the match. As long as God and his human allies keep the upper hand in cosmic warfare, satanic victories in minor battles are not only tolerable but are in fact what keeps the cogwheel going, as they make the search for divine empowerment and protection ever relevant and necessary. In the case of dull church meetings, the victory of Satan does not testify to the limited powers of God, but only to the frailty of his human subjects, who do not always seek his presence wholeheartedly. Thus members of the EPC sometimes speak of the importance of maintaining their own spiritual fortress through praying, fasting, Bible reading, and participation in worship so that they may resist the attacks of Satan.

While members of the EPC insist that human beings are fundamentally powerless and dependant on God, I have in some of the preceding chapters tried to illustrate how their notions of agency are in fact complex. Adding the Devil to the picture does not simplify matters. On the one hand Pentecostal understandings of the openness of the subject to sacred interference and control are contradictive to modernist rationalist notions of the individual as a bounded and autonomous agent. On the other hand, blaming Satan for a dull church meeting is not merely a way of neglecting human responsibility. Pentecostals do not perceive themselves as puppets that are passively moved by sacred forces. The ability of Satan to sabotage blessings is to a large extent dependant upon how much room God allows him.[5] But this allowance is ultimately dependant upon human actors who can contribute to the marginalisation of Satan by wholeheartedly seeking and activating divine power. Or they can, wittingly or (mostly) unwittingly, make room for Satan, allowing him to win a few rounds by failing to stay close to God. Thus a significant measure of human responsibility and agency is involved in Pentecostal understandings of spiritual warfare, even if the role of humans mainly consists in seeking divine power and protection. Such understandings of satanic sabotage to blessings and ideal Christian states of affairs, and of human beings as being open to sacred interference, yet at the same time exercising responsibility and agency in spiritual warfare, are also prevalent in discourses on internal conflicts and tensions in Pentecostal churches.

---

[5] Pentecostals sometimes refer to the book of Job to illustrate this point.

Satan in the Church: Imitations and Conflicts

In July 2002, a young man from the EPC in Valparaíso received a visit from his mother and aunt, Andrea and Elena, who lived in Santiago where they were also active congregants. After a church meeting I was invited to have tea with them in the home of another congregant. Since they were far away from their home congregation, they apparently felt it was safe to gossip about their fellow 'sisters' in Santiago. They told us about a particular woman from their congregation who refused to preach on the street in her own neighbourhood. This woman was a repeated source of tension and disharmony in the women's group (*las dorcas*) of the congregation. When they had tea together she would sometimes leave the table in the middle of a conversation and demonstratively start washing the dishes. Or she would look at Andrea and Elena in a depreciative way, and they had further been told that she frequently gossiped about them! They were convinced that this woman was possessed and manipulated by demons, a conviction that was confirmed when Andrea had a dream where she saw the woman standing outside of the church blocking the door. Elena's youngest son had been given an extraordinary spiritual vision, a divine gift that enables a person to detect spiritual presence.[6] This gift is commonly given to children, as their childish innocence supposedly make them more sensitive to spiritual matters, a view that finds certain resonance with a more widespread belief in Chile, namely that young children are more likely to be able to detect the presence of ghosts of deceased inhabitants in old houses. Elena's son (who, by the way, lost his spiritual vision a few years later when he became a teenager) had seen that this woman was surrounded by demons. However, some blame was also placed on the woman herself for not recognising that the demons were working in her.

The fact that Pentecostals gossip about each other does not distinguish them from members of any other human community on the planet. What is interesting in the present context is how tensions and conflicts within Pentecostal churches are often addressed in terms of diabolic forces. It follows that the study of diabologies may also provide

---

[6] Spiritual vision may also be given by the Devil. Dora, a woman from the EPC, told me that another church member who had this gift had seen a divine white light surrounding her (Dora's) head. Whenever Dora ran into Gypsy women on the street they tried to avoid her, and she concluded that they could probably also see this light and consequently knew that she would be immune to their demonic powers.

a window onto Pentecostal sociality and micro-politics. In looking for ways of exploring Pentecostal gossiping and intra-church tensions I have found that the anthropological literature on African witchcraft is a helpful place to start.

Discourses on witchcraft address themes of envy, morality, and the perceived failure of others to live up to common standards for adequate, decent conduct. In classical functionalist studies, witchcraft beliefs are partly seen as a media through which social norms are reinforced, as accusations and suspicions of witchcraft provide an efficient sanction against socially inadequate conduct (Evans-Pritchard 1937). In a study of the Ukaguru of east central Tanzania Thomas O. Beidelman sees witchcraft as 'rooted in the idea of the uncontrollable person, the person free to reject social norms' (1963: 63). Early as well as contemporary scholars of witchcraft have emphasised the need to construct sociologies of witchcraft attribution, as the direction of accusations and suspicions often point to inherent micro-political tensions in a community in question. Thus Beidelman notes how accusations often occur between different wives of the same husband or between kinsmen who refuse to meet important obligations (ibid.: 74). More recently Peter Geschiere has related the omnipresence of witchcraft among the Maka in Cameroon to a fundamental contradiction between an egalitarian ideology and unequal practices. In a society organised around kinship obligations and reciprocal exchange, personal ambitions and excessive accumulation are likely to foster resentment, which may inspire suspicions of witchcraft (1997). Other scholars such as Geschiere and Francis Nyamjoh (1999) or James Ferguson (1999) have demonstrated how envy, unfulfilled expectations in redistribution of wealth, and perceptions of urban arrogance result in tensions between urban migrants and people from their rural villages in contemporary Africa, which may again foster suspicions and fear of witchcraft.

Though Africa and Chile are far apart, parallels can be explored between witchcraft suspicions and Pentecostal gossiping in terms of demonic powers. A link between gossiping and witchcraft has been made by James Scott, who argues that gossip can be seen as the linguistic equivalent and forerunner of witchcraft, which is a second step in the escalation of social hostilities. Gossip is basically about social norms that have been violated, and in a way gossip reinforces such norms by teaching what kinds of conduct are likely to be despised (Scott 1990: 142–3). Like witchcraft, Pentecostal demonologies provide a negative cultural mirror of the ideal Christian person but also of the ideal Christian community, where un-Christian, contaminating factors such as envy and arrogance, feelings of superiority and desires to show off should be absent.

Once again complex questions of agency and intentionality emerge. In Africa, witches are in most, but not all, cases perceived as intentional agents who deliberately deploy their powers to harm others. Likewise members of the EPC recognise that someone may wittingly use demonic powers for evil and destructive purposes. But people who wittingly ally themselves with evil powers and even knowingly practice witchcraft are mostly believed to be outsiders. Congregants mostly see possible demonic influence within the church as manipulation, which is not actively desired but is nevertheless facilitated by the failure to stay close to God.

Like suspicions and accusations of witchcraft in African societies, suspicions of demonic presence and infl uence within the EPC do in many cases point towards certain inherent tensions in the community. In the following I will highlight what I see as three fundamental contradictions, namely between (1) the ideal of spiritual equality and the unequal distribution of spiritual manifestations during church meetings, (2) the priesthood of all believers and highly hierarchical church structures, and (3) a community of spiritual equals and inequality, in terms of social 'worldly' status.

According to members of the EPC, imitating the work of God is one of Satan's favourite tactics. In addition to initiating the planting of dubious neo-Pentecostal prosperity ministries, Satan is also known to infiltrate true Pentecostal churches like the EPC. As mentioned in the previous section, satanic presence and interference during church meetings can be detected when the atmosphere is dull and participants appear indifferent. But another diabolic strategy is to imitate the work of the Holy Spirit in order to create confusion and disorder. Like God, Satan is known to manifest himself through dreams, visions, and sudden intuitions and in effusive expressions of trance and ecstasy. And similar to how God can use one Pentecostal as an instrument by giving him or her a message to deliver to another, Satan is known to let himself be heard through human instruments such as false prophets. Thus a central ambivalence pervades Pentecostal life. Whenever a congregant receives a message from God, confirmation must be sought as a precaution against both satanic imitations and human self-deception. A message received in a dream may be confirmed through a human instrument or vice versa, or one human instrument can confirm what was said by another. Most families in the EPC keep a little box with small pieces of paper with quotations from the Bible in their home (this box is called *pan de vida*—'bread of life'), and they may pick an arbitrary piece in order to seek and find confirmation of a previously received message or simply to find advice, guidance, and answers to questions and requests made to God. In searching for confirmation of a previously received message, Pentecostals may also open the Bible at random, trusting that God will lead them to a relevant passage.

The distribution and verification of spiritual manifestations during church meetings are quite sensitive issues in the EPC. Being taken by the Lord is a much desired experience, but it is often the same persons who start screaming, dancing, jumping, and speaking in tongues, whereas many others only report sensations of internal *gozo*. Ironically, it is during ritual experiences of spontaneous communitas where structural differentiation is temporarily annulled (see page 132) that inequality in terms of spiritual manifestations can be observed. Congregants occasionally question the authenticity of the most observable spiritual manifestations in others. Inauthentic manifestations may be ascribed to both satanic imitations and human emotions. In the case of older, long-term congregants who are known and respected as committed Christians, too frequent spiritual manifestations are mostly ascribed to human self-deception, resulting from a strong desire to experience divine presence. Referring to Francisco, a long-term congregant in his seventies who frequently started weeping, shouting, and embracing his fellow congregants during meetings, a young woman from the church explained to me, 'He is getting older and has become more sentimental. Sometimes the Lord uses him in magnificent ways. But sometimes he gets carried away by his own emotions.' Suspicions of satanic imitations of divine manifestations are either directed at strangers who sometimes enter the church and behave as if they were touched by the Holy Spirit, or at congregants who are suspected of being uncommitted and having sinned. A visit by the Holy Spirit is a gift that should fall upon committed and sanctified Pentecostals. Satan, on the other hand, is only able to imitate spiritual manifestations if he uses persons who have failed to stay close to the Lord. Suspecting someone of being manipulated by diabolic forces during a church meeting is, in fact, the same as suspecting him or her of being a bad Christian.

One middle-aged woman, Eloisa, showed up for meetings in the EPC on Thursdays, though she never became a committed member and never joined the *dorcas* (the women's group). She told me that she also attended another Pentecostal church that had no activities on Thursdays, which was why she visited the EPC on that particular day. But her hair remained short, making it clear that she was not committed to the codes and norms of the EPC. On more than one occasion she started behaving as if the Holy Spirit had touched her during meetings, but several members commented that such behaviour could probably be ascribed to the influence of Satan, and that Eloisa might even be sorcerer who intentionally infiltrated the church with wicked spiritual forces.

Another woman, Lorena, was a regularly attending congregant, who dressed according to church norms and had long hair. She was nevertheless considered to be a negative and disharmonious element within the women's group. Rumour had it that she, a single woman, could be quite flirtatious with some of the married men in the church. Lorena frequently started dancing and shouting during meetings, but these manifestations were debated by other congregants. On several occasions Lorena was the only person who started to behave in this way. Besides, her dancing movements were semi-aggressive and reminiscent of a military march, and many congregants intuitively sensed that this could not be manifestation of the love, peace, and harmony of God. While some believed that she was unknowingly being manipulated by demons, others thought that she was, in fact, a witch who deliberately used spiritual forces to create disharmony.

Whenever Lorena started dancing and shouting one man came forward to the pulpit to kneel down and pray, explaining to me he did this so that God would neutralise the demonic powers that were present in the church. As mentioned, spiritual manifestations are an integral part of church meetings, and when someone starts screaming, jumping, weeping, or dancing, the rest of the congregation react by standing up and singing a hymn in order to welcome the Holy Spirit and encourage its continued presence. But after meetings some congregants would also sometimes explain the need of collective singing in more defensive terms, as a strategy of marginalizing the Devil whenever he appeared to be present.

In a study of deliverances and perceptions of demonic presence in a North American Vineyard church, Jon Bialecki (2011: 271) argues that analytical models that foreground language use, embodiment, and experience in ritual need to be complemented by a focus on internal beliefs and particularised understandings of what is occurring.

Bialecki focuses on unmarked prayers asking for an emotion or physic state of an afflicted person to be gone. In such prayers, the demonic is not mentioned, but Bialecki discovered that the one who prays sometimes considers the act to be one of deliverance, even if the afflicted does not understand it in this way. Such 'quiet deliverances' also take place in the EPC, where praying for the sick and afflicted rarely include any mentioning of demonic forces but may nevertheless be perceived as an act of deliverance by those who pray. In a similar vein, perceptions of demonic presence in ritual life are almost never outspoken during meetings, but only commented upon afterwards in private settings. I had, in fact, been doing fieldwork in this church for more than two months before I realised certain spiritual manifestations may be perceived in this way by some congregants.

According to Bialecki, framing a prayer as deliverance can be seen as a reflexive act of self-classification, or 'of seeing oneself as someone who is knowledgeable about Charismatic activity and skilled in its practice' (2011: 268). Though members of the EPC insist that the gifts of discernment and expulsion of demons can only be given by God, they also believe that the ability to perceive and understand what really occurs during meetings, and to act accordingly, comes with experience. Claiming to be able to identify and combat demons during meetings is also an assertion of spiritual growth and maturity. The credibility of such an assertion is dependant upon the social status that follows from being a committed congregant and an exemplary Christian.

Now, to complicate matters, it should be noted that too much suspicion and gossiping about inauthentic spiritual manifestations can also be ascribed to diabolic manipulation. One of the Devil's most hardworking servants, especially within the church, is believed to be the spirit of envy (*el espíritu de envidia*). It is common knowledge in the EPC that the envious sentiments that this spirit inserts into people are often directed at divine manifestations in others. One man from the EPC told me other congregants sometimes questioned the authenticity of his spiritual manifestations in meetings, and whenever that happened, he felt that an evil power was at work, trying to sabotage his blessings. On one occasion two men felt touched by the Holy Spirit in a meeting and started dancing and embracing each other. A third congregant, Joaquin made a sarcastic comment, insinuating a possible homosexual relationship between his two dancing brothers. A fourth congregant, Skandard overheard this comment but claimed that nobody else did, as he was the only one standing close to Joaquin.

Skandard did not tell anyone about this incident (except the visiting anthropologist), but a week later the pastor removed Joaquin from a post he had been holding in the church. Skandard concluded that this was probably a punishment from God, since making derogatory comments about the work of the Holy Spirit is a serious sin. The spirit of envy had clearly been at work, but as in the case with Elena and Andrea, who suspected their sister of being manipulated by demons, Skandard also placed some responsibility on Joaquin for allowing such manipulation.

Willy, an ex-member of the Methodist Pentecostal Church in Valparaíso, explained to me how he had left his church because Satan made other congregants question his spiritual manifestations. Though he was a relatively new congregant God soon started to use him in magnificent ways as a prophet, preacher, and a competent bass player in the church band. When he was preaching God would loosen his tongue and let inspirational words flow from his mouth, and the presence of the Holy Spirit could be felt in the church room. He saw his rapidly acquired musical skills as nothing less than a miracle, as he had never received any training. But though Willy humbly insisted on giving God all the credit for his contributions to congregational life, some of the long-term congregants were annoyed that a newcomer should be given such spiritual privileges. Not only did they start questioning the authenticity of Willy's spiritual experiences as well as his source of inspiration during preaching; they further accused him of having tried to seduce some of the married women in the church. Finally Satan became so successful in sabotaging Willy's blessings that he found himself compelled to leave the church.

The data presented in this section point to the complexity of Pentecostal ritual. Scholars such as Victor Turner have emphasised the ability of ritual to resolve the contradictions and paradoxes of social life (1969) whereas others have argued that ritual works by shaping and systematizing otherwise diffuse and unsystematic cultural orientations and meanings (Ortner 1978; Geertz 1973). However, the above descriptions clearly show that diverging and conflicting interpretations of the meaning of events are possible in Pentecostal ritual (see also Bialecki 2011) and that compromises, harmony, and interpretive consensus are not necessarily reached at the end of a meeting. Furthermore we can see how Pentecostal ritual sometimes generates its own tensions and contradictions or contributes to the escalation—rather than the resolution—of existing ones (see also Csordas 2011).

Demonologies and suspicions of demonic influence of others reveal a good deal about Pentecostal sociality, micro-politics, and status parameters. Judging whether an effusive manifestation during a church meeting should be ascribed to divine inspiration, human emotionality, or satanic imitation is partly a matter of observing and intuitively evaluating the behaviour in question, as Pentecostals insist that divine manifestations should always produce a sensation of peace and harmony. But such a judgement is also in large part dependant upon the status of the person who acts and whether he or she is believed to be entitled to receive a spiritual visit. Finally the credibility of such a judgment is dependant upon the social status of the person who makes it. An unjustified suspicion of inauthentic spiritual manifestations may itself be seen by others as a result of demonic manipulation.

A second fundamental contradiction, sometimes leading to conflicts that can be conceptualised as satanic interference, is between spiritual individualism and hierarchical church structures. Like most Pentecostals, members of the EPC take the priesthood of all believers seriously, and the individual and unmediated contact with God/Jesus/Holy Spirit fosters a certain individualism and sense of autonomy. On the other hand the structure of the EPC as of many other Pentecostal churches is quite hierarchical, and submission to pastors and other persons holding leadership positions is the general norm. Besides the pastor, the leaders and suppliant leaders of local church buildings, where meetings are held twice a week, hold some authority over fellow congregants. Though individual initiative, mostly explained in terms of direct divine inspiration, is common, some church leaders assert their own authority to control, authorise, and forbid activities like evangelising, street preaching, and visiting the sick. Pedro and Victoria, a middle-aged couple from the EPC once told me that they used to go to a public hospital to evangelise among patients on their own initiative until Satan prevented them from continuing to do so. When I asked them to be a little more specific they explained that Satan had successfully injected other congregants with envious sentiments that were directed at Pedro's and Victoria's initiative and at the spiritual blessings and privileges they were receiving by carrying out divinely ordained work at the hospitals. Eventually one person, who was in a position to do so, forbade Pedro and Victoria to evangelise without his authority.

There was little doubt in their mind that this person had been used as an instrument of Satan.

The tensions that occasionally occur when Pentecostals feel other congregants try to control them and prevent them from doing something, which God has inspired them to do, have, without doubt, been a source of numerous schisms and the backsliding of individuals in Chile as elsewhere. The very first schism in the history of Chilean Pentecostalism occurred in 1913, when members of the Methodist Pentecostal Church—the first Pentecostal denomination in the country, which was founded in 1909—were dissatisfied with the interruption of spiritual manifestations during meetings by the ringing of a bell. They decided to leave and found their own denomination, Church of the Lord (Kessler 1967: 296). In the EPC congregants are well aware that human interruptions of divine manifestations is problematic, and during church meetings leaders are careful not to interrupt spiritual manifestations, but rather let them die out little by little (see chapter 7).

During field trips to Chile in 2007 and 2008–9 I interviewed Pentecostals from a variety of denominations, many of whom had shifted churches at least once because of perceived incompatibilities between submission to pastoral authority and individual guidance by the Holy Spirit. One woman from the prosperity ministry, Christ Your Only Hope, told me she had left another Pentecostal church after the pastor had scolded her for attending an interdenominational revival seminary in Santiago without his permission. In the Assemblies of God I met a woman in her thirties who was a former member of the EPC. She explained to me she had felt that her womanness was being annulled in the EPC, and that she was simply not convinced God did not want her to wear jeans or use make up. On one occasion she had cut her hair to shoulder length. She was confident her personal relationship with God did not depend on the way she cut her hair. But other congregants were annoyed, and the following week she was told she would not be allowed to participate in an excursion with the unmarried girls from the church. Given the theological emphasis on spiritual warfare, it should come as no surprise that Pentecostals commonly ascribe the lack of Pentecostal unity and the many individual drop outs to the influence of Satan.

Differences in terms of secular social or 'worldly' status represent a third source of tension within the EPC. Chile is one of the most unequal societies in the world, and research has shown that a majority of Chileans regard the gaps between rich and poor as the greatest conflict

in the country (Manzi & Catalán 1998: 532). In the EPC material prosperity and educational mobilisation are generally conceived of as divine
blessings, yet congregants also emphasise that materialism can distract
Christians from spiritual matters. An anecdote I heard told on more
than one occasion concerned an unnamed congregant who bought a
new car and drove it to church, only to spend the better part of the
meeting worrying someone might steal or vandalise it instead of paying attention to the word of God.

Humility, modesty, and simplicity (*sencillez*) are considered important behavioural virtues in the EPC. *Una persona sencilla* (a simple person) may be intelligent, rich, and successful, but he or she is not
extravagant, ostentatious, pretentious, or arrogant. Pentecostal dress
codes, hair codes, and the ban of cosmetics are clear manifestations of
the ideal of simplicity. For members of the EPC, humility and simplicity indicate that a person is more concerned with spiritual than 'worldly'
material matters and does not think too highly of him- or herself, but
modestly gives God the credit for any success in life.

In the EPC, there was one man, Alec, in his fifties, who held a university degree and had a well-paid job. He was a third-generation congregant and in 1999 the only person in the church—and in 2008 the
only person older than 32 years—with a higher education. He lived in
a beautiful house in an upper middle-class neighbourhood and was
able to pay for the university education for both his children. Being a
long-term congregant, he was occasionally asked to preach. His preaching was quite atypical as he rarely spoke about human powerlessness
and divine omnipotence—an otherwise recurring theme in sermons—
nor about the difference between life with God and the 'world.' Instead
he would offer thorough biblical teachings, supplemented with anecdotes from his own trips all over the world. Also, he sometimes made
references to philosophers and non-Christian figures like Gandhi. He
often greeted me loudly in English so that everyone could hear that he
spoke a foreign language. On several occasions I had conversations
with him, where he took great pains to distance himself intellectually
from his fellow brothers and sisters in Christ (though never in their
presence).

The position of Alec in the church was ambiguous. On the one hand
he enjoyed considerable respect. When congregants were constructing
a new church building, he was in charge of the construction plans, and
on a few occasions he represented the church in meetings with political
authorities concerning building permits. But his superior social status

and atypical preaching also made him an object of gossip and resentment. Humberto, an unemployed man from the church, told me he was annoyed because the pastor frequently invited Alec to his home. The pastor had also expressed intentions of inviting Humberto home for tea at a time when he was still working, holding a good position in a company. But then he quit his job, and the invitation was never repeated. Though it would be contrary to church norms to discriminate on the basis of social status, Humberto suspected that the pastor's declining interest in having him home for tea was related to his unemployment.

Humberto further told me that he and Alec had once met in a work context and that a conflict had developed as Alec accused Humberto of dishonesty. A few days later, Humberto started feeling uncomfortable at work. He was sweating all the time and lost his appetite. Eventually he got too sick to work, and he decided to quit his job and almost immediately started feeling better. He spoke with a woman from another Pentecostal church who, after having received a message from God, warned him that someone from his church was sabotaging his spiritual growth as well as his career. During church meetings Humberto sometimes felt the church was charged with an evil energy. On one occasion he felt touched by the Holy Spirit and started dancing, but afterwards other congregants questioned whether or not this spiritual manifestation was authentic. Humberto suspected that Alec had, consciously or unconsciously, been attacking him with demonic powers and that he had also influenced other congregants, who started questioning the authenticity of Humberto's spiritual experiences. Maybe Alec felt threatened because Humberto, despite having a lower level of education and earning a much lower salary, had been a respected and upcoming worker in a rival company. Besides, Humberto had always felt Alec was a person who could not be trusted, since he was arrogant and did not display the kind of humility that is expected from Pentecostals. The warning, given by the woman from another Pentecostal church, confirmed his suspicions. When I returned to Chile in July 2002, Humberto had left the church and returned to secular life. During my previous field trips, I had spent a lot of time with him, but whenever he saw me speaking to Alec, which I did on several occasions, he was annoyed and apparently felt that I was being disloyal.

Like all stories about human conflicts, there was more than one version of this one. Alec never gave me his version of the story, but other congregants ascribed the work-related conflict and the strained relationship between the two to Humberto's envy of Alec's superior education and higher salary. The spirit of envy had clearly been successful in manipulating Humberto, but (as in the other cases) his personal responsibility for allowing such manipulation was also emphasised.

Attitudes towards social and educational mobilisation are complex and ambivalent in the EPC. It is widely accepted, appreciated, and indeed perceived as a result of divine blessings, that a younger genera-tion of congregants now goes to university, holds degrees, and is enter-ing the middle class. The presence of educated middle-class people within the church indicates that traditional Pentecostalism, contrary to the perception of many middle- and upper-class Catholic Chileans and of more moderate Pentecostals, is not simply the irrational and fanatic religion of the poor, ignorant masses. On the other hand, the contrast between the privilege of salvation and a low status according to 'worldly' standards forms an important part of an oppositional religious identity. Thus the advantage of spiritual over material blessings is repeatedly stressed in sermons and witnessing. When congregants are born-again Christians with a testimony of salvation and spiritual growth but who also make little effort to disguise their 'worldly' status, the important contrast loses some of its persuasiveness. Young students and profes-sionals are believed to be blessed by God, but they are also expected to display humility and simplicity, as 'worldly' status parameters should, in principle, be irrelevant in a community of spiritual equals. Alec was quite atypical for a member of his generation. His lack of humility and his frequent attempts to bring his 'worldly' status into the church, for instance by speaking English or referring to his journeys and to phi-losophers, were viewed with considerable ambivalence by other con-gregants. Humberto suspected the pastor preferred to have Alec as a guest because of his of superior social status. The sensation that 'worldly' standards are, after all, relevant and important within the church is a source of tension and resentment that can be addressed in terms of demonic powers.[7]

---

[7] Victor, an ex-member of another Pentecostal church in Valparaíso, told me of a somewhat inverse experience, though also one where Satan had successfully taken advantage of church members' concern with social status. Being a poor man with no education beyond primary school, and making his living as a vendor at a street market, Victor joined a church where several of the members were professionals and belonged to the middle class. Victor was regularly asked to preach in church, which he always did with a humble attitude, insisting that any wise words flowing from his mouth should be ascribed to divine inspiration. But then Satan interfered and Victor soon felt that some of the better off and more intellectual church members were annoyed

A further glance at the anthropological literature on African witch-craft demonstrates how accusations and suspicions can be directed both upwards and downwards in social hierarchies (Geschiere 1997; Geschiere & Nyamnjoh 1999). On the one hand, witchcraft is com-monly associated with weak members of a society who are believed to be envious because of the prosperity of others. On the other, those who have accumulated wealth rapidly can be accused of having done so through witchcraft, and often at a high price such as the death or zombification of a relative (Comaroff & Comaroff 1999; Lindhardt 2009*b*). In a similar vein, suspicions of demonic influence in Pentecostal churches can move in various directions. We have seen that both those who appear to be privileged in terms of spiritual manifestations and those who are too busy questioning the authenticity of such manifesta-tions can be suspected of being manipulated by diabolic forces. While social mobilisation is mostly seen as a divine blessing, the attempt to bring 'worldly' standards into the church can be ascribed to demonic manipulation, as can the envy directed towards the superior 'worldly' status of others.

The agency of Satan and his demons are often detected in different kinds of tension that threaten the integrity of the Christian community. In this section I have demonstrated how patterns of diabolic/ demonic strategies negatively mirror Pentecostal ideals of intra-church sociality and harmony between spiritual equals. Thus the diabolic/demonic pro-vides a language for speaking about states or affairs that are not ideal— or about the impossibility of achieving a perfect divine order in the here and now, even within the confines of the church. But diabolic/ demonic disturbances can also be detected in tensions and confronta-tions between congregants and 'worldly' non-Pentecostals, who do not understand and appreciate the spiritual privileges of Pentecostals. It is to such tensions and confrontations that I will now turn.

Satanic Attacks through Non-Pentecostal 'Worldly' Others

In chapter 7 I described how ritual language is sometimes perceived by both speaker and listeners as originating from God. I noted that it is

---

because a humble man was granted such privileges. His 'brothers' in Christ were obvi-ously unable to abstract from the 'worldly' status of a preacher and focus on the divine message that was being articulated through him. Eventually a conflict became inevita-ble, and Victor left the church.

highly uncommon to congratulate a preacher on a sermon, however beautiful and inspirational it might have been, as preachers are mainly seen as messengers of the divine. Besides, most Pentecostals have stories to tell about how God has spoken to them through instruments, or how they have themselves been used as instruments. By this is meant that God uses one Pentecostal to speak to another about a personal matter concerning the listener and of which the speaker could only have gained knowledge through divine inspiration. Congregants from the EPC do not ascribe the ability to do significant things with words— to produce truly inspirational and consequential speech—to the creativity of human speakers but rather to divine agency.

Speech is one of several areas in which the interference of God in human affairs resembles that of his opponent. Several Pentecostals (from the EPC and other churches) told me that a favourite tactic of the Devil is to let himself be heard through the mouth of human instruments. While a certain lack of control of the uttered word characterise both satanic and divine inspiration in speech, there are also important differences between the two. Humans cannot decide when God should speak through them, but divine inspiration is nevertheless conditioned by the human will to surrender and openness. The most compelling imposition of a divine 'I' upon a human speaker, for instance in prophecies, glossolalia, and affectively marked performances of sermons and testimonies mostly occur within controlled ritual contexts and only after an intense ritual atmosphere has been produced by initial singing and praying. By contrast Pentecostals mostly describe satanic interference in human speech in terms of manipulation.

Pentecostals may themselves, in retrospect, detect diabolic control of their own speech. Marco, a young man from the EPC explained to me that he occasionally argued with his wife and daughter, and that he would afterwards be shocked when they reminded him of the ugly words that had come out of his mouth. He was convinced that Satan or some demon had been controlling his speech. Such accounts are, however, quite rare. Explaining one's own behaviour and thoughts in terms of demonic manipulation is not a way of neglecting personal responsibility, as Pentecostals insist that such manipulation is only possible if a person has failed to stay close to God. The Devil is known to be a very persistent sacred other, and members of the EPC consider the humble recognition of one's own human frailty and imperfection to be a fundamental Christian virtue. Hence the acknowledgement of occasional diabolic manipulation of unarticulated thoughts and emotions is not only acceptable but to some extent normative (claiming to be totally immune to diabolic attacks can be associated with arrogance). But admitting diabolic control of speech and other kinds of manifest behaviour is basically the same as admitting to being a bad Christian. It is more common for Pentecostals to suspect each other of being used as diabolic instruments (which, similarly, is really the same as suspecting others of being bad Christians).

But Pentecostals believe that the human instruments through which Satan and his demons are most easily able to speak are non-Pentecostals, people from the 'world'. I once talked about my research with a Chilean Baptist. He explained to me that the EPC was the worst and most conservative Pentecostal church in Chile, and he suggested I do my research elsewhere. When I later told some members of the EPC about this conversation they immediately concluded that the Devil had been speaking directly to me through the mouth of this Baptist.

I was often told that new converts and especially younger men for whom conversion implies giving up all kinds of 'worldly' pleasures such as partying, drinking, drug abuse, womanising, going to discos and concerts, etc., are particularly vulnerable to Satanic attacks through non-Pentecostal friends who still live in the 'world'. Leonardo, a young man from the church explained to me how 'worldly' spirits had tried to keep him away from God and the church after conversion.

> You know the 'worldly' spirits; the legions of Satan are flying in the air, doing what they can to corrupt people. I played the guitar in a rock band. It was one of these underground circles. But the Lord saved me. I lived in the 'world', in this sub-world. I was blind. I had many friends who drink, take drugs, have so many vices, and the Lord took me away from these circles. But Satan put many obstacles in my way. My friends said to me, 'Hey, how can you leave the band? Are you not going to play the guitar anymore? What about the concerts? What about the applause of the audience?' All this was very painful for me; I was really suffering. Those were the instruments that the Devil used to make me stray from the path of the Lord.

Eventually Leonardo lost contact with his old friends, and he married a woman from the church. But during his first months as a 'saved' Pentecostal, ties to old non-Pentecostal friends were still strong, and in retrospect he ascribes their harshly outspoken lack of comprehension to satanic manipulation.

For many members of the EPC, the sensation of being misunderstood and regarded as fanatic, irrational, and too self-righteous by non-Pentecostals from the 'world' is a source of some resentment, yet also a fundamental part of an oppositional religious identity. Thus the failure of the people from the 'world'—who are often better off financially—to understand and appreciate the spiritual blessings of Pentecostals is a recurring theme in sermons, witnessing, and informal conversations.

In Pentecostal terminology, Satan and his spirits are the rulers of the 'world'. When non-Pentecostals criticise members of the EPC as being too fanatic, narrow-minded, and conservative, the former often interpret such criticism as satanic attacks. Consider the following excerpt from a sermon in the EPC:

> The enemy tries to disturb us, for instance when we are preaching on the street and we are distracted if people try to sell us things. And the enemy attacks us and tries to make us feel ridiculous. For instance: when people tell us that we are weird and fanatic. The enemy says, 'Don't go to church again; you are too fanatic,' or 'How can you dress like that, so old-fashioned?'

We have seen that Pentecostals ascribe truly inspirational and consequential ritual speech that touches the hearts of listeners to divine inspiration. Similarly, the ability of 'worldly' non-Pentecostals to produce negatively consequential speech, that is, speech that has the potential to inspire doubt and question religious doctrines and identities, is often associated with the agency of another sacred other, the Devil.

Satanic Attacks on the Human Mind

Manuel, a young unemployed man from the EPC (whom we also met in chapter 6 on conversion) once told me, as we were sitting and chatting in the church building one late afternoon, that he was going through a kind of spiritual crisis. When I asked him to be more specific, he first said that he did not want to tell me because I would probably not understand him anyway. But after a while, he eventually started telling me, and then remarked:

> Well, you understood me perfectly well. It can be good to talk about things sometimes. The enemy says to you, 'Don't tell him; he won't understand you; he will just laugh at you.' But you understood me.

Serious demonic crises when possessed persons scream, vomit, and shake violently are a rarity in the EPC, as well as in other Chilean Pentecostal churches I have visited. But, like Manuel, who retrospectively ascribed his own anticipation that I would not understand him to the enemy (the Devil) having manipulated his thoughts, many Chilean Pentecostals regularly express their concerns that God's main opponent is constantly trying to attack their minds. The Devil does so by sending sinful images and sceptical, inappropriate, and confusing thoughts. As Pentecostals believe that God holds the upper hand in spiritual warfare, such minor satanic attacks do not inspire panic or paranoia. But they do remind Pentecostals of the need to keep their eyes on God and protect their minds against an external but potentially intruding otherness.

On the one hand Pentecostals frequently point out that real spiritual struggles only start after conversion as there is really no need for Satan to bother the people from the 'world' who are already under his dominion. Yet they believe that from time to time non-Pentecostals can become victims of serious demonic attacks. Some of the most dramatic testimonies of salvation are stories about strong depressions, suicidal tendencies, and other mental disturbances, which—in retrospect—are attributed to demonic manipulation of the mind (see chapter 6).

Devoted and long-term Pentecostals feel relatively immune to such serious attacks. But they often perceive themselves as targets of minor satanic/demonic disturbances in the form of emotions and inappropriate desires, images, and thoughts. The kinds of thoughts most likely to be identified with satanic manipulation of the mind are negative, envious, and resentful thoughts against other persons—a clear deviation from the Christian ideal of loving one's neighbour—and, not least, sceptical thoughts that question Pentecostal 'truths', values, doctrines, and the authenticity of religious experiences.

Though saved by God and empowered by the Holy Spirit, Pentecostals still live in the 'world' of sin, saturated with aggressive demonic forces. Attempting to stay close to God in order to gain immunity from spiritual attacks is an important way of disciplining the Christian self on an everyday basis. André, a newly converted young man from the EPC (whom we also met in chapter 6), described his daily struggles with the Devil as follows:

> Now I am always trying to keep my eyes on the Lord, not to look at other things that can distance me from him. For instance: if you see a beautiful girl, and your mind starts working immediately. Before, I didn't realise it, but now I realise that it is impossible for a man to dominate his own thoughts. Because if I am not concentrated, suddenly all these thoughts come upon me, thoughts against other persons. So he is working with the mind. And if the Devil is controlling you, he is constantly injecting all kinds of thoughts in you. That's what the Devil does, he puts thoughts in

you, thoughts that are really not your thoughts. You don't understand why you are thinking such things, but he injects you with these thoughts.

In a later conversation André elaborated a little further on his internal struggles with diabolic forces.

> When you are a servant of God, there is always this internal struggle … to control the thoughts that come to your head. Because the mind is like a battle field; if you don't control the thoughts, they will turn into vices and habits. So every day you are fighting with these thoughts that are bad for you. And if you fast and pray, it is easier to control these thoughts.

It has been argued more than once by scholars that Pentecostal-charismatic Christians find the Devil and his demons good to think with about a number of issues (Csordas 1994; Meyer 1999; Robbins 2004). For Chilean Pentecostals the biblical metanarrative about a cosmic war between God, trying to enact his plan of salvation, and Satan, trying to sabotage it, serves as a model of and for reality (Geertz 1973: 93) through which meaning is attributed to experience, and possible courses of action are outlined. World historical as well as quite trivial everyday events can be integrated as episodes within this metanarrative. Many Pentecostals see natural disasters such as earthquakes, the global power, and expansion of the Catholic Church or the unification of European countries in the EU as signs of satanic control of world history. At the same time they sometimes ascribe minor episodes in everyday life, such as getting stuck in traffic and arriving late for a church meeting or encounters with sceptical non-Pentecostal others to demonic attacks. In the excerpt above we can see how André also perceives this cosmic war as being fought at an intra-subjective level. The only way of keeping the Devil at arm's length is to seek divine power and protection. It is striking how André describes thoughts and images as having an external origin, as something the Devil puts into his head. Satanic presence is detected when certain thoughts and images are perceived as both inappropriate and autonomous, as an intruding and uncanny otherness within the self.

How do Pentecostals develop this kind of awareness towards certain aspects of their own thought processes? As noted by Tanya Luhrmann, the emphasis among many contemporary Christians on experiencing God in one's mind and body creates a problem of discernment. While this problem has a long tradition within Christianity, its theological role has greatly increased in the kind of Christianity in which God's communication is vivid, real, and concrete. Writing on a Californian Vineyard church, Luhrmann proposes a simple definition

of discernment as the 'attempt to distinguish between God's communi-
cations and the congregant's own ideas' (2006: 9). She further notes
(though she does not elaborate on that point) that congregants seem to
develop familiarity with God and with demonic spirits in a similar way
(2006: 27).

Unlike the Vineyard church studied by Luhrmann, the EPC has no
courses on how to search for and identify the presence of sacred others
in the everyday flow of awareness. But preachers frequently warn their
audience about possible satanic manipulations of the mind. Besides,
many congregants are fond of reading Christian books and comics,
many of which are produced in the United States (and translated into
Spanish) and sold cheaply in Evangelical bookshops. Some Evangelical
comics vividly illustrate how demons create confusion, doubt, and
insecurity in Christians.[8]

The extent to which literature and comics influence the self-
awareness of Pentecostal readers is difficult to measure, though I should
emphasise that I have noticed a remarkable correspondence between
the explanations provided in the comics and the ones given to me by
Pentecostals. Nevertheless, I argue here for the relevance of a point
made by Peter Berger and Thomas Luckmann, namely that subjective
reality is mainly produced and sustained through conversation with
significant others (1972: 177). Drawing on these scholars and others,
I argued in chapter 6 that conversion and continuing growth in faith
over time can be seen as processes of narrative self-construction in
which Pentecostals situate their own life course and particular experiences within a shared biblical metanarrative of a struggle between God
and the 'world' or the Devil. In large part, Pentecostal narrative processes consist in discerning the presence and intervention of sacred
others in different situations and thus in transforming seemingly mundane incidents into episodes within a biblical metanarrative. For
instance God or the Devil can be identified as the ultimate link in a
causal chain, as when Pentecostals tell themselves, each other, and visiting anthropologists that the Devil was the real author of words spoken by a 'worldly' other or that he was in fact the one who made them
get stuck in traffic so that they arrived late for a church meeting.

---

[8] Many of these comics are available online. See Jack T. Chick, 'A Devil's Nightmare',
Chick Publications, 1972 <http://www.chick.com/reading/tracts/0004/0004_01.asp>;
or Jack T. Chick, 'A Demon's Nightmare' [Spanish translation], *Chick Publications*, 1972
<http://www.chick.com/reading/tracts/0519/0519_01.asp>.

I further argued that conversion and growing in faith are also processes of learning to pay attention to emotions, bodily states, and
streams of consciousness in specific ways. As noted by Luhrmann, this
process requires the acquisition of new linguistic cognitive knowledge
(2004: 527) or of specific models for interpreting evidence of sacred
presence (2007: 6). As Pentecostals become more conscious of possible
communication with sacred others— a likely result of participating in
worship, praying on a regular basis, and listening to the stories of fellow
congregants—passing thoughts, intuitions, or sensations, which they
earlier would have regarded as their own may be interpreted as divine
messages. In a similar vein Pentecostals learn to look for and identify
the presence and voice of the Devil. When constructing their testimony
of salvation they may, encouraged or at least inspired by others, start to
interpret previous thoughts, emotions, fears, and attitudes as signs of
diabolic manipulation. In chapter 6 I described how Manuel, through
conversations with his father, came to realize that his pre-conversion
fears and suicidal inclinations were really caused by evil spirits. The
awareness of possible diabolic attacks is also in large part cultivated
through gossiping about occult forces. The circulation of gossip about
fellow congregants functions in several ways. It teaches which kinds of
conduct are likely to be despised (display of arrogance, envy, too much
scepticism) while at the same time provides congregants with a constant incitement to reflect upon their own behaviour, attitudes, and
thoughts. It also provides a cognitive model for interpreting certain
behaviours, attitudes, and thoughts as evidence of satanic presence.

Self and the Diabolic Other

In order to pursue the analysis of Pentecostal experiences of an uncanny
diabolic other imposing itself on the human mind a little further I will
briefly summarise the theoretical perspectives on the human self that
were introduced in chapter 2. What I hope to demonstrate here is that
the ways in which scholars such as Csordas and in particular Mead
have addressed issues such as self-distance, self-reflection, and self-
objectification can shed some important light on Pentecostal understandings and interpretations of their own mental activity as arenas of
spiritual struggle.

In chapter 2 I referred to the work of Csordas, who proposes a
cultural phenomenological view of self-processes as grounded in

embodiment. Drawing on Merleau-Ponty Csordas argues that the human body is not, in the first place, an object, but an integral part of the perceiving subject, and that consciousness should in the first place be seen as a body projecting itself into the world. Perception starts pre-objectively with the body in the world, and the constitution of objects, including the objectification of the body, of the self, and of other humans is a secondary product of socially conditioned reflective think-ing. Csordas further stresses that the pre-objective, while pre-reflective, is not pre-cultural, and he finds Bourdieu's concepts of habitus and the socially informed body helpful in terms of explaining the grounded-ness of culture in the body (1990: 10–12) and consequently of account-ing for commonalities within the pre-objective.

Applying this theoretical framework in a study of demon pos-session and deliverance among North American Catholic charis-matics, Csordas makes a distinction between demons as culturally reified objects and their experiential manifestations as concrete self-objectifications in religious participants (1990: 15). As cultural objects in a behavioural environment, demons are conceptualised as intelli-gent beings with purposes and functions. At a representational level, demonologies can be seen as a negative mirror of the ideal Christian person (Csordas 1994: 225). But Csordas argues that persons who are victims of demon attacks do not in the first place perceive a demon as a culturally reified object inside themselves. What is sensed is some thought pattern, behaviour, emotion, or aspect of one's personality as being outside of control or as being a controlling factor (Csordas 1994: 225). This pre-objective sense of lack of control—which is not pre-cultural since standards of personal control derive from culture and are inscribed in the habitus—may then secondarily be explored and discerned as demonic presence in religious practice. Csordas presents examples of charismatic healing in which the healer as a specialist in cultural objectification discerns whether or not a given problem is of demonic origin. By contrast my Chilean Pentecostal informants often diagnose their own thoughts, emotions, attitudes, and internal images as resulting from satanic manipulation.

According to Csordas the condition of possibility of sacred (demonic or divine) presence is an alterity of the self that is an essential feature of embodied existence. Drawing on the work of Richard M. Zaner (1981) he notes how the autonomous functioning of our bodies imposes limits on our being and leaves us with a sense of inescapable contingency (Csordas 1994: 158). Csordas defines the sacred as 'an existential encounter with Otherness that is a touchstone of our humanity' and then adds that this sense of otherness is itself 'phenomenologically grounded in our embodiment' (ibid.: 5). In chapter 7 I noted how Csordas sees the otherness of language, which makes it apt for certain mystifications as divine presence and control, as a result of language being part of our embodied existence. But the essential bodily otherness that may at times be objectified as divine presence can also be 'magnified to cosmological proportions as the uncanny presence of evil spirits' (ibid.: 226).

Considering that the personal experience of the sacred is a core feature of Pentecostal-charismatic religiosity, it is hardly surprising that phenomenology has been a theoretical favourite in much of the existing scholarly literature. Many scholars of Pentecostalism and charismatic Christianity have been inspired by Csordas (see Coleman 2000a; Collins & Coleman 2000; Ryle 2010, 2011), and others who do not explicitly identify themselves as phenomenologists have nevertheless focused extensively on the ways in which encounters with God are produced through bodily practice (Albrecht 1999; Steven 2002; Luhrmann 2004). In a similar vein, other authors, apart from Csordas, have emphasised how the other sacred others, Satan and his demons, become manifest in certain bodily experiences, symptoms, and behaviours (see for example Meyer 1998; Lindhardt 2009a, 2010). Thus, Dorothy Hodgson conceives of the possession of Maasai women by diabolic spirits, resulting in different kinds of bodily distress, as an embodiment of the contradictions of modernity, such as increased marginalisation and transformation of gender relationships (1998).

The value of phenomenology and, more broadly, of a focus on bodily practice and experience for an understanding of Pentecostal-charismatic religiosity is not disputed here. Any reader who has managed to struggle through the preceding chapters of this book should have little doubt concerning my personal indebtedness to the work of Csordas (see also Lindhardt 2009a, 2011). Besides, some of the points he makes concerning the constitution of demons as cultural objects through culturally specific objectifications of sensations of lack of control are highly relevant and applicable in an analysis of reported experiences and diagnosis of demonic presence in the EPC. But given the strong emphasis that congregants place on Satan as becoming manifest in internal conversation and scepticism, I suggest that a partial shift in focus from embodiment and bodily experience to questions of language and reflective thought may be useful.

I have in earlier chapters (6, 7) argued that an analysis of the cultivation of a personal relationship between Pentecostal individuals and
God as a daily companion and partner of conversation can benefit
from the application of a Meadian perspective on the human self as a
site of internal responsiveness. According to Mead, reflective thought
takes the form of an internal dialogue between the 'I' and the 'me'. The
latter is conditioned by the response of the generalised other, which is
constituted through the internalisation of the generalised response of
different human others. The 'me' belongs to the organisation of the
community and mirrors the general values of the group, whereas the
response of the 'I' constitutes the individual adjustment to the social
environment. The self is constituted out of multiple selves, as the objectified 'me' is identified with a number of past actions and experiences
with different others. It is the 'I' that creates a unity among different
aspects of the self and activates them in different social contexts. Mead
further emphasises the importance of language for the development of
the self, as it is only through linguistic behaviour that the individual
can internalise the attitudes of others and fully become an object to
himself. It follows that external conversations must be prior to the
internal ones.

What I argue now is that Mead's perspective of the self is also useful
in terms of understanding Pentecostal experiences of the Devil as
imposing himself upon thought activity. Like Csordas, Mead conceives
of the self as an ongoing and socially conditioned process of reflection,
objectification, and adjustment to the social, cultural world. A difference between them is that Csordas sees the otherness of the self as
grounded in our embodied existence. For Mead, on the other hand, the
otherness that is a prerequisite of self-distancing does not derive from
the body but from society and is constituted as an object of reflection
through an internalisation of social processes. While neither Csordas
nor Merleau-Ponty is blind to the role of others in self-objectification
or to the importance of language for the constitution of the self, I think
that the essentially social, linguistic conditioning and dialogical nature
of the self and reflective thought are more aptly captured by Mead.
According to members of the EPC, the Devil attacks by telling them
certain things, by sending them inappropriate, confusing, and sceptical
confusing thoughts. Consider the following explanation from Edgardo,
an unskilled worker from the church:

> You know, the Devil is trying to tell us things all time, to put all kinds of
> thoughts into our head. He may say to you, 'Come on, do you really think

that God is going to keep his promises to you?' or 'Now you are praying again, it is not necessary to pray so much, you are too fanatic,' or maybe you are praying and suddenly you receive an image of a naked girl. In that case the only thing to do is to ask the Lord for protection or to open the Bible and read the Word.

Following Csordas we can say that what happens when Pentecostals like Edgardo and André experience such diabolic attacks is that certain images or thoughts are in the first place *sensed* as being disturbing or outside of control and secondarily objectified in a culturally specific way. So far so good! But in order to grasp the origin of thoughts that are discerned as demonic presence I think we may be well served by turning to the work of Mead. In Mead's view reflective thinking always implies an otherness, which is ultimately the presence of society, or the generalised social perspectives of others, within the self. Now, we may compare the first part of Edgardo's explanation with the last excerpt in the earlier section of this chapter, 'Satanic Attacks through Non-Pentecostal "Worldly" Others' (page 215), where a preacher describes how the Devil works through the commentaries of non-Pentecostal, human others who tell Pentecostals that they are too fanatic. The difference is that in Edgardo's description it is an internal rather than an external flesh-and-blood other that brings him this disturbing message. This internal other is the internalised generalised response of sceptical non-Pentecostal others. Similar to how diabolic attacks can be discerned in the responses and negative recognition of external human others, the Devil is here identified with the internal other, the 'me' that arises through the taking of attitudes of external others.

Mead's emphasis on the constitutive role of the attitudes of others for the development of the self has been echoed by the Canadian philosopher Charles Taylor. Challenging views on identity as based primarily on free choice and creative self construction, Taylor argues that to a large extent identities are formed by the ways in which persons or groups are recognised—or not recognised or misrecognised—by others (1994). But the work of Taylor also provides an important supplement to the theories of Mead as he points out that the extent to which social recognition by others can shape identities is influenced by power relationships and status parameters. The way in which majorities or powerful political actors within a society recognise a religious/ethnic/racial minority may affect identity processes among the latter in significant ways, for instance by fostering minority complexes, resentment, and defiant radicalism.

Pentecostalism is a minority religion in Chile and does not have the same public status as Catholicism. Members of the EPC take pride in belonging to a traditional Pentecostal church where a particularly strict discipline prevails. But they are also well aware that both 'worldly' others and more moderate Pentecostals regard them as fanatic and extremely conservative. Negative social recognition can be internalised so that members of the EPC start reflecting upon themselves from the perspective of a generalised 'worldly' sceptical other. Such reflection and scepticism towards oneself and the norms and standards of the religious community with which one identifies may be experienced as involuntarily confusing and disturbing and hence as representing a threat of fragmentation to the integrity of the self. Because of this perceived threat it is understandable that Pentecostals culturally objectify certain thoughts as demonic attacks.

'Satan Makes You Question Things'

Pentecostals also from time to time find themselves questioning the necessity of religious commitments as well as the authenticity of religious experiences and manifestations. Such questioning, which is also commonly ascribed to Satanic manipulation of the mind, was mostly but not exclusively reported to me by a younger and more educated generation of congregants. I have mentioned that a number of younger and native congregants from the EPC are now pursuing higher education or hold degrees. During my latest fieldwork in Chile in 2007 and 2008–9 I interviewed thirty members of a youth group of the Assemblies of God and attended several youth meetings in this church. This group consists of around forty to fifty persons between eighteen and thirty-two. More than 80 per cent of them have Pentecostal parents and approximately 75 per cent study at universities or professional institutes or hold degrees. While acknowledging theological similarities, the youth of the Assemblies of God also perceive themselves as quite distinct from traditional Pentecostals. Unlike the EPC, the Assemblies of God does not have strict dress and hair codes. For this new generation of young and educated Pentecostals the theological dualism between the church and the 'world' of sin has lost some of its importance.

As university students, Pentecostals who abstain from parties, getting drunk, discos, pre-marital sexual relationships, concerts, and popular secular music with erotic lyrics do feel different from their class mates. Many of my younger informants told me that their most intimate friendships were with fellow congregants and that romantic partners should also be sought within the confines of the church. In both the EPC and the Assemblies of God youth meetings on Saturday nights, followed by informal gatherings, provide important social alternatives to parties or a night out in town. Yet attitudes towards other aspects of 'worldly' culture such as consumerism, fashion, television, cinema, the internet, sports, going to the beach, politics, or—in the case of the Assemblies but *not* of the EPC—even the occasional consumption of a glass of wine, etc. are more relaxed among the younger and more educated congregants than among the preceding generations. Though generally faithful to the norms and doctrines of their church many of the younger congregants also negotiate their religious identities on a more individual basis, adapting to popular culture and seeking inputs through Christian and secular literature, the mass media, academic studies, etc.

Many of my younger Pentecostal informants reported how Satan sometimes attacked their mind with different kinds of thoughts. Marcelo, a high school student from the Assemblies of God, told me how he once stayed up all night preparing for a test on a Friday morning. He performed well but was very exhausted when he afterwards remembered that he had to prepare for a Sunday school class he was teaching for the children in the church. But then the Devil started manipulating with his mind, making him question if it was really necessary to put the same effort into a religious task. After all, he would receive no grade for his performance in the Sunday school, and his secular career would not depend on it. He finally decided to take the Saturday off and give the material he was supposed to be teaching a quick glance on the bus on his way to church Sunday morning. After giving a poor and uninspired Sunday school lecture, he was eventually able to identify the origin of his thoughts. Several young Pentecostals from both churches also explained to me how the Devil sometimes made them wonder if certain religious experiences such as feelings of warmth and energy streaming through their bodies; divine inspiration in preaching, teaching, and testifying; or being used as instruments to give messages to others, were in fact authentic or should rather be attributed to psychological self-deception. Guillermo, a young man from the EPC who had recently finished high school, gave me the following explanation:

> You have this experience, the Lord manifests himself, but then the enemy starts manipulating your mind. He says, 'Was that really the Lord? Maybe it was just something psychological!'

Guisela, a twenty-nine-year-old school teacher from the Assemblies of God explained to me how being used as an instrument by God was a beautiful and faith-confirming experience, yet also an open door for satanic attacks. On one occasion God had given her a message to deliver to another member of the youth group, Pablo:

> He [Satan] begins to put fear in you, to work with your mind: 'No, God did not give you that message; how are you going to deliver to that message to this person; it was not from God; you are just fooling yourself.' Well, now I have learnt not to pay too much attention to him, but Satan works a lot with these kinds of thoughts. He makes you question things. For instance what happened with Pablo was that God used me as an instrument. But Satan makes you question things. So I hesitated, but when I finally decided to give that message to Pablo, God confirmed that it did indeed come from him.

It has become commonplace to assert that processes of social identity formation can be complex and ambiguous in modern societies as individuals are confronted with different and sometimes contrasting value systems and structures of plausibility. According to Robert Hefner, in the course of their lives individuals develop real or imagined reference groups which serve as anchors for their sense of self and other. In modern society reference group orientations tend to be plural, and religious allegiances may very well conflict with other allegiances, leading to forced reflection (1993: 25–6). Reference group theorists do not see human identity as wholly socially determined but rather as emerging from ongoing and contingent socio-psychological interactions. The precise effect of culture in the creation of self is always mediated by the dispositions of individuals, that is, by 'their dispositions in a particular social world, and their ongoing efforts—never themselves fully culturally programmed—to assess the meaning and value of all that goes on around them' (Hefner 1993: 26). This point is consonant with Mead's definition of the social self as made up of the 'me', shaped by the attitudes of a generalised other and the 'I', the subjective attitude of response to and reflection upon this experience.

Historical research has demonstrated that religious self-doubt and the wish for signs from God to confirm one's faith stances are not peculiarities of late modern individuals whose inner worlds reflect the complexity and arbitrariness of the external social world in which they orient themselves.[9] Nevertheless it seems reasonable to relate many of the doubts concerning religious commitments and experiences, as reported by young Pentecostals, and not least their frequent evocation of 'psychology' as a possible interpretive framework for explaining such experiences, to their navigation between different reference groups (the church, the school/university, workplace). Their identities are never fully determined by the culture or structure of plausibility of a particular group but emerge in ongoing processes of interaction, reflection, and negotiation of meaning and 'truth'. This point does to some extent apply to all or most Pentecostals. But young professionals or students are more likely to develop identities that conflict with Pentecostal identities. It is notable that the defence of biblical truths is of little concern to older Pentecostals with low levels of education, whereas several younger Pentecostals put a good deal of effort into reconciling religious beliefs with scientific knowledge, for instance by studying creationist science textbooks. It is when forced reflection results in too much uncertainty and confusion concerning religious commitments and communication with the divine, on which a substantial part of Pentecostal self-identity is based, that diabolic presence can be discerned.

Conclusion: Making an Incomplete Break with the 'World'

Nosotros vivimos en el 'mundo' pero no pertenecemos al 'mundo'.
(We live in the 'world', but we do not belong to the 'world'.)

Nosotros estamos en el 'mundo'. Que el 'mundo' no esté en nosotros.
We live in the 'world'. The 'world' should not be in us.

These statements, both made during sermons in the EPC, encapsulate the dilemma in which many Chilean Pentecostals find themselves while at the same time express an ideal state of affairs that can only be strived towards through daily struggle. On the one hand Pentecostals describe personal salvation as a moment of rupture, a movement away from the 'world' and towards the realm of God. On the other hand, they are bound to live and participate in the 'world' and to deal with the daily challenges that such participation implies. Rather than a

---

[9] For an intriguing study of religious self doubt among seventeenth- and eighteenth-century Puritans in America, see Hall (2004).

once-and-for-all achieved state, rupture becomes an ongoing and essentially incomplete life project (see Lindhardt 2009*a*, 2011). On one occasion I attended the funeral of an old woman from the EPC. The preacher stated that death should actually be seen as a victory for Pentecostals and added that this was obviously not the way people from the 'world' would generally see it. Only now that she had died was the old woman on the safe side, whereas being alive implied an ever-present risk of losing salvation by sliding back into the 'world.'

Reviewing the scholarly literature on global Pentecostalism/charismatic Christianity, Robbins notes that Pentecostals/charismatics tend to ritualise discontinuity in different post-conversion rituals of rupture such as deliverance, healing, and spiritual in-filling where disjunction is emphasised (2004*b*: 128). In her work on Ghanaian Pentecostalism, Meyer demonstrates how the diabolic provides converts with a language and set of practices by use of which they can articulate the difficulty of making a complete break with the past. Meyer found that many Ghanaian Pentecostals were haunted by family spirits, defined as diabolic agents, after conversion. She sees this spiritual ambiguity as corresponding to a perceived conflict between identity in terms of membership of an extended family and the striving for modern individualism (1998: 340). By emphasizing the active role played by the Devil and his demons in human affairs, Pentecostalism provides 'a bridge over which converts can move back and forth and hence discursively and ritually return to their past' (1999: 215).

In this chapter I have illustrated how the Devil comes into the picture when Pentecostals experience ongoing tensions with the 'world' of sin. Though conversion implies leaving the 'world' behind, the latter often seems unwilling to let the convert go. Pentecostals are confronted with the 'world' in the form of non-Pentecostal sceptical others, who ridicule them, question their doctrines, or remind them of 'worldly' pleasures. They further encounter the 'world' in the form of secular structures of plausibility that are contradictive to Pentecostal religious 'truths', in the mass media and more generally in a decadent but tempting mainstream culture. At times non-Christian sentiments and behaviours and 'worldly' standards of social status infiltrate the Pentecostal church community and create tensions. Finally, Pentecostals sometimes experience that the 'world' or the Devil is present within them as a confusing and sceptical part of their own mental activity.

In the last part of the chapter I argued that the analysis of Pentecostal experiences and cultural objectifications of the sacred, in this case the

Devil, can gain much from a pragmatist perspective on the self and reflective thought. The advantage of this perspective is that it enables us to see the diabolic other, which imposes itself on the mind and becomes an uncanny, conflictive, and sceptical part of the self, as deriving from wider society or from the 'world' that Pentecostals perceive themselves as having a tense and oppositional relationship to. It is when a non-Pentecostal 'worldly' society, which does not understand and appreciate the spiritual blessings and religious commitments of Pentecostals and does not accept the validity of religious experiences and 'truths', enters into the thinking of the individual in the form of the generalised other that satanic presence may be discerned. A Meadian perspective of the self as emerging through the interplay between inter- and intra-subjective processes may, in other words, help us understand how the devil Satan manages to make the passage from society to mind.

CHAPTER ELEVEN

ANOTHER END OF HISTORY

Eschatology, Conspiracy Theories, and Global Imagination

Like many other Pentecostals around the world, congregants from the EPC see global processes and world history as saturated with diabolic forces. Pentecostal understandings of spiritual warfare not only inform interpretations of many of the challenges and misfortunes of everyday life, as described in the previous chapter. Spiritual warfare also occupies a central position in a Pentecostal eschatological metanarrative within which world historical events and global processes are integrated as episodes or parts.

Eschatology, the theological concern with the end of the world and the final events in history, forms part of official Pentecostal teachings in the EPC as in other Pentecostal churches. In this chapter I explore eschatological readings of world history. And I attempt to demonstrate how Pentecostal historical awareness and global orientations are to a large extent constituted and shaped by the less-official eschatological subgenres of rumour and conspiracy theories. These subgenres belong to what I have earlier described as the third level of Pentecostal discourse (see chapter 2). They only circulate in private contexts and never find their way into sermons, Sunday school lessons, or homilies directed to potential converts on the street. Positioning Pentecostals as persecuted victims of globally stretching satanic conspiracies, these genres tend to follow a paranoid style of thought, defined by the American historian Richard Hofstadter as a 'way of seeing the world and of expressing oneself' in which 'the feeling of persecution is central, and it is indeed systematized in grandiose theories of conspiracy' (1965: 4). Hofstadter adds that 'the paranoid mentality is far more coherent than the real world, since it leaves no room for mistakes, failures of ambiguities' (ibid.: 36). Drawing on the work of Hofstadter in a study of religious conflict in Nigeria, Nils Kastfelt sees the paranoid style as providing 'a master story which unites visible and invisible forces into a unified, coherent and all-embracing pattern' (2005: 45). In the case of the EPC this master story is about God trying to unfold

his plan of salvation and Satan trying to sabotage it and gain world
dominion for himself. Within this broad storyline of sacred forces
struggling against each other there is plenty of room for human actors
and institutions. As will be shown, Pentecostal rumours and conspiracy theories present the Catholic Church, North American enterprises,
cartoons, and the internet as the allies or instruments of the Devil. The
role of Pentecostals is that of persecuted victims of global conspiracies.
They further see themselves as allies of God and, very importantly, as
activators of his transformative power that will ultimately secure victory
and prepare the world for the Second Coming of Christ, the Reign of the
Millennium, and the Great Day of Judgment, though the road may be
long and bumpy.

In the scholarly literature popular conspiracy theories and other
rumours are often portrayed as forms of subaltern communication that
are distinguished from other discourses by being authorless, anonymous, ambiguous, opaque, and network-like in their circulation (Guha
1983; Spivak 1987; Scott 1990; Coombe 1997). In Homi Bhaba's view,
the indeterminate circulation of meaning as rumour or conspiracy
constitutes an intersubjective realm of revolt and resistance (1994:
200). As they have no signature or origin and do not belong to anyone,
rumours are difficult to control and dispute, but at the same time they
constitute powerful and pervasive cultural narratives, which articulate
an alternative version of social reality and reshape the world as well as
the place of the subject within it (Bubandt 2002: 4).

In what follows I explore how rumours, conspiracy theories, and
more generally the eschatological metanarrative that informs these
genres allow Pentecostals to symbolically reposition themselves in the
social world while at the same time constitute a sense of global spiritual
agency. In addition to the literature on rumour, sketched above, the
analysis I pursue is inspired by a recent body of literature focusing on
Pentecostal-charismatic Christianity from a global perspective. Several
scholars have demonstrated how Pentecostal-charismatic organiza-
tions socialize their adherents into a specifically global orientation
(Coleman 2000; Corten & Marshall-Fratani 2001; Lindhardt 2010,
2011). Thus Birgit Meyer argues that Pentecostalist churches in Ghana
take their members beyond the scope of local culture by placing more
emphasis than other churches on their being a world religion (1999*b*:
159–60). In a similar vein Ruth Marshall-Fratani points to the ability of
Nigerian Pentecostalism to create new moral, physical geographies and
global imagined communities (2001: 82–4). Pentecostal subjectivity,

she argues, is partly constructed through projections on a global scale (ibid.: 89) or through negotiations between global and local (ibid.: 83). In a study of the Swedish charismatic ministry Word of Life, where strong emphasis is placed on being part of a global revival movement, Simon Coleman draws on Ronald Robertson's definition of globalization as 'both the compression of the world and the intensification of consciousness of the world as a whole' (1992: 8, quoted from Coleman 2000*a*: 50). The advantage of this definition, so Coleman argues, is that it does not limit the understanding of globalization to economic, social, and communicative interconnections, but includes changing forms of reflexivity of perception (ibid.; see also Appadurai 1996).

Drawing on important insights from these two bodies of literature, I see Pentecostal eschatology, rumours, and conspiracy theories as particular discursive practices that redefine the meaning and direction of global historical processes as well as the roles of Pentecostal subjects within them. By engaging in such discourses, congregants from the EPC project themselves into a global order, creating what Coleman refers to as a 'multidimensional yet cultural specific sense of reaching out into an unbounded realm of action and identity' (2000: 6).

Satanism, Foreign Enterprises, and Popular Culture

Many rumours and conspiracy theories focus on the presence and cultural impact of North American enterprises in Chile. Thus several congregants from the EPC explained to me that Microsoft, McDonalds, Citibank, and the producers of the shampoo 'Head and Shoulders' are committed to Satanism and donate high percentages of their profit to satanic churches. All these enterprises or their products can be found in Chilean society, with Citibank having several local branches all over the over the country. I never heard similar rumours about national enterprises.

In a fascinating study of rumours about origins and meanings of corporate trademarks in the United States, Rosemary Coombe (1997: 250) argues that such rumours are created and used by consumers to make audible a sense of powerlessness and lack of control in a ubiquitous world of commercial media culture. As production and distribution become more globally organized, feelings of alienation and lack of control over local events develop. Coombe (1997: 270) adds that the presence of corporate power is pervasive and incorporeal in that both production and origin is invisible, hidden behind the play of media signifiers. Thus corporate powers are often surrounded by an aura of mystery, indeterminacy, and inaccessibility. In a similar vein, Pentecostal rumours linking foreign North American enterprises with Satanism point to ambivalent sentiments towards the presence and power of such enterprises in Chile. In addition to being a symbol or embodiment of global inequality, foreign enterprises present a perceived threat to local control over the production of meaning and values.

Pentecostal rumours further link foreign mass-mediated cultural genres to diabolic forces. 'Worldly' music such as heavy metal, hard rock, or any kind of popular music performed by artists with non-human, semi-monstrous appearances such as Marilyn Manson or the American group KISS is seen as a powerful instrument by use of which the Devil influences youth culture. Members of the EPC also believe that the physical appearance of demons is remarkably reminiscent of non-human fictive figures such as the Ninja Turtles, Freddy Kruger, monsters from Japanese cartoons, or Gollum from *The Lord of the Rings*. It is a little unclear whether the producers of movies or cartoons have deliberately allied themselves with the Devil or whether the latter has managed to infiltrate popular mainstream culture in subtle ways, providing producers with demonic models for popular fictive figures in order to contaminate an audience that mainly consists of children and youth.

Either way, such rumours reflect perceptions of popular mass-mediated products as positing challenges to Pentecostal projects of evangelisation and purification of society. Due to their immaturity children and youth are seen particularly vulnerable to different popular cultural inputs that may distract them from spiritual matters. In the EPC as in other Pentecostal churches, a number of (native Pentecostal) teenagers have a hard time accommodating to church standards and find it difficult to denounce some of the 'worldly' pleasures enjoyed by their classmates in school. Congregants sometimes comment that their children are bored during church meetings and that it is a great challenge for a Pentecostal parent to teach children and not least teenagers to focus on God rather than on 'worldly' temptations such as television. The demonisation of different popular cultural genres points to the perceived difficulty of fully controlling the socialization of children and youth in a modern globalised and mass-mediated society where parents have to compete with a variety of other inputs and social influences in everyday life.

Catholicism and Anti-Evangelical Conspiracies

I once asked José, a young man from the EPC, about his opinion of the Catholic Church. Knowing that I was married to a Catholic woman, he was first a little hesitant in answering, but then decided that he better be straight forward with me. He told me he was convinced that the Catholic Church was the wife of Antichrist, the famous prostitute that appears in Revelation, chapter 17. Like many other congregants, he suspected the Catholic Church had infiltrated society at different levels and that its numerous spies registered and observed the conduct of all Evangelicals:

> José: You know if a pastor [of an Evangelical church] starts speaking up against the Catholic Church, this pastor will soon get into serious trouble. The Catholic Church has spies all over the world. Do you know the Jesuits?
>
> ML: Yes!
>
> José: They are working as spies all over the world. They know everything; they know about all Christian members of Evangelical churches in the whole world. They know the name of each one; they know what all Evangelicals are doing, and if someone starts criticising [the Catholic Church] he will soon get into serious trouble.

Other congregants explained to me that the Jesuits are trying to infiltrate Pentecostal churches in different parts of the world and had already been successful in doing so in England.[1] In addition to the Jesuits, congregants of the EPC also see the Catholic integralist movement Opus Dei as one of the most dangerous enemies of Chilean Pentecostalism. The perceived political and economic power of this movement, combined with the lack of transparency that characterises its work, structures, and actual influence in Chilean society nourish the ground for

---

[1] At the beginning of my second fieldwork in June 2000 a friend from the EPC said that he had something very funny to tell me. After I had left Chile in 1999 one of the older church members had expressed suspicion that I might be a Jesuit spy, who reported everything I saw and heard in the church to the Catholic authorities. After we had both laughed at this suspicion he looked at me and asked cautiously, 'Well, you aren't a Jesuit spy, are you?'

the creation and circulation of rumours about its possible anti-Evangelical agenda.

The main villain in Pentecostal rumours and conspiracy theories is not foreign enterprises or cartoons but the Catholic Church. Like many other Chilean Pentecostals, congregants from the EPC associate the Catholic Church with social inequality and unequal access to political power, the mass media, and proper education in Chilean society. The church runs several universities and primary and secondary schools, which are all expensive and hence inaccessible to persons from the lower social sectors.

However, the Catholic Church is more than a symbol and embodiment of inequalities within Chilean society. Theories of Catholic conspiracies against the world's Evangelical population are grounded in and constitutive of a more global and eschatological orientation and imagination. Members of the EPC very rarely make comments about particular Chilean bishops or other specific national Catholic authorities. The Catholic persecution of Evangelicals is perceived to be a global project, organised by the Vatican. While resentful of the privileged economic and political position of the Catholic Church within Chilean society, members of the EPC are in fact much more concerned with the globally stretching powers and threats of Catholicism, and they frequently comment upon the secrecy, greed, and excessive wealth of the Vatican. Luis, a man in his forties from the EPC explained himself as follows:

> I read a book that says that the all the gold that was stolen from the Jews during the Second World War can be found in the Vatican. Whenever the Germans stole in some country, it all went to the Vatican.... I have heard that with all the gold in Vatican, there is enough to erase world poverty and to solve all the problems in the world. That's how much the Vatican has, but they have their accounts in the best banks in Switzerland, so they are really powerful.

In a similar vein, Armando, a retired worker from the EPC described the power, wealth, and influence of the Catholic Church in Chile and beyond:

> In the Vatican there are millions and millions of dollars and gold. Here in Chile, they have millions of dollars, the ministers. Here in Chile the Roman Catholic Church has everything. The politicians all support the ministers, the Christian Democrats, all of them. And they give millions to the Catholics. The Evangelicals don't receive anything. In the Catholic schools, the parents must pay, and the schools also receive money from

the politicians; all that money goes to the Vatican. Millions of dollars annually to that pagan church.... You know, in the supermarket, Santa Isabel, when they ask you if you want to donate 10 pesos to *Hogar de Cristo*[2], all that money goes directly to the Vatican.... They have always persecuted the Evangelicals.

Like foreign enterprises, the Catholic Church is associated with economic and political inequality. Members of the EPC further perceive the Catholic Church as being surrounded by an aura of mystery, indeterminacy, inaccessibility, and elitist secrecy. The Vatican is seen as a particularly dangerous and secretive political–religious centre, where important decisions affecting people in distant parts of the world are made behind closed doors.

In August 1999 a photocopy with a message that had supposedly been downloaded from the Internet by an anonymous church member somewhere in Chile circulated in the EPC in Valparaíso. The photocopy contained a warning to all Evangelicals that the Pope had allied himself with a powerful Arabic league and with the United States in order to gain world dominion and make the US dollar a universal currency, wiping out all national currencies. It further said that the Catholic Church was about to initiate a brutal crusade, prepared for almost two hundred years, against the world's Evangelical churches. Non-Catholics would be threatened to convert to Catholicism and killed if they refused. A few days earlier, a prophecy, given in the EPC, had included a warning about a proximate persecution of Evangelicals. Since two similar warnings within a few days could hardly be ascribed to mere coincidence, and since it was considered unlikely that the old woman who prophesied should have been surfing on the Internet, most congregants believed that the message of the photocopy was valid.

Given that prophecies are given several times each year in the EPC, and that they more often than not include warnings that congregants should prepare themselves for hard times and persecutions, I did not find this coincidence particularly alarming. But for some days, the atmosphere in the church was characterised by certain anxiety and alertness. After a week, the immediate anxiety had diminished. Stories of possible Catholic conspiracies and persecution of the Evangelical population were, after all, old news. Similar to how most Chileans have

---

[2] *Hogar de Cristo* is a Catholic charity organisation that provides food and shelter to orphans and old people. In the national supermarket Santa Isabell, customers are encouraged to donate small change to this organisation.

learnt to live with the ever-present risk of earthquakes, every day life of Pentecostals is not seriously disrupted by the circulation of conspiracy theories. But in the weeks following the circulation of the photocopy, congregants from the EPC frequently discussed the Catholic–US plan to gain world dominion, occupy Jerusalem, and make all nations adopt the US dollar as a compulsory common currency. The unification of European countries in the EC and the introduction of the euro as a common European currency were seen as important first steps towards the establishment of a Catholic–US world government and the universalisation of the US dollar.

The photocopy did not indicate the website where this alarming information had been found,[3] and the congregant who found the message apparently felt no need to identify him- or herself and take the credit for his or her discovery. Like most other rumours, this one was characterised by mystery, indeterminacy, and lack of any traceable origin. One Pentecostal friend of mine even suspected that someone had made up this story to pull the legs of the Pentecostals and create an atmosphere of panic, but he did not tell other congregants about this suspicion.

Eschatological rumours associating the Catholic Church with satanic conspiracies against the world's Evangelical population are not a Chilean peculiarity, though they connect particularly well with local Pentecostal resentment towards Catholicism. The content of the photocopy was clearly informed by widespread Christian eschatological narratives on the final moments of earth's history. Such narratives are articulated in mass-mediated products such as North American Christian literature, books, comics, and small tracts, which are translated into Spanish and numerous other languages.[4] In Chile this material is sold, cheaply, in Evangelical bookshops. North American literature presents the Catholic Church as the wife of the Antichrist and points to close historical alliances between the Church and Nazi and

---

[3] At the time most congregants were not familiar with the Internet, and no one considered doing an advanced google search to find the web page with the message.

[4] Especially the North American Protestant editorial, *Chick Publications*, has specialised in anti-Catholic propaganda, which is translated into Spanish and distributed all over Latin America. See 'Where to Get Chick Tracts Worldwide', *Chick Publications*<http://www.chick.com/distrib.asp>; Jack T. Chick, 'The Last Generation', *Chick Publications*, 1992 <http://www.chick.com/reading/tracts/0094/0094_01.asp>; or Jack T. Chick, 'The Beast', *Chic Publications*, 1988 <http://www.chick.com/reading/tracts/0007/0007_01.asp>.

Communist regimes. It further describes how the return of Christ will be preceded by times of intense and bloody persecution of the world's Evangelical population.

Pentecostal/Fundamentalist Christian eschatology draws on particular passages of the Bible. The interpretation of the unification of European countries as an apocalyptic sign finds support in the book of Daniel, which speaks of a political leader from a reunited Roman Empire (7: 24) who will make a peace contract with the nations of the earth for seven years (9: 27).[5] Revelation chapter 13 speaks of 'a beast coming up out of the sea' (verse 1), and then predicts that 'all people living on earth will worship it' (verse 8) and that it 'will cause as many as do not worship the image of the beast to be killed' (verse 15). North American Evangelical tracts predict that this beast will rule the world from the Vatican.[6] Revelation 18: 4 is interpreted as a warning to all Catholics that they need to leave their church: 'Come out, my people! Come out of her! You must not take part in her sins.' The 'she' that supposedly refers to the Catholic Church is 'the famous prostitute,' (17: 1), the 'Great Babylon, the mother of all prostitutes and perverts in the world' (17: 5) or 'the great city that rules over the kings of the earth' (17: 18).

Globalization does not imply a homogenising diffusion of cultural forms, values, and ideas but heterogeneous global flows of social, economic, cultural, and communicative streams that are locally appropriated and recast in multiple ways (see Appadurai 1996). Like other Chilean Pentecostals, congregants from the EPC consider North American literature to be important sources of knowledge about Catholicism and satanic conspiracies. But in addition to reproducing the views of North American literature, Chilean Pentecostal conspiracy theories articulate local resentment towards the Catholic Church as well as an ambivalent view of the political, economic, and cultural power of the United States. Congregants from the EPC consider the present de facto and the (imagined) future formal universalisation of

---

[5] See 'The European Union and the WEU', *Watchman Bible Study*, 27 November 2009 <http://www.watchmanbiblestudy.com/Topics/Europe/EuropeanUnion.htm>; Don Koenig, 'The Rise of Europe and the New Holy Roman Empire', *Prophetic Years*, <http://www.thepropheticyears.com/reasons/The%20rise%20of%20the%20new%20roman%20empire.HTM>, and 'According to the Book of Revelations the Anti-Christ Is: Is It Obama?' *Godlike Productions* [discussion board] <http://www.godlikeproductions.com/forum1/message557672/pg2>.

[6] See 'Information on Roman Catholicism', *Chick Publications* <http://www.chick.com/information/religions/catholicism/>.

the US dollar to be an important part of Catholic–satanic plans of gaining world dominion. The introduction of the euro as a common
European currency is merely seen as a first step in this process.

What struck me about the rumour on the photocopy was that it circulated less than two months before the new law of equal legal status to
Evangelical churches was finally passed, after years of discussion and
pressure from Evangelical leaders (see chapter 3). Though separated
from the Chilean state in 1925 the Catholic Church did until 1999
enjoy a privileged position in Chile, whereas Evangelical churches had
the same legal status as organisations such as neighbourhood associations. At the time of the rumour, congregants knew the legal position
of the church was about to improve. While they generally approved of
that, many also expressed scepticism, stressing that the salvation of
souls did not depend upon political processes, and that Pentecostals
should never repeat the serious mistake of the Catholic Church by
getting too involved in 'worldly' matters such as politics. Though the
timing might be a pure coincidence, the rumour certainly served as a
reminder that formal legal equality did not change the position of
Pentecostals as a persecuted minority, and that the Catholic Church
was still to be considered a powerful and dangerous enemy of the
world's Evangelical population. A couple of weeks after the circulation
of the photocopy, I had the following exchange with Alberto, an
unskilled worker in his forties from the EPC:

> Alberto: Not long ago it said on the Internet that the Pope wants to gather
> all the presidents in the world in order to unite all the churches and create
> one universal currency. And do you remember that the Revelation says
> that there will be one governor in the world, and it says that it will be the
> United States? The United States is the beast, you know. And the Pope
> will rule the whole world. And now there is this currency, the euro.
>
> ML: Yeah, but that is just European.
>
> Alberto: Well, but afterwards it will be the dollar, and the Pope and the
> United States will rule the world. They are persecuting the churches all
> over the world; they are killing the Christians. Now in Chile, they will
> pass the new law of religious freedom, but they can change that; you
> should never trust the politicians.

In addition to testifying to a heartfelt distrust in national politicians
(see also chapter 3 and 5), this excerpt also illustrates how the dangers
of Catholicism are conceived of in global terms. It follows that a new
law of religious equality in Chile is not perceived as a serious obstacle
to the omnipresent threat of global Catholicism and the United States.

According to Coombe, the indeterminacy of rumours about corporate trademarks reflects the indeterminacy of the media that they combat (1997: 270). In a similar way the mystery and indeterminacy of the rumour on the photocopy can be seen as reflecting Pentecostal perceptions of the mysterious secrecy, indeterminacy, and omnipresence of the Catholic Church and its global influence.

The Dangers of the Internet

During my initial fieldwork in the EPC in 1999, the Internet figured prominently in rumours of satanic revival and Catholic conspiracies. Most web sites start with 'www', and 'w' can, with a little goodwill, be seen as the contraction of a 'v' and an 'i'. In the Roman system of numbers, 'vi' is 6, which means that 'www' can be read as '666', the number of the Antichrist. Congregants pointed to the fact that pornography, suicidal recipes, heavy metal music (which is believed to satanic), and other sinful materials are all available on the Internet as proofs that this is indeed a favourite medium, used by the Devil to contaminate Chilean youth. It was even suggested to me by a man in the church that Bill Gates, the owner of Microsoft and supposedly one of the richest persons in the world might be the Antichrist. According to popular theories, the Devil would in time use the Internet to brainwash the population of the entire world. At the moment computers were too expensive and the Internet too inaccessible to a great number of people for the Devil to carry out his plan, but in time everyone would have access to this medium. All the world's computers would then be connected to one big supercomputer, already constructed in the Vatican, and in some versions of the story with the co-operation of Microsoft.

While a globally pervasive and tremendously powerful medium of communication, the Internet is also characterised by incorporeality and unlocalizability. The streams of information that flow globally through the net can pop up on specific computers all over the world. But at the same time they are detached from specific localities and places of origin and hence surrounded by an aura of mysterious omnipresence. Like rumour itself, the perceived dangers of the Internet are everywhere but do not inhabit a specific site. The rumour that Bill Gates might be the Antichrist may be explained in terms of resentment and feelings of alienation and impotence in relation to the concentration of wealth and power that he and Microsoft represent. But the rumour could also be seen as representing an attempt to localise the indeterminate and incorporeal dangers of the Internet.

Two years later, in 2001, things were changing at a remarkable rate. While the great majority of the congregants of the EPC still did not have access to the Internet, and many still expressed a certain ambivalence and scepticism towards this medium, some of the younger members were now using the net from computers at work, in educational institutions, or even, in a few cases, at home. When I returned to Valparaíso in 2007, cheap Internet cafes had opened up all over the city.

The Internet had in other words become more familiar and accessible, and as young members were clearly requiring some accommodation of church doctrines to modern technology, a continued demonisation of this medium would be problematic. The same man who suspected that Bill Gates could be the Antichrist was now considering taking a computer course and learning about the Internet, as he was convinced that this would improve his career opportunities. During my last fieldwork in 2001, 2002, 2007, and 2008–9, the satanic nature of the Internet was no longer a topic of conversation. Though congregants still commented that it could be used for evil purposes such as distribution of pornography, the Internet itself was no longer intrinsically associated with Satan. Within the last few years I have received many emails from Pentecostal friends.

In 2002, 2007, and 2008–9 rumour still had it that the world's largest computer, the size of a three-storey building, had been constructed in the Vatican, containing all the information in the world. In the latest version of this story, the 666 richest and most powerful men on the planet had participated in this project with the ultimate aim of gaining world dominion and making the US dollar a universal currency. But it was no longer commented that the Devil and Catholic leaders would use the Internet to brainwash and control the population of the entire world.

Pentecostal World History

For members of the EPC, history is loaded with signs and indexes of sacred interference. In April 2003 I received an email from a Pentecostal friend who warned me that the war in Iraq was a sign that the second coming of Christ is near. He urged me to consider where I wanted to spend eternity. Congregants further see natural catastrophes like the tsunami in East Asia in 2004, the heavy rains in Central Europe in the summer of 2002, or the earthquakes in Turkey in 1999 (since Chile is an earthquake zone, such news are usually of particular interest) as signs that history is approaching its end. Some Pentecostal acquaintances have warned me that earthquakes and other disasters will hit Denmark within a foreseeable future. My secular scientific arguments that Denmark is located far away from the world's earthquake zones did not convince anyone. In the last days, I was told, all kinds of natural disasters would occur in parts of the world where such phenomena have never occurred before. Other signs of the proximate return of Christ are the recent global economic crisis and the unification of European countries in the EU.

On a national level, apocalyptic signs include increasing accessibility of pornography, political corruption, children who disobey their parents, drug and alcohol problems, the emergence of new pubs and discotheques, heavy metal music, increased acceptance of homosexuality, sexual liberalisation, etc. In the view of many Pentecostals, one particular disturbing symptom of a contemporary moral and apocalyptic chaos was the visit of the Canadian photographer Spencer Tunick in Santiago on 30 June 2002 (see chapter 3, page 51). Within Chile's religious field the lack of unity among Pentecostals, the fact that some churches have become less ascetically focused, and the proliferation of new dubious prosperity ministries and other religious movements all indicate that human history might be over soon.

Congregants from the EPC generally saw the terrorist attacks in New York on 11 September 2001 as one more, though a particularly dramatic and bloody, example of the chaos that characterises the final moments of earth's history, but also as a result of the United States having distanced itself from God. Many congregants have some knowledge about European and North American church history, and some of them explained to me how the United States in the early days of colonization had been an exemplary Protestant nation. As a result the country was blessed materially by God. But in time sin made its entrance like the snake in Paradise, and New York especially, with its great gay population, is seen as a centre of moral corruption. Some congregants speculated that the terrorist attacks might be nothing less than a divine punishment, while others believed that God had not planned the attacks but that he had somehow permitted them and allowed Satan to let different sinners punish each other. A few congregants also argued that 11 September could have positive effects if it inspired Americans to seek God, as when George W. Bush appeared on television and encouraged his fellow Americans to pray for the nation.

By grasping current and historical signifiers and making them refer to alternative signifieds, Pentecostals do not read history—they write it! Much like the personal testimony of salvation, eschatological metanarratives are constructed through processes of emplotment where single events are integrated into a coherent storyline and chains of causality are constructed (see also chapter 6). Pentecostal eschatological metanarratives defy secular versions of history and on a more general level represent what Susan Harding refers to as a 'constant dissent, disruption and critique of modern thought' (1994: 66). By narrating historical and current events as parts of a cosmic struggle between God and Satan, Pentecostals further constitute themselves as important historical actors, as their own mission to evangelise and activate the power of God through ritual practice and thus prepare the world for the Second Coming becomes central to the unfolding of world history.

Despite the frequent identification of eschatological signs I only heard very few specificpredictions concerning the timing of the Second Coming. Most Pentecostals agree that the last days could be a long period, and long-term planning, for example, in terms of education or aspirations to buy a house, is not suspended by the conviction that human history will soon be over. Besides, they firmly believe that the Second Coming will be preceded by a great revival where millions of souls will be saved.

During my initial fieldwork in Chile between 1999 and 2002, members of the EPC frequently expressed their hopes that the one-hundred-year anniversary of the church and of Chilean Pentecostalism in February 2009 would coincide with or at least mark the beginning of a great second revival (the first revival being the one that gave birth to Chilean Pentecostalism in 1909) that would prepare the world for the Second Coming.[7] These hopes were partly inspired by a certain disappointment because the new building, constructed with much effort and paid for by congregants themselves, was rarely more than half-full during meetings. During my latest fieldwork in November and December 2008, hopes for a proximate revival had vanished. Several congregants now seemed stressed and frustrated because of all the work they had

---

[7] The EPC separated itself from the Methodist Pentecostal Church in 1934 (see chapter 3), but members of the EPC see themselves as the legitimate heirs of the first Pentecostal revival in Chile.

to put into the planning and organisation of a big one-week-long conference—with participation of pastors and officials from a number of local congregations of the EPC in Chile and beyond—to celebrate the anniversary. In 2008 I heard no specific predictions concerning the timing of the revival and the Second Coming. Congregants still eagerly emphasised that the revival would occur sooner or later, but now added that only God knew when and how. 'The Lord will revive his church and initiate a great revival,' the pastor said during a sermon in December 2008. He then continued, 'I do not know how he will do it, but he will do it.' As the last phrase produced some excitement among members of the congregation, many of whom started shouting, 'Amen', the pastor repeated it three times.

Domesticating Globalisation

As particular cultural genres, rumours and conspiracy theories articulate sensations of marginalization and powerlessness towards globally dominant institutions and forces. But more than a desperate and irrational cry from otherwise voiceless and powerless sectors, who do not find themselves on the happy side of globalization's dialectic of inclusion and exclusion, these genres also represent cultural strategies of domesticating forces of globalization. Through rumours and conspiracy theories, the powers of Catholicism, the United States, the Arab world, the Internet and foreign enterprises, etc. are encompassed by and contained within an eschatological metanarrative where the God of Pentecostals is the ultimate victor. While the possibility of Catholic–US–Arab plans becoming realized inspires fear and anxiety, such plans are ultimately seen as integral episodes or parts of this metanarrative, the culmination of which is the return of Christ, the defeat of the Devil, the reign of the Millennium, and the Great Day of Judgement.

In eschatological metanarratives, God and Satan are the real actors, the former being the source of all good things and the latter being in control of the 'world' of sin and constantly working to sabotage the work and blessings of his opponent. But though predetermined by God, the unfolding of world history and the realization of the plan of salvation are also to some extent dependant upon Pentecostal ritual and evangelising agency through which new souls are won, divine power activated, and the scope of the Devil limited.

Scholars have noted how the realm of darkness provides an important point of integration between biblical master narratives and local concerns of struggles (Cortén & Marshall-Fratani 2001: 10; Lindhardt 2011: 17, 28). The Devil who manifests himself in Japanese and North American cartoons and mobilises the Catholic Church, the United States, foreign enterprises, Arabic countries, and the EU in order to gain world dominion is the same Devil that haunts Chilean Pentecostals in their everyday lives, who dominated them before conversion (see chapter 6), and whom they continuously manage to fight off in minor battles by staying close to God and actively seeking his power and protection (see chapter 10). Thus minor struggles and practices aiming at controlling and dealing with particular local realities become parts of a global, universal warfare between good and evil.

Rumours, conspiracy theories, and eschatological metanarratives articulate an alternative version of social reality and redefine the position and agency of Pentecostal subjects within it. As subaltern genres, they represent a cultural strategy for gaining a symbolic, categorical control over global processes and world history. Through rumours, conspiracy theories, and eschatological metanarratives Pentecostals respond locally to processes of globalization while at the same time projecting themselves into a global order as they redefine world history as *their* history.

CHAPTER TWELVE

CONCLUSION

The predictive inadequacy of the classical secularisation thesis has for some time been strikingly clear. A quick glance at the present world order makes it almost impossible to assert that religion has outplayed its own role and become irrelevant in the modern world. On the contrary scholars have begun to focus attention on the ways in which worldwide, though highly heterogeneous, processes of social transformation, often associated with neoliberal capitalist modernity, have created symbolic voids and opened new spaces for the upsurge of religious movements and discourses on the occult (Bernice Martin 1998; Comaroff & Comaroff 1999; Meyer 1999*b*; Cortén & Marshall-Fratani 2001; Lindhardt 2009*b*). Rather than hard-lived remains from a premodern past, current religious and spiritual phenomena are increasingly being portrayed not only as active and creative responses to ambiguous and contradictory processes of modernisation and globalisation but also as implicated in and shaping those same processes.

It has become commonplace to conceive of religious fundamentalism as a rebellious child of post-enlightenment modernity. Bruce Lawrence has described religious fundamentalists as modern people who reject a particular modernist version of the world (1989: 1, 17). They are modern in that they find themselves and their world in a state of ambiguity, disintegration, contradiction, and anguish. They understand that the world is changing, and they wittingly embrace many features of modernity such as technology and bureaucratic forms of organisation. On the other hand they reject modernism as a holistic and ideological framework with deep roots in the enlightenment (ibid.: 1–2). David Lehmann has later added that while religious fundamentalists share a global orientation with other modern people, the former are not cosmopolitans who valorise difference (1996: 222). Rather they insist on absolute and divine truths on the basis of which they can interpret events, make moral judgements on the present state of affairs, and outline appropriate courses of future action.

The present study has attempted to shed some light on the ways in which members of a particular fundamentalist group, a traditional Chilean Pentecostal church, symbolically insert themselves into an ambiguous modern world. I have argued that we can best understand the ability of Pentecostalism to open up new and alternate realms of meaning and identity by focusing carefully on different aspects of religious practice. By continuously engaging in ritual and everyday, discursive, embodied, and reflective practice, traditional Pentecostals constitute and unfold a re-enchanted vision of social reality and project themselves into it. More specifically I have argued that congregants from the EPC, through the ritual and discursive unfolding of a theology of human impotence and dependence upon divine power, in fact cultivate a sense of empowerment and spiritual agency. By emphasising their own powerlessness and at the same time establishing an intimate and embodied relationship with transformative divine power, congregants indirectly grant themselves a significant measure of power to shape the social world.

The Pentecostal power of powerlessness is not put to use in political or militant struggles that aim at structural transformations of Chilean society. Rather it is a subjective and intersubjective power that enables congregants to defy the logic of a dominant socio-cultural system, to construct new and meaningful biographies and to symbolically appropriate world history and make it their own. It is a power to create a sense of sacred order in an otherwise messy and ambiguous world (or 'world'). It is the power of congregants to constitute themselves as theological and ritual experts or as the blessed and privileged children of God—instead of merely being defined by their 'worldly' social status. And it is a power to transform domestic spheres by altering patterns of consumption and relationships between spouses. I hope to have demonstrated that the Pentecostal otherworldliness does not represent a simple withdrawal from the surrounding social world. Rather it represents ongoing attempts to devise a well-defined position within that world and to reach out for and act upon it with authority, mercy compassion, and responsibility. A question that remains to be addressed is whether a traditional Pentecostal church like the EPC will remain a site of imaginary symbolic reversal of the social order. Or, might the critical consciousness of the present 'worldly' state of affairs and the sensations of power, agency, and responsibility to act upon the world, cultivated through Pentecostal practice, contain seeds that could grow into future political action?

Pentecostalism and Political Culture

A good deal of scholarly writing on Latin American Pentecostalism has been concerned with the movement's impact on political culture in the region. Historical declarations of support from Pentecostal leaders to authoritarian regimes such as Pinochet's military regime in Chile (see chapter 3) seem to support a view on Pentecostalism as an inherently conservative religion whose anti-'worldliness' finds consonance with political systems where popular mobilisation is discouraged. Writing mainly on Central America, David Stoll (1990) points out how North American political interests and concerns—in particular with the influence of liberation theology—have inspired support for missionary activities and the growth of apolitical Evangelical churches in the region. On the other hand, the waves of democratisation that have swept Latin America within the last couple of decades have been accompanied by continuous Pentecostal growth and proliferation of denominations, making it difficult to assert any narrow association between the thriving of Pentecostalism and particular political climates. Research shows that many Latin American Pentecostals have positive attitudes towards democracy though their actual political participation is still limited (Freston 1993; Christian Smith 1994; Dodson 1997; Anthony Gill 2004; Fediakova & Parker 2009).

Scholars have for some time more or less unanimously been arguing that participation in Pentecostal churches results in cultural transformations in the private, domestic spheres and enables Latin Americans to adapt to insecure and flexible labour markets (Ossa 1991; Bernice Martin, 1995, 1998; David Martin 1990, 1991, 1995*b*, 2001; Mariz 1994). A question that has generated more division is whether or not the transformative potential of Pentecostal religion may in time be transferred onto other spheres, inspiring political, democratic participation. The early and pioneering works of Christian Lalive d'Epinay (1968) and Emilio Willems (1967) stake out two positions in a scholarly debate on the potential contribution of Pentecostalism to popular mobilisation and processes of democratisation in Latin America (see chapter 3; for extensive summaries of this debate see Sepúlveda 1988; Dodson 1997; Robbins 2004*b*). Without using a Marxist vocabulary Lalive d'Epinay came close to an 'opiate of the masses' position in his portrayal of Pentecostal communities as introverted, authoritarian, and highly restrictive of congregants' participation in political and other secular organisations. He further noted that Pentecostal pastors (who participated in a survey) showed a striking disinterest in and ignorance of political themes and events. The lack of interest and involvement in politics made Lalive d'Epinay describe Pentecostalism as a social strike with little potential to bring about broader social, political transformations (1968: 170). Willems, on the other hand, adopted a more positive stance, arguing that the adaptation to Pentecostal rigorous standards for consumption, personal behaviour, and appearance could be seen as a creative response to insecure and impoverished urban life conditions. In Willems' view Pentecostalism not only provided cultural strategies for individual advancement; he further argued that the emphasis on spiritual egalitarianism and the organisational and rhetoric skills acquired through active lay participation in congregational life would in time prepare Pentecostals for democratic participation (1967: 91–3).

The debate was revived in the 1990s with scholars such as Jean Pierre Bastian (1993) and later Evguenia Fediakova and Christian Parker (2009) echoing Lalive d'Epinay's description of Pentecostal congregations as being too authoritarian to cultivate democratic dispositions. Others have argued that the Pentecostal emphasis on spiritual causality directs attention away from political struggles (Stoll 1990; Deiros 1991; Brouwer, Gifford & Rose 1996) or pointed out that Pentecostals tend to have a fundamentally individualist and non-structural approach to social change (Christian Smith 1994; Smilde 1998). Pentecostals tend to explain social problems in terms of a distance between humans and God. The main strategy for achieving societal transformation must therefore be evangelisation and the conversion of large numbers of individuals rather than the political imposition of new laws and structural reforms.

Sharing Willem's optimism, the British sociologist David Martin has presented a more positive view on the potential contribution of Pentecostalism to the emergence of a democratic liberalist culture in the traditionally Catholic and authoritarian Latin America (1990, 1995b, 2001). In Martin's view the Protestant growth in the region represents a break with an autocratic, monopolistic, and organic Catholic culture. With the upsurge of Protestant and especially Pentecostal denominations, the religious structure of Latin America has become more pluralistic and voluntarist (1990: 265–6, see also Christian Smith 1994: 130–3). Martin further explores parallels between Latin American Pentecostalism and nineteenth-century Anglo-American Methodism, arguing that both movements foster voluntarism, ideals of equality, strict personal discipline, decent appearance, and sobriety. While many

Methodist and Pentecostal churches have hierarchical structures, they also value active lay participation and emphasise the equality of each person before God. In Latin American Pentecostal churches women are given semi-public positions, and the relationship between Pentecostal spouses tends to be based on dialogue and consensus rather than male tyranny. Similar to nineteenth-century Methodism, Latin American Pentecostalism has emerged in the form of alternative cultural spaces in which people from marginal sectors of society have been able to develop a sense of personal autonomy (resulting from each believer's direct line to heavenly powers), self-worth, discipline, and self-government, in addition to organisational and rhetorical skills. These cultural spaces tend to be apolitical and characterised by withdrawal from the surrounding society. But the point made by Martin (1990: 44, 1995b) and later repeated by numerous other scholars (Mariz 1992; Burdick 1993; Smith 1994; Dodson 1997; Fediakova 2004) is that religious values, skills, and models of initiative and autonomy may in time be transferred into other, for example, political spheres. According to Martin religious skills and forms of self-consciousness may be carried by individuals moving between spheres, but he also foresees that Pentecostal ideals of personal and cultural development can become enlarged and diffused to whole populations in Latin America (1990: 286).

My own research in the EPC, as in other Pentecostal churches, has so far provided me with little incitement to join the chorus of scholars who see Pentecostalism as 'an anticipation of liberty' (Martin 1990: 44) and celebrate its potential contribution to processes of democratisation in Latin America (Harrison 1992; Berger 2009). This is not because I concur with the point made by Lalive d'Epinay and later Bastian, namely that Latin American Pentecostals learn to be submissive and obedient rather than critical and reflexive. In my own experience such an argument might be supported by a narrow analysis of sermons and interactions between church leaders and lay people, but it fails to stand up to a more thorough empirical scrutiny. Some churches like the EPC do try to restrict and control the behavior, physical appearance, and evangelising initiatives of members. But as described (chapter 9 and 10), restrictions and control sometimes clash both with younger congregants' desire for more freedom and with the Pentecostal emphasis on the unmediated individual inspiration from the Holy Spirit. Such clashes often inspire discontent and critical reflection and even lead persons to drop out and maybe look for new churches. With the proliferation of denominations and the increased mass mediation of religion in Chilean society and beyond, the religious monopoly and power of socialisation of particular churches and pastors are to an increasing extent being challenged. Contemporary Pentecostals are able to construct their religious self-identities on a more individual basis by 'shopping around' in the religious market and critically choosing from a variety of inputs. I have met several Pentecostals who have shifted denomination several times and who tend to identify more with individual beliefs, values, and a personal relationship with God than with institutional attachments and submissive relationships to particular pastors.

But will the religious pluralism, voluntarism, and individualism that characterise contemporary Chilean society inspire people to actively exercise their individuality and power of decision making within the political sphere? Making predictions about the future is always an insecure business. On the other hand Pentecostalism and religious pluralism have been around in Chile for quite some time now. And so far there are very few indications that Pentecostalism has contributed in any significant ways to an overall cultural transformation of Chilean society or that any significant number Pentecostals have attempted to bring their values and skills into the political sphere. In a survey conducted by Fediakova and Parker in 2008, 1.1 per cent of Evangelical respondents expressed interest in joining a political party and 3.5 per cent claimed to have a high level of interest in participating in political discussions (2009: 55, 62). In my own experience Pentecostals do feel that a moral transformation of Chilean society is necessary. But only a minority believes that such a transformation can be achieved through political struggle, and of the few Pentecostals (all from other churches than the EPC) I have spoken to who did believe that, no one expressed an actual interest in becoming politically active.

Max Weber has taught us that social change can be initiated from within religious spheres (1967). But he also taught us that different religious movements have the potential of contributing to different kinds of social change and, equally importantly, that the possibility of that potential being realised always depends upon complex interplays with wider social and material forces. The prediction made by David Martin and others, that Pentecostalism may contribute to the emergence of a liberalist democratic culture in Latin America by fostering specific attitudes and skills, is highly speculative and has yet to be supported by substantial empirical or historical research. Acquiring a sense of self-worth and new skills in public address is not necessarily equivalent to learning the arts of political dialogue, negotiation, pragmatism, and the seeking of compromises. And as demonstrated in this work, the sense of individual autonomy that is fostered through religious practice in a traditional Pentecostal Church like the EPC practice is grounded in notions of human insufficiency and dependence upon God and differs markedly from the notions of individual autonomy that inform modernist ideologies of democracy and citizenship.

Pentecostal churches do not provide platforms for debates about national or international politics, and the openness that many Pentecostals (but again, not from the EPC) show towards political participation is accompanied by very little actual incitement or encouragement from congregations. As argued by David Smilde, people who experience upward social mobility are more likely to adopt a religious frame that contains a more mundane sense of agency (1998: 300). In so far as a younger generation of well-educated 'native' Pentecostals has a more open-minded stance towards political participation than the preceding generations within their churches, that difference should probably be ascribed more to the sense of agency that the former have acquired in educational institutions and as professionals than to the influence of their churches.

If we turn to the interplay between Pentecostal religion and wider social forces it cannot be ignored that Pentecostalism has continued to grow, thrive, and renew itself in a historical period characterised by increasing individualism, low levels of popular political participation and a declining confidence in politicians and political parties (see chapter 3; see also Parker 1998; Portales 2000; Moulián 2002; Larraín 2001, 2005; Tironi 1999, 2005; Paley 2001, 2004). As Christian Smith has pointed out, the Pentecostal individualistic approach to social change (that is, the belief that a large number of individual conversions will lead to societal transformation) does not necessarily rule out the opportunity that Pentecostals may consider political action to be the most appropriate way of addressing certain social problems, though this often appears to be the case (1994: 129–30, see also Dodson 1997: 33). But in the case of contemporary Chile, the interplay between Pentecostalism and other societal tendencies does to large extent appear to be shaped by an ideological congruence between, on the one hand, individualistic-theistic understandings of social change and a view of politics as a corrupt and 'worldly' matter and, on the other hand, a neoliberal order where political disenchantment is widespread and where individualism and conformism prevail over social and political mobilisation. If popular perceptions of politics in Chile were to change in more positive directions Pentecostals might react by becoming more open to political participation. And in so far as Pentecostals who have experienced upwards mobility come to think of the 'world' as a not-all-that-horrible place and become open to participating in its political institutions they will probably bring their values, visions, and mundane senses of agency into their churches (some of them have already done so). But whether Pentecostalism could *in itself* become a decisive cultural motor in processes of democratisation and the strengthening of Chilean and Latin American civil societies in any foreseeable future is another question. Making general conclusions about Latin American Pentecostalism based on a single case study would be a questionable endeavour. But the analysis of traditional Pentecostal practices, discourses, and understandings of transformative power presented in this book does not lead me to conclude that a denomination like the EPC will contribute in any significant way to the cultivation of democratic skills and values or inspire political participation. Rather, it leads me to concur with Fediakova and Parker's description of Chilean Pentecostals as constituting a restricted cultural citizenship that acts much more on the basis of religious than on national identities (2009: 72).

While I suspect that its political impact will be limited, I have little doubt that Pentecostalism has come to stay and, in its numerous variants, will continue to renew itself and play a very important role on the religious scene in Chile, Latin America, and other parts of the world for decades to come. Its appeal and cultural force will lie in the ability of the movement to draw its adherents into encompassing and multidimensional systems of knowledge of practice and thereby to provide them with sources of identity, empowerment, and sensations of control. As people's search for such sources is unlikely to diminish in an ambiguous, modern, and globalised world so is the relevance of Pentecostalism.

REFERENCES

Abu-Lughod, Lila. 1990. The romance of resistance: tracing transformations of power through Bedouin women. *American Ethnologist* 17 (1): 41–55.

Albrecht, Daniel E. 1999. *Rites in the spirit: A ritual approach to Pentecostal-charismatic spirituality.* Sheffield: Sheffield Academic Press.

Ammerman, Nancy T. 1994a. The dynamics of Christian fundamentalism: An introduction. In *Accounting for fundamentalisms*, edited by Martin E. Marty and R. Scott Appleby. Chicago: University of Chicago Press.

——. 1994b. Accounting for Christian fundamentalisms: Social dynamics and rhetorical strategies. In *Accounting for fundamentalisms*, edited by Martin E. Marty and R. Scott Appleby. Chicago: University of Chicago Press.

Andrade Cardemil, Rosa. 2008. Manos que sanan. Experiencia de Salud en Mujeres Pentecostales chilenas *Revista Cultura y Religión* 2.3 26–41

Appadurai, Argon. 1996. *Modernity at large: Cultural dimensions of globalization.* Minneapolis: University of Minnesota Press.

Asad, Talal. 1993. *Genealogies of religion.* London: John Hopkins University Press.

Austin, John L. 1975. *How to do things with words.* 2d ed. Cambridge, MA: Harvard University Press.

Austin-Broos, Diane. 2003. The anthropology of conversion: An introduction. In *The anthropology of religious conversion*, edited by Andrew Buckser and Stephen D. Glazier. Oxford: Rowman & Littlefield.

Bastian, Jean-Pierre. 1993. The metamorphosis of Latin American Protestant groups: A sociohistorical perspective. *Latin American Research Review* 28 (2): 33–61.

Beckford, James A. 1978. Accounting for conversion. *British Journal of Sociology* 29 (2): 249–62.

Beidelman, Thomas O. 1963. Witchcraft in Ukaguru. In *Witchcraft and sorcery in East Africa*, edited by John Middleton and E. H. Winter. London: Routledge.

Bell, Catherine. 1992. *Ritual theory, ritual practice.* Oxford: Oxford University Press.

Bengoa, José. 2000. La Desigualdad. In *La Desigualdad*, edited by José Bengoa, Francisca Márquez, and Susana Aravena. Santiago: Ediciones Sur.

Berger, Peter L. 1974. *Religion, samfund og virkelighed.* Copenhagen: Lindhardt og Ringgolf.

——. 2009. Born-again modernity. *American Interest* (July–August).

Berger, Peter L., and Luckmann, Thomas. 1972. *Den samfundsskabte virkelighed.* Copenhagen: Lindhardt og Ringgolf.

Bernstein, Richard B. 1972. A sociolinguistic approach to socialization: With some reference to educability. In *Directions in sociolinguistics*, edited by J. J. Gumperz and D. Hymes. New York: Holt, Rinehart & Winston.

Bhaba, Homi K. 1994. *The location of culture.* London: Routledge.

Bialecki, Jon. 2011. Quiet deliverances. In *Practicing the faith: The ritual life of Pentecostal-Charismatic Christians*, edited by Martin Lindhardt. New York: Berghahn Books.

Billig, Michael. 1995. *Banal nationalism.* London: Sage Publications.

Bloch, Maurice E. F. 1998. *How we think they think: Anthropological approaches to cognition, memory, and literacy.* Boulder, CO: Westview.

Bonino, José Miguez. 1995. *Faces of Latin American Protestantism.* Cambridge: Cambridge University Press.

Boone, Kathleen C. 1989. *The Bible tells them so: The discourse of Protestant Fundamentalism.* New York: State University of New York Press.

Booth, Wayne C. 1995. The rhetoric of fundamentalist conversion narratives. In *Fundamentalism comprehended*, edited by Martin E. Marty and R. S. Appleby. Chicago: University of Chicago Press.

Borzutzky, Silvia. 2006. Social security and health policies. In *After Pinochet: The Chilean road to democracy and the market*, edited by Silvia Borzutzky and Lois Hecht Oppenheim. Gainesville: University Press of Florida.

Bourdieu, Pierre. 1977. *Outline of a theory of practice*. London: Routledge.

——. 1986. *Distinction: A social critique of the judgement of taste*. Cambridge: Cambridge University Press.

——. 1990. *In other words*. Cambridge: Polity.

——. 1991. *Language and symbolic power*. Cambridge: Polity.

Boyer, Pascal. 2001. *Religion explained: The human instincts that fashion God, spirits and ancestors*. London: William Heinnemann.

Brouwer, Steve, Paul Gifford, and Susan Rose. 1996. *Exporting the American gospel: Global Christian fundamentalism*. London: Routledge.

Brown, Karen M. 1994. Fundamentalism and the control of women. In *Fundamentalism and gender*, edited by John Stratton Hawley. Oxford: Oxford University Press.

Bruce, S. 1987. The Moral Majority: The policies of fundamentalism in secular society. In *Studies in religious fundamentalism*, edited by John Stratton Hawley. Hong Kong: Macmillan.

Brusco, Elizabeth. 1995. *The Reformation of machismo: Evangelical conversion and gender in Colombia*. Austin: University of Texas Press.

Bubandt, Nils. 2002. Rumour politics: Mobilisation and anonymous discourse in violent conflicts. Paper presented at the 7th Biennial Conference for the European Association for Social Anthropologists (EASA), Copenhagen, 14–17 August.

Burdick, John S. 1993. Struggling against the Devil: Pentecostalism and social movements in urban Brazil. In *Rethinking Protestantism in Latin America*, edited by Virginia Garrad-Burnett and David Stoll. Philadelphia: Temple University Press.

——. 1996. *Looking for God in Brazil: The progressive Catholic Church in urban Brazil's religious arena*. Berkeley and Los Angeles: University of California Press.

Butler, Judith. 1990. *Gender trouble: Feminism and the subversion of identity*. London: Routledge.

——. 1993. *Bodies that matter: On the discursive limits of "sex."* London: Routledge.

Canales Guevara, Hermes. 2000. *Firmes y Adelante*. Santiago: Barlovento Impressores.

Canales, Manuel, Samuel Palma, and Hugo Viella. 1991. *En Tierra Extraña ll: Para una sociología de la religiosidad popular protestante*. Santiago: Amerindia.

Cancino, Hugo. n.d. *Den chilenske venstrefløj mellem tradition, fornyelse og tilpasning til den nye orden*. Unpublished manuscript.

Cancino, Rita. n.d. *Universiteter og studenterbevægelse i Chile: Fra statsligt undervisningsmonopol til undervisningsindustri*. Unpublished manuscript.

Carr, David. 1991. Discussion: Ricoeur on narrative. In *On Paul Ricoeur: Narrative and interpretation*, edited by David Wood. London: Routledge.

Chesnut, R. Andrew. 2003. *Competitive spirits: Latin America's new religious economy*. Oxford: Oxford University Press.

Chong, Kelly. 2011. Healing and redomestication: Reconstitution of the feminine self in South Korean Evangelical cell group ritual practices. In *Practicing the faith: The ritual life of Pentecostal-charismatic Christians*, edited by Martin Lindhardt. New York: Berghahn Books.

Christensen, Steen Fryba. n.d. *Chiles Økonomiske udvikling, 1973–2009*. Unpublished manuscript.

Christoffani, Pablo. n.d. *Modernitet og Forbrugskultur i Chile*. Unpublished manuscript.

Cleary, Edward L. 1997. Introduction: Pentecostals, prominence, and politics. In *Power, Politics and Pentecostals in Latin America*, edited by Edward L. Cleary and Hanna W. Stewart-Gambino. Boulder, CO: Westview Press.

Cleary, Edward L., and Juan Sepúlveda. 1997. Chilean Pentecostalism: Coming of age. In *Power, politics and Pentecostals in Latin America*, edited by Edward L. Cleary and Hanna W. Stewart-Gambino. Boulder, CO: Westview Press.

Cole, Jennifer. 2008. Fashioning distinction in urban Madagascar. In *Figuring the future: Globalization and the temporalities of children and youth*, edited by Jennifer Cole and Deborah Durham. Santa Fe, NM: School for Advanced Research Press.

Coleman, Simon. 2000a. *The globalization of Charismatic Christianity: Spreading the gospel of prosperity*. Cambridge: Cambridge University Press.

——. 2000b. Moving towards the millennium? Ritualized mobility and the cultivation of agency among Charismatic Protestants. *Journal of Ritual Studies* 14 (2): 16–27.

——. 2003. Continuous conversion? The rhetoric, practice, and rhetorical practice of Charismatic Protestant conversion. In *The anthropology of religious conversion*, edited by Andrew Buckser and Stephen D. Glazier. Oxford: Rowman & Littlefield.

Coleman, Simon, and Peter Collins. 2000. The 'plain' and the 'positive': Ritual, experience and aesthetics in Quakerism and Charismatic Christianity. *Journal of Contemporary Religion* 15 (3): 317–29.

Collier, Simon, and William F Sater. 1996. *A history of Chile, 1808–1995*. Cambridge: Cambridge University Press.

Comaroff, Jean. 1985. *Body of power, spirit of resistance: The culture and history of a South African people*. Chicago: University of Chicago Press.

Comaroff, Jean, and John Comaroff. 1993. Introduction to *Modernity and its malcontents: Ritual and power in postcolonial Africa*, edited by Jean and John Comaroff. Chicago: University of Chicago Press.

——. 1999. Occult economies and the violence of abstraction: Notes from the South African postcolony. *American Ethnologist* 26 (2): 279–303.

——. 2001. Millennial capitalism: First thoughts of a Second Coming. In *Millennial Capitalism and the culture of neoliberalism*, edited by Jean and John Comaroff. London: Duke University Press.

Comte, Auguste. 1974. *The positive philosophy*. New York: AMS Press.

Coombe, Rosemary. 1997. The demonic place of the 'not there': Trademark rumours in the postindustrial imaginary. In *Culture, power, place: Explorations in a critical anthropology*, edited by Akhil Gupta and James Ferguson. Durham, NC: Duke University Press.

Corvalán, Oscar. 2009. Distribución, crecimiento y discriminación de los evangélicos pentecostales. *Revista Cultura y Religión* 3 (2): 76–97.

Cortén, André, and Ruth Marshall-Fratani. 2001. Introduction to *Between Babel and Pentecost: Transnational Pentecostalism in Africa and Latin America*, edited by André Cortén and Marshall-Fratani. London: Hurst Publishers; Bloomington: Indiana University Press.

Cristi, Marcela, and Lorne L. Dawson. 1996. Civil religion in comparative perspective: Chile under Pinochet 1973–1989. *Social Compass* 43 (3): 319–338.

Csordas, Thomas. 1990. Embodiment as a paradigm for anthropology. *Ethos: Journal of the Society for Psychological Anthropology* 18 (1): 5–47.

——. 1994. *The sacred self: A cultural phenomenology of Charismatic healing*. Berkeley and Los Angeles: University of California Press.

——. 1997. *Language, charisma, and creativity: The ritual life of a religious movement*. Berkeley and Los Angeles: University of California Press.

——. 2007a. Introduction: Modalities of transnational transcendence. *Anthropological Theory* 7 (3): 259–72.

——. 2007b. Global religion and the re-enchantment of the world: The case of the Catholic Charismatic renewal. *Anthropological Theory* 7 (3): 295–314.

——. 2011. Ritualisation of life. In *Practicing the faith: The ritual life of Pentecostal-charismatic Christians*, edited by Martin Lindhardt. New York: Berghahn Books.

de Certeau, Michel. 1984. *The practice of every day life*. Berkeley and Los Angeles: University of California Press.

Deiros, Pablo. 1991. Protestant Fundamentalism in Latin America. In *Fundamentalism observed*, edited by Martin E. Marty and R. Scott Appleby. Chicago: University of Chicago Press.

Dodson, Michael. 1997. Pentecostals, politics, and public space in Latin America. In *Power, politics and Pentecostals in Latin America*, edited by Edward L. Cleary and Hanna W. Stewart-Gambino. Boulder, CO: Westview Press.

Drogus, Carol Ann. 1997. Private power or public power: Pentecostalism, base communities, and gender. In *Power, politics and Pentecostals in Latin America*, edited by Edward L. Cleary and Hanna W. Stewart-Gambino. Boulder, CO: Westview Press.

Durkheim, Emile. 1995/1915. *The elementary forms of religious life*. New York: Macmillan.

Engelke, Matthew. 2004. Discontinuity and the discourse of conversion. *Journal of Religion in Africa* 34 (1): 82–109.

Evans-Pritchard, E. E. 1976/1937. *Witchcraft, oracles and magic among the Azande*. Oxford: Clarendon Press.

Ezzy, Douglas. 1998. Theorizing narrative identity: Symbolic interactionism and narrative identity. *Sociological quarterly* 39 (2): 239–52.

Fabian, Johannes. 1983. *Time and the other: How anthropology makes its object*. New York: Columbia University Press.

Fediakova, Evguenia. 2002. Separatismo o Participación: Evangélicos chilenos frente a la política. *Revista de Ciencia Política* 27 (2): 32–45.

——. 2004. 'Somos parte de esta sociedad': Evangélicos y política en el Chile post autoritario. *Política* 1 (43): 254–284.

Fediakova, Evguenia, and Christian Parker. 2009. Evangélicos en Chile Democrático (1990–2008): Radiografía al Centetismo Aniversario. *Revista Cultura y Religión* 3 (2): 48–75.

Fenn, Richard K. 1982. *Liturgies and trials: The secularisation of religious language*. Oxford: Basil Blackwell.

Ferguson, James. 1999. *Expectations of modernity: Myths and meanings of urban life on the Zambian Copperbelt*. Berkeley and Los Angeles: University of California Press.

Fleet, Michael, and Brian H. Smith. 1997. *The Catholic Church and democracy in Chile and Peru*. Notre Dame, IN: University of Notre Dame Press.

Foucault, Michel. 1972. *The archaeology of knowledge*. London: Tavistock.

——. 1981. The order of discourse. In *Untying the text: A post-structuralist reader*, edited by Robert Young. London: Routledge.

Freston, Paul. 1993. Brother votes for brother: The new politics of Protestantism in Brazil. In *Rethinking Protestantism in Latin America*, edited by Virginia Garrad-Burnett and David Stoll. Philadelphia: Temple University Press.

——. 2001. *Evangelicals and politics in Asia, Africa and Latin America*. Cambridge: Cambridge University Press.

——. 2004. *Protestant political parties: A global survey*. Aldershot: Ashgate.

——. 2006. *Evangelical Christianity and democracy in Latin America*. Oxford: Oxford University Press.

Geertz, Clifford. 1963. *The interpretation of cultures*. New York: Basic Books.

Geschiere, Peter. 1997. *The modernity of witchcraft*. Charlottesville: University Press of Virginia.

Geschiere, Peter, and Francis Nyamnjoh. 1999. Witchcraft as an issue in the 'politics of belonging': Democratization and urban migrants' involvement with the home village. *African Studies Review* 41 (3): 69–91.

Giddens, Anthony. 1994. *Modernitetens konsekvenser*. Copenhagen: Hans Reitzels Forlag.

——. 1996. *Modernitet og selvidentitet*. Copenhagen: Hans Reitzels Forlag.

Gill, Anthony. 2004. Weber in Latin America: Is Protestant growth enabling the consolidation of democratic capitalism? *Democratization* 11 (4): 42–65.

Gill, Lesley. 1990. 'Like a veil to cover them': Women and the Pentecostal movement in La Paz. *American Ethnologist* 17 (4): 798–821.

Goffman, Erving. 1961. *Asylums: Essays on the social situation of mental patients and other inmates*. Chicago: Aldine.

Gooren, Henri. 2007. Conversion careers in Latin America: Entering and leaving church among Pentecostals, Catholics and Mormons. In *Conversion of a continent: Religious identity and change in Latin America*, edited by Timothy J. Steigenga and Edward L. Cleary. Brunswick, NJ: Rutgers University Press.

———. 2010 Conversion Narratives. In: *Studying Global Pentecostalism: Theories and Methods*, edited by Allan Anderson, Michael Bergunder, André Droogers, and Cornelis van der Laan. Berkeley and Los Angeles: University of California Press.

Greil, Arthur L., and David R. Rudy. 1984. What have we learned from process models of conversion? An examination of ten case studies. *Sociological Focus* 17 (4): 305–23.

Guha, Ranajit. 1983. *Elementary aspects of peasant insurgency in colonial India*. Oxford: Oxford University Press.

Haas, Liesl. 1999. The Catholic Church in Chile: New political alliances. In *Latin American religion in motion*, edited by Christian Smith and Joshua Prokopy. London: Routledge.

Hall, David A., ed. 2004. *Puritans in the New World: A critical anthology*. Princeton, NJ: Princeton University Press.

Hallowel, A. Irving. 1955. *Culture and experience*. Philadelphia: University of Pennsylvania Press.

Harding, Susan F. 1987. Convicted by the Holy Spirit: The rhetoric of fundamental Baptist conversion. *American Ethnologist* 14 (1): 167–181.

———. 1994. Imagining the Last Days: The politics of apocalyptic language. In *Accounting for fundamentalism*, edited by Martin E. Marty and R. Scott Appleby. Chicago: University of Chicago Press.

Harrison, Lawrence E. 1992. *Who prospers? How cultural values shape economic and political success*. New York: Basic Books.

Harrold, Francis, Raymond Eve, and John Taylor. 2004. Creationism, American style: Ideology, tactics and rhetoric in a social movement. In *The cultures of creationism: Anti-Evolutionism in English speaking countries*, edited by Simon Coleman and Leslie Carlin. Aldershot: Ashgate.

Hastrup, Kirsten. 1992. Writing ethnography: State of art. In *Anthropology and autobiography*, edited by Judith Okely and Helen Callaway. London: Routledge.

Hawley, John. S., and Wayne Proudfoot. 1994. Introduction to *Fundamentalism and gender*, edited by John S. Hawley. Oxford: Oxford University Press.

Haynes, Jeff. 1995. *Religion, fundamentalism and ethnicity: A global perspective*. United Nations Research Institute for Social Development. Discussion paper.

Hebdige, Dick. 1979. *Subculture: The meaning of style*. London: Routledge.

Hefner, Robert W. 1993. World building and the rationality of conversion. In *Conversion to Christianity: Historical and anthropological perspectives on a great transformation*, edited by Robert W. Heffner. Berkeley and Los Angeles: University of California Press.

Hodgson, Dorothy. 1998. Embodying the contradictions of modernity: Gender and spirit possession among the Maasai in Tanzania. In *Gendered encounters: Challenging cultural boundaries and social hierarchies in Africa*, edited by Maria Grosz-Ngate and Omari H. Kokole. London: Routledge.

Hofstadter, Richard. 1965. *The paranoid style in American politics and other essays*. New York: Knopf.

Hollenweger, Walther. 1972. *The Pentecostals*. London: SCM.

———. 1997. *Charismatisch-pfingstliches Christendum Herkunft, Situation ökumenische Chancen* Göttingen: Vandenhoeck & Ruprecht.

Hoover, Mario. 2002. *El movimiento pentecostal en Chile del siglo XX*. Santiago: Eben-Ezer.

Hoover, Willis C. 1977. *Historia del avivamiento pentecostal en Chile*. Santiago: Eben-Ezer.

Hughes-Freeland, Felicia, and Mary M. Crain. 1998. Introduction to *Recasting ritual: Performance, media, identity*, edited by Felicia Hughes-Freeland and Mary M. Crain. London: Routledge.

Humphrey, Caroline, and James Laidlaw. 1994. *The archetypal actions of ritual: A theory of ritual illustrated by the Jain rite of worship*. Oxford: Clarendon.

Hurtado, Josefina. 1993. Mujer pentecostal y vida cotidiana. *Huellas, seminario mujer y antropología*. Santiago: CEDEM.

Ingstad, Benedicte. 1990. The cultural construction of AIDS and its consequences for prevention in Botswana. *Medical Anthropology Quarterly* 4 (1): 28–40.

Jackson, Michael. 1983. Knowledge of the body. *Man* 18 (n.s.): 327–45.

Kamsteeg, Frans H. 1998. *Prophetic Pentecostalism in Chile: A case study of religion and developmental policy*. Maryland and London: Scarecrow Press.

——. 1999. Pentecostalism and political awakening in Pinochet's Chile and beyond. In *Latin American religion in motion*, edited by Christian Smith and Joshua Prokopy. London: Routledge.

Kastfelt, Nils. 2005. History, religion and political culture in northern Nigeria: The contexts of a recent Bachama-Muslim conflict. In *The 'traditional' and the 'modern' in West African (Ghanaian) history: Case studies on co-existence and interaction*, edited by Per Hernæs. Trondheim: Norwegian University of Science and Technology.

Keesing, Roger. 1992. *Custom and confrontation: The Kwaio struggle for cultural autonomy*. Chicago: University of Chicago Press.

Kessler, J. B. A. Jr. 1967. *A study of the older Protestant missions and churches in Peru and Chile: With special reference to the problems of division, nationalism and native ministry*. Goes: Oosterbaan & Le Cointre.

Klein, Naomi. 2007. *The shock doctrine*. London: Penguin Books.

Kristensen, Dorthe Brogaard. 2008. *The shaman or the doctor: Patient, power and culture in southern Chile*. PhD dissertation, University of Copenhagen.

Lagos Schuffeneger, Humberto. 1988. *Crisis de la Esperanza: Religión y autoritarismo en Chile*. Santiago: Presor.

——. 2001. *El General Pinochet y el Mesianismo Político*. Santiago: Lom Ediciones.

Lalive d'Epinay, Christian. 1968. *El refugio de las masas: Estudio sociológico del protestantismo chileno*. Santiago: Editorial Del Pacifico.

Larraín, Jorge. 2001. *Identidad Chilena*. Santiago: LOM ediciones.

——. 2005. *América Latina moderna? Globalización e identidad*. Santiago: LOM ediciones.

Lavigna, Robert. 2002. Neoliberal Chile: A sketch. *Terra Incognita* (3) <http://www.terraincognita.50megs.com/neoliberal.html>.

Lavín, Joaquín. 1987. *Chile: La Revolución Silenciosa*. Santiago: Zig-Zag.

Lawrence, Bruce. 1989. *Defenders of God: The fundamentalist revolt against the modern age*. New York: Tauris.

Leder, Drew. 1990. *The absent body*. Chicago: University of Chicago Press.

Lehmann, David. 1996. *Struggle for the spirit: Religious transformation and popular culture in Brazil and Latin America*. Cambridge: Polity.

——. 1998. Fundamentalism and globalism. *Third World Quarterly* 19 (1): 607–34.

León, Arturo, and Javier Martínez. 1998. La estratificación social chilena hacia fines del siglo XX. In *Chile en los noventa*, edited by Christián Toloza and Euginio Lahera. Santiago: Dolmen Ediciones.

Liechty, Mark. 2003. *Suitably modern: Making middle-class culture in a new consumer society*. Princeton, NJ: Princeton University Press.

Lies, William M. 2006. A clash of values: Church-state relations in democratic Chile. In *After Pinochet: The Chilean road to democracy and the market*, edited by Silvia Borzutzky and Lois Hecht Oppenheim. Gainesville: University Press of Florida.

Liesl, Haas. 1999. The Catholic Church in Chile: New political alliances. In *Latin American religion in motion*, edited by Christian Smith and Joshua Prokopy. London: Routledge.

Lindhardt, Martin. 2009*a*. The ambivalence of power: Charismatic Christianity and occult forces in Urban Tanzania. *Nordic Journal of Religion and Society* 22 (1): 37–54.

——. 2009*b*. More than just money: The faith gospel and occult economies in contemporary Tanzania. *Nova Religio: Journal of Emergent and Alternative Religions* 13 (1): 41–67.

——. 2010. 'If you are saved you cannot forget your parents': Agency, power and social repositioning in Tanzanian born-again Christianity. *Journal of Religion in Africa* 40 (3): 240–72.

——. 2011. Introduction to *Practicing the faith: The ritual life of Pentecostal-charismatic Christians*, edited by Martin Lindhardt. New York: Berghahn Books.

Lira, Elizabeth. 2006. Human rights in Chile: The long road to truth, justice, and reparations. In *After Pinochet: The Chilean road to democracy and the market*, edited by Silvia Borzutzky and Lois Hecht Oppenheim. Gainesville: University Press of Florida.

Lofland, John, and Rodney Stark. 1965. Becoming a world-saver: A theory of conversion to a deviant perspective. *American Sociological Review* 30 (6): 862–75.

Loveman, Brian. 2001. *Chile, the legacy of Hispanic capitalism*. Oxford: Oxford University Press.

Luhrmann, Tanya M. 2004. Metakinesis: How God becomes intimate in contemporary US Christianity. *American Anthropologist* 106 (3): 518–28.

——. 2005. The art of hearing God: Absorption, dissociation, and contemporary American spirituality. *Spiritus* 5 (2): 133–57.

——. 2006. Learning religion at the Vineyard: Prayer, discernment and participation in the divine. *Religion and Culture Web Forum*. Martin Marty Center. University of Chicago.

Mansilla, Miguel Ángel. 2007*a*. La construcción de la masculinidad en el pentecostalismo chileno. *Revista Polis* 5 (16).

——. 2007*b*. El neopentecostalismo chileno. *El Cotidiano* 22 (143): 106–114.

——. 2008. Pluralismo, subjetivización y mundanización: El impacto de secularización en el neopentecostalismo chileno. *Revista Polis* 19.

——. 2009. Pentecostalismo y ciencias sociales: Reflexión en torno a las investigaciones del pentecostalismo chileno (1968–2008). *Revista Cultura y Religión* 3 (2): 26–47.

Manzi, Jorge, and Carlos Catalán. 1998. Los cambios en la opinión pública. In *Chile en los noventa*, edited by Christián Toloza and Euginio Lahera. Santiago: Dolmen Ediciones.

Mardsen, George. 1991. *Understanding fundamentalism and evangelicalism*. Grand Rapids, MI: Eerdmans.

Mariz, Cecília Loreto. 1992. Religion and poverty in Brazil. *Sociological Analysis* 53: 63–70.

——. 1994. *Coping with poverty: Pentecostals and Christian base communities in Brazil*. Philadelphia: Temple University Press.

Mariz, Cecilia Loreto, and Maria das Dores Campos Machado. 1997. Pentecostalism and women in Brazil. In *Power, politics and Pentecostals in Latin America*, edited by Edward L. Cleary and Hanna W. Stewart-Gambino. Boulder, CO: Westview Press.

Marshall-Fratani, Ruth. 2001. Mediating the global and local in Nigerian Pentecostalism. In *Between Babel and Pentecost: Transnational Pentecostalism in Africa and Latin America*, edited by André Cortén and Ruth Marshall-Fratani. London: Hurst Publishers; Bloomington: Indiana University Press.

Martin, Bernice. 1995. New mutations of the Protestant ethic among Latin American Pentecostals. *Religion* 25 (2): 102–17.

——. 1998. From pre- to postmodernity in Latin America: The case of Pentecostalism. In *Religion, modernity and postmodernity*, edited by P. Heelas. Oxford: Blackwell.

——. 2011a. Latin American Pentecostalism: The ideological battleground. In *Pentecostal power: Expressions, impact and faith of Latin American Pentecostalism*, edited by Calvin Smith. Leiden and Boston: Brill.

——. 2011b. Interpretations of Latin American Pentecostalism: 1960s to the present. In *Pentecostal power: Expressions, impact and faith of Latin American Pentecostalism*, edited by Calvin Smith. Leiden and Boston: Brill.

Martin, David. 1990. *Tongues of fire: The explosion of Protestantism in Latin America*. Cambridge: Basil Blackwell.

——. 1991. The economic fruits of the spirit. In *The culture of entrepreneurship*, edited by Bridgitte Berger. San Francisco: Institute for Contemporary Studies.

——. 1995. Evangelical religion and capitalist society in Chile: Historical context, social trajectory and economic ethos. In *Religion and the transformations of capitalism: Comparative approaches*, edited by Richard H. Roberts. London: Routledge.

——. 1996. *Forbidden revolutions*. London: SPCK.

——. 2001. *Pentecostalism: The world their parish*. Oxford: Blackwell.

Martínez, Javier, and Alvaro Díaz. 1996. *Chile: The great transformation*. Geneva: United Nations' Research Institute for Social Development.

Marty, Martin E. 1992. Fundamentals of fundamentalism. In *Fundamentalism in comparative perspective*, edited by Lawrence Kaplan. Amherst: University of Massachusetts Press.

Marty, Martin E., and R. Scott Appleby. 1992. *The glory and the power: The fundamentalist challenge to modernity*. Boston: Beacon.

Mauss, Marcel. 1973. Techniques of the body. *Economy and Society* 2 (1): 70–88.

Maxwell, David. 2002. A youth religion? Born-again Christianity in Zimbabwe and beyond. In *Africa's young majority*. Centre of African Studies, edited by Barbara Trudell, Kenneth King, Simon McGrath, and Paul Nugent. Edinburgh: University of Edinburgh.

——. 2006. *African gifts of the spirit: Pentecostalism and the rise of a Zimbabwean transnational religious movement*. Oxford: James Currey.

Mead, George Hebert. 1962. *Mind, self and society*. Chicago: University of Chicago Press.

Merleau-Ponty, Maurice. 1962. *The phenomenology of perception*. Evanston, IL: Northwestern University Press.

Meyer, Birgit. 1992. 'If you are a devil you are a witch and if you are a witch, you are a devil': The integration of 'pagan' ideas into the conceptual universe of Ewe Christians in southeastern Ghana. *Journal of Religion in Africa* 22 (2): 98–132.

——. 1998. 'Make a complete break with the past': Memory and postcolonial modernity in Ghanaian Pentecostalist discourse. *Journal of Religion in Africa* 28 (3): 316–49.

——. 1999a. *Translating the devil: Religion and modernity among the Ewe in Ghana*. Edinburgh: Edinburgh University Press.

——. 1999b. Commodities and the power of prayer: Pentecostalist attitudes towards consumption in contemporary Ghana. In *Globalization and identity: Dialectics of flow and closure*, edited by Peter Geschiere and Birgit Meyer. Oxford: Blackwell.

Montecino, Sonia, and Alexandra Obach. 2002. Caminar con el Espíritu: Perspectivas de género en el movimiento Evangélico Pentecostal. *Estudio: Centro De Estudios Públicos* 87: 73–103.

Moulian, Tomás. 1998. *El consumo me consume*. Santiago: Lom Ediciones.

——. 2002. *Chile Actual: Anatomia de un mito*. Santiago: Lom Ediciones.

Neitz, Mary Jo. 1987. *Charisma and community: A study of religion in American culture.* New Brunswick: Transaction.

Neitz, Mary Jo, and James V. Spickard. 1990. Steps towards a sociology of religious experience: The theory of Mihaly Csikszentmihalyi and Alfred Schutz. *Sociological Analysis* 51 (1): 15–33.

Norris, Rebecca Sachs. 2003. Converting to what? Embodied culture and the adoption of new beliefs. In *The anthropology of religious conversion,* edited by Andrew Buckser and Stephen D. Glazier. Oxford: Rowman & Littlefield.

Orellana U, Luis. 2008. *El fuego y la nieve: Historia del movimiento Pentecostal en Chile 1909–1932.* Concepción: Ceep Ediciones.

Orellana Rojas, Zicri. 2009. La Iglesia Pentecostal: Communidad de mujerers. *Revista Cultura y Religión* 3 (2): 119–131.

Ortner, Sherry B. 1978. *Sherpas through their rituals.* Cambridge: Cambridge University Press.

———. 1990. *Narrativity in history, culture and lives.* Paper presented at the annual meeting of the American Anthropological Association. New Orleans.

———. 1995. Resistance and the problem of ethnographic refusal. *Comparative Studies in Society and History* 37 (1): 173–93.

Ossa, Manuel. 1991. *Lo ajeno y lo propio: Identidad Pentecostal y trabajo.* Santiago: Rehue.

———. 1996. La identidad Pentecostal. *Revista Persona y Sociedad* 10 (1).

Østergård, Uffe, and Jan Ifversen. 1996. *Begreb og Historie.* Aarhus: Det Humanistiske Fakultets Trykkeri, University of Aarhus.

Oviedo, David. 2009. Neopentecostalismo en el Chile contemporáneo: Ruptura religiosa y asimilación social. In *Voces del Pentecostalismo Latinoamericano ll: Identidad, teologia, historia,* edited by Daniel Chiquete and Luis Orellana. Concepción: Relep.

Paley, Judith. 2001. *Marketing democracy: Power and social movements in post-dictatorship Chile.* Berkeley and Los Angeles: University of California Press.

———. 2004. Accountable democracy: Citizens' impact on public decision making in post-dictatorship Chile. *American Ethnologist* 31 (4): 497–513.

Parker, Christian. 1998. Religion y cultura. In *Chile en los noventa,* edited by Christián Toloza and Euginio Lahera. Santiago: Dolmen Ediciones.

Peel, J. D. Y. 1995. For who hath despised the day of small things? Missionary narratives and historical anthropology. *Comparative Studies in Society and History* 37 (3): 581–607.

Percy, Marty. 1996. *Words, wonders and power: Understanding contemporary Christian fundamentalism and revivalism.* London: SPCK.

Peste, Jonathan. 2006. Radical Israeli settler: Ultimate concerns, political goals and violence. In *Exercising power: The role of religions in concord and conflict,* edited by Tore Ahlbäck and Björn Dahla. Åbo, Finland: Donner Institute for Research in Religious and Cultural History.

Pfeil, Gretchen. 2011. Imperfect vessels: Emotion and rituals of anti-ritual in American Pentecostal and Charismatic devotional life. In *Practicing the faith: The ritual life of Pentecostal-charismatic Christians,* edited by Martin Lindhardt. New York: Berghahn Books.

Pierce, C. S. 1940. *The philosophy of Pierce: Selected writings.* Edited by J. Buchler. London: Routledge.

Pilmark, Kristina Biilman. n.d. *Genopfindelsen af det chilenske højre.* Unpublished manuscript.

Portales, Felipe. 2000. *Chile: Una democracia tutelada.* Santiago: Editorial Sudamericana.

Rambo, Lewis. 1993. *Understanding religious conversion.* New Haven, CT: Yale University Press.

Rappaport, Roy A. 1999. *Ritual and religion in the making of humanity.* Cambridge: Cambridge University Press.

Reyes, Praxedes Peña. 1986. *Incorporación y Fé en la Iglesia Metodista Pentecostal: Un estudio antropológico de cinco casos*. MA thesis, Universidad de Chile, Santiago.

Ricoeur, Paul. 1984, 1985, and 1987. *Time and narrative*. 3 vols. Chicago: University of Chicago Press.

Riesebrodt, Martin. 1993. *Pious passion: The emergence of modern fundamentalism in the United States and Iran*. Berkeley and Los Angeles: University of California Press.

Riesebrodt, Martin, and Chong, Kelly. 1999. Fundamentalisms and patriarchal gender politics. *Journal of Women's History* 10 (4): 55–77.

Riobó Pezoa, Enrique. 2010. La evolución del discurso de la teología de la liberación durante la dictadura chilena: El caso de los periódicos clandestinos No Podemos Callar y Policarpo. *Revista Cultura y Religión* 4 (2): 39–56.

Robbins, Joel. 2001. Ritual communication and linguistic ideology: A reading and partial reformulation of Rappaport's theory of ritual. *Current Anthropology* 42 (5): 591–614.

——. 2003. On the paradoxes of global Pentecostalism and the perils of continuity thinking. *Religion* 33 (3): 221–31.

——. 2004a. *Becoming sinners: Christianity and moral torment in a Papua New Guinean society*. Berkeley and Los Angeles: University of California Press.

——. 2004b. The globalization of Pentecostal and Charismatic Christianity. *Annual Review of Anthropology* 33: 117–143.

——. 2007. Continuity thinking and the problem of Christian culture: Belief, time and the anthropology of Christianity. *Current Anthropology* 48 (1): 5–38.

——. 2011. The obvious aspects of Pentecostalism: Ritual and Pentecostal globalization. In *Practicing the faith: The ritual life of Pentecostal-charismatic Christians*, edited by Martin Lindhardt. New York: Berghahn Books.

Robertson, Roland. 1992. *Globalization: Social theory and global culture*. London: Sage Publications.

Rolim, Francisco Cartaxo. 1979. Pentecostisme et societé au Brazil. *Social Compass* 26 (2): 345–72.

Ruana, Edgar Moros. 1995. La Iglesia Católica ante el desafío Pentecostal. In *En la fuerza del Espíritu: Los pentecostales en América Latina. Un desafío a las iglesias históricas*, edited by Benjamin F. Guiterrez. Mexico City: AIPRAL.

Ryle, Jacqueline. 2010. *My God, my land: Interwoven paths of Christianity and tradition in Fiji*. Aldershot: Ashgate.

——. 2011. Laying our sins on the altar: Ritualising Charismatic Catholic reconciliation and healing in Fiji. In *Practicing the faith: The ritual life of Pentecostal-charismatic Christians*, edited by Martin Lindhardt. New York: Berghahn Books.

Schultze, Quentin J. 1994. Orality and power in Latin American Pentecostalism. In *Coming of age: Protestantism in contemporary Latin America*, edited by Daniel Miller. Boston: University Press of America.

Schutz, Alfred, and Thomas Luckmann. 1973. *The structure of the life world*. Evanston, IL: Northwestern University Press.

Scott, James. 1985. *Weapons of the weak: Everyday forms of peasant resistance*. New Haven, CT: Yale University Press.

——. 1990. *Domination and the arts of resistance: Hidden transcripts*. New Haven, CT: Yale University Press.

Sepúlveda, Juan. 1988. Pentecostalismo y Democracia: Una interpretación de sus relaciones. In *Democracia y Evangelio*, edited by Arturo Chacón. Santiago: Rehue.

——. 1992. Die Pfingstbewegung und ihre Identität als Kirche. *Jahrbuch Mission*: 145–53. Hamburg: Missionshilfe Verlag.

——. 1996. Reintepreting Chilean Pentecostalism. *Social Compass* 43 (3): 299–318.

——. 1999a. Indigenous Pentecostalism and the Chilean experience. In *Pentecostals after a century: Global perspectives on a movement in transition*, edited by Allan H. Anderson and Walter J. Hollenweger. Sheffield: Sheffield Academic Press.

———. 1999*b*. *De Peregrinos a Ciudadanos: Breve historia del cristianismo evangélico en Chile*. Santiago: Fundación Honrad Adenanuer.

Shupe, Anson, and Jeffrey K. Hadden. 1992. Is there such a thing as global fundamentalism? In *Secularisation and fundamentalism reconsidered: Religion and the political order*, edited by Jeffrey K. Hadden and Anson Shupe. New York: Paragon.

Sjørup, Lene. 1995. *Fundamentalisme eller fattigdomsbekæmpelse? Pentekostalismen i Latinamerika*. Copenhagen: Center for udviklingsforskning.

———. 2008. *Pinochets Gud og de fattiges teologiske modstand*. Copenhagen: Museum Tusculanums Forlag.

Slootweg, Hanneke. 1991. Mujeres Pentecostales Chilenas: Un caso en Iquique. In *Algo más que opio: Una lectura antropológica del pentecostalismo latinoamericano y caribeño*, edited by Barbara Boudenwijnse, André Droogers, and Franz Kamsteeg. San José, Costa Rica: Editorial DEI.

Smilde, David A. 1998. 'Letting God govern': Supernatural agency in the Venezuelan Pentecostal approach to social change. *Sociology of Religion* 59: 287–303.

———. 2007. *Reason to believe: Cultural agency in Latin American Evangelicalism*. Berkeley and Los Angeles: University of California Press.

———. 2011. Public rituals and political positioning: Venezuelan evangelicals and the Chávez government. In *Practicing the faith: The ritual life of Pentecostal-charismatic Christians*, edited by Martin Lindhardt. New York: Berghahn Books.

Smith, Brian H. 1982. *The church and politics in Chile: Challenges to modern Catholicism*. Princeton, NJ: Princeton University Press.

———. 1998. *Religious politics in Latin America: Pentecostal vs. Catholic*. Notre Dame, IL: University of Notre Dame Press.

Smith, Christian. 1994. The spirit and democracy: Base communities, Protestantism, and democratization in Latin America. *Sociology of Religion* 55 (2): 119–43.

Snow, David A., and Richard Machaleck. 1983. The convert as a social type. *Sociological Theory* 1: 259–89.

Snow, David A., and Cynthia L. Phillips. 1980. The Lofland-Stark conversion model: A critical reassessment. *Social Problems* 27 (4): 430–7.

Spittler, Russel P. 1994. Are Pentecostals and Charismatics fundamentalists? A review of American uses of these categories. In *Charismatic Christianity as a global culture*, edited by Karla Poewe. Columbia, SC: University of South Carolina Press.

Spivak, Gayatri Charakvorty. 1987. *In other worlds: Essays in cultural politics*. New York and London: Methuen.

Sørensen, Ulla Britt. 1993. *Befrielsesteologi og demokrati i Chile: Kirkens rolle i gendemokratiseringen af det chilenske samfund i periode fra sidste halvdel af 1980erne til i dag*. MA thesis, Faculty of Theology, University of Copenhagen.

Steigenga, Timothy J., and Kenneth M. Coleman. 1995. Protestant political orientations and the structure of political opportunity: Chile 1972–1991. *Polity* 27 (3): 465–82.

Steigenga, Timothy, and Edward L. Cleary. 2007. Understanding conversion in the Americas. In *Conversion of a continent: Religious identity and change in Latin America*, edited by Timothy J. Steigenga and Edward L. Cleary. New Brunswick, NJ: Rutgers University Press.

Steven, James H. S. 2002. *Worship in the Spirit. Charismatic worship in the Church of England*. Carlisle, UK: Paternoster Press.

Stewart-Gambino, Hannah. 1992. Redefining the changes and politics in Chile. In *Conflict and competition: The Latin American church in a changing environment*, edited by Edward L. Cleary and Hannah Stewart-Gambino. London: Lynne Rienner.

Stoll, David. 1990. *Is Latin America turning Protestant? The politics of Evangelical growth*. Berkeley and Los Angeles: University of California Press.

Stromberg, Peter G. 1985. The impression point: Synthesis of symbol and self. *Ethos: Journal of the Society for Psychological Anthropology* 13 (1): 56–74.

——. 1993. *Language and self-transformation: A study in Christian conversion narrative*. Cambridge: Cambridge University Press.

Susumu, Shimazono. 1986. Conversion stories and their popularization in Japan's new religions. *Japanese Journal of Religious Studies* 13 (2–3): 157–75.

Tambiah, Stanley J. 1979. A performative approach to ritual. *Proceedings of the British Academy* 65, London.

——. 1996. *Leveling crowds: Ethnonationalist conflict and collective violence in South Asia*. Berkeley and Los Angeles: University of California Press.

Tan Bercerra, Reinaldo. 2010. Tres miradas de ser católico: Jóvenes, adultos y adultos mayores católicos chilenos. ¿Encuentro o desencuentro? *Revista Cultura y Religión* 4 (2): 192–210.

Taylor, Charles. 1994. The politics of recognition. In *Multiculturalism: Examining the politics of recognition*, edited by Amy Gutman. Princeton, NJ: Princeton University Press.

Tironi, Eugino. 1999. *La irrupción de las masas y el malestar de las élites: Chile en el cambio de siglo*. Santiago: Grijalbo.

——. 2005. *El sueño chileno: Comunidad, familia y nación en el bicentenario*. Santiago: Taurus.

Tokman, Victor E. 2001. *De la informalidad a la modernidad*. Mexico City: Oficina internacional del trabajo.

Tripp, Ali Mari. 1997. *Changing the rules: The Politics of liberalization and the urban informal economy in Tanzania*. Berkeley and Los Angeles: University of California Press.

Turner, Victor. 1969. *The ritual process*. London: Routledge.

——. 1982. *From ritual to theatre: The human seriousness of play*. New York: PAJ Books.

Valdés, Teresa. 1998. Entre la modernización y la equidad: Mujeres, mundo privado y familias. In *Chile en los noventa*, edited by Christián Toloza and Euginio Lahera. Santiago: Dolmen Ediciones.

Weber, Max. 1947. *The theory of social and economic organization*, edited with an introduction by Talcott Parsons. New York: Oxford University Press.

——. 1967. *The Protestant ethic and the spirit of capitalism*. Translated by Talcott Parsons, with a foreword by R. H. Tawney. London: Unwin.

——. 1968. *Max Weber on charisma and institution building*, edited by S. N. Eisenstadt. Chicago: University of Chicago Press.

——. 1995. The sociology of charismatic authority. In *From Max Weber: Essays in sociology*, edited by H. H. Gerth and C. Wrigth Mills. London: Routledge.

Weiss, Brad. 2004. Introduction to *Producing African futures*, edited by Brad Weiss. Leiden and Boston: Brill.

Willems, Emilio. 1967. *Followers of the new faith: Culture change and the rise of Protestantism in Brazil and Chile*. Nashville: Vanderbilt University Press.

Williams, Cyril G. 1981. *Tongues of the spirit: A study of Pentecostal glossolalia and related phenomena*. Cardiff: University of Wales Press.

Willis, Paul. 1977. *Learning to labour: How working class kids get working class jobs*. New York: Colombia University Press.

Winn, Peter. 2004. The Pinochet era. In *Victims of the Chilean miracle: Workers and neoliberalism in the Pinochet era, 1973–2002*, edited by Peter Winn. Durham, NC: Duke University Press.

Zaner, Richard M. 1981. *The context of the self: A phenomenological inquiry using medicine as a clue*. Athens: Ohio University Press.

INDEX